THE ANCIENT MIND
AND ITS HERITAGE

THE ANCIENT MIND
AND ITS HERITAGE

VOLUME II

EXPLORING THE HEBREW, HINDU, GREEK AND CHINESE CULTURES

BY ELMER G. SUHR

FOREWORD BY PROFESSOR VAN L. JOHNSON
Department of Classics
Tufts University

An Exposition–University Book

EXPOSITION PRESS   NEW YORK

Exposition Press Inc., 386 Park Avenue South, New York 16, N.Y.

FIRST EDITION

to

RICHARD   EUGENE   HAYMAKER

amicitiae causa

FOREWORD

In this second volume of *The Ancient Mind and Its Heritage* Professor Suhr continues and concludes his comparative study of ancient civilizations. Once more he succeeds in outlining the central facts and isolating the chief factors of interest to us. The relation of man to his universe is again the dominant, unifying theme behind some vivid portraits of the Hebrew nomad in trusting covenant with a single god; of the brooding Hindu quietly resolving barriers between the finite and the infinite; of the restless Greek whose curiosity is never satisfied till he has organized experience and found eternal forms within it; of the Chinese peasant carefully accommodating life to nature with inherited observances and changeless rules of human behavior.

This volume, like its predecessor, demonstrates that the art historian has certain advantages in the realm of comparative history: His language, the language of art, is a universal one and gives all of us easier access to civilizations otherwise beyond our understanding or very difficult to comprehend through other media. Moreover art often expresses more precisely, cogently, and simply what is of most significance to us in matters seemingly remote and vastly complicated. Professor Suhr has kept this well in mind and he always reads the monuments for our instruction, refining and delineating what there is for us in a study of ancient civilizations. The faith of the Hebrew, the introspection of the Hindu, the intelligence of the Greek, and even the rigid formality of the Chinese emerge as things pertinent to the democratic man. I myself have found the chapters on the Hebrew and the Hindu particularly rewarding; perhaps there is too much to say of the Greek and too little to say of the

Chinese, but such is the nature of the evidence, all nicely reflected in the truthfulness of the author's account.

PROFESSOR VAN L. JOHNSON
Department of Classics
Tufts University, Medford, Mass.

PREFACE

In this volume, as in the first, I have included a brief historical survey and only as much of the religion, thought, literature, and art of each culture as I deemed necessary to understand its viewpoint—how each man looked at his world and fellow man, in what respect he advanced or retarded the cause of democracy.

The Egyptian created the most self-sufficient world perspective in the Mediterranean area, so secure and certain he had no desire to improve on it. The Mesopotamian, finding the solace of security and certainty beyond the grasp of his powerful hand, sensed a tragic significance threading its way through the pattern of his life. As a by-product of his covenant the Hebrew contributed a sense of moral responsibility. That the Greek was directly influenced by either the tragic implications of Mesopotamian thought or the morality of the Hebrew is questionable, but his contacts with his two adjacent neighbors certainly bore fruit in the fields of art and religion; the static forms of Egypt gave the Greek artist a point of departure for his future achievements, while the Mesopotamian contributed something of the matrix of power manifested in the spiral, the vortex, the volute, and the spindle, all figuring strongly in the creation of the cosmos and of fertility in that cosmos in terms of earth, air, fire, and water. Beyond these obvious marks of contact the Greek seems to have generated most of the impetus that brought forth his democratic viewpoint.

With the exception of Pythagoras and Plato there is little indication of direct influence emanating from the Hindu to Hellas. The Chinese produced a beautiful but lonesome flower in a sheltered garden, a flower whose fragrance still lingers with us; eventually it wilted and shed its petals on the grave of its own creator. The influence of China was and still is tremendous without offering any more support to democratic thought than the land of the Nile. The achievements of ancient viewpoints can, however, be of great value in the formation of a modern world perspective, and here the ancient Hindu's contribution of tolerance will be a decided asset. If we admit that the development of human personality is cumulative, the ancient past is as much a part of us as our children or yesterday's nightmare. On the negative side there is the obsessing fear of the primitive and his subjective concentration, the philosophy of expediency, the mania for certainty and security, the abuse of power and religious intolerance; on the other side are the assets of a democratic viewpoint we have already mentioned. All this is a part of our past, of what we are and hope to be, all or any one of these can play a prominent role in the process of learning more about ourselves and how we can deal with our world in terms of fairness.

In addition to the acknowledgements made in the first volume I wish to express my gratitude to the committee on grants-in-aid of the University of Rochester for assistance in defraying incidental expenses. Thanks are also due to Miss Janet McAdam, to Miss Marilyn Johnson, and to my wife for reading the manuscript.

ELMER G. SUHR
Rochester, N.Y.

CONTENTS

THE ANCIENT MIND
AND ITS HERITAGE

THE HEBREW

BECAUSE WE HAVE in their writings a record of their past, the history of the Hebrew people is often considered easy to trace, but this assumption is not necessarily true. The Old Testament is primarily a history of a people's religious experience in which the sequence of events was intended to throw additional light on Yahweh's leadership and protection throughout the centuries of the Hebrews' wanderings, their conquests, their kingdoms, and their persecutions; it is also important to remember that different writers have recorded certain traditions or attempted to compromise conflicting traditions handed down from the past. Until the advent of archaeology into Palestine and its neighborhood, the literature, taken by itself, brought as much confusion as clarification into the picture of their past, some authorities going so far as to put certain authors down as deliberate liars. Strange as it may seem, after the spade had uncovered a number of sites, the chronology and sequence of events of the Bible turned out to be surprisingly intelligible, a fact so much the more surprising in that so much reliance was laid on oral transmission from one generation to another. The archaeologist has, then, elucidated to a certain degree what the literature had made confusing or conflicting to the modern reader. The intermediate position of the Hebrews between the Egyptians on the one side and the Mesopotamians on the other has shed some light, especially on the periods following the conquest; for the early periods of their wanderings the records of the Nile and Euphrates valleys are none too helpful. They do inform us, by inference, how much the Hebrews borrowed from the older civilizations and also impress us with the remarkable advance made on what they borrowed. It is this contribution of the Hebrew viewpoint in which we are especially interested.

The earliest patriarch to appear on the pages of history, so says the Bible, was Abraham, whom we find with his family and flocks, most likely not in Ur but in the region of northern Mesopotamia. From there he wandered with a Hurrian migration into and out of Canaan as well as through the semidesert territory to the south, settling temporarily here and there to take advantage of pasture and water supplies. When famine threatened the country, his descendant Jacob and his children took refuge in Egypt, where Joseph had found favor in the eyes of the pharaoh. Here the Hebrews prospered and increased greatly in number. In the course of time a pharaoh ascended the throne who, knowing nothing about Joseph, subjected the Hebrew people to hard labor and persecution to the point where they decided to seek a new home. In this plight they put their trust in a new leader, Moses, escaped from the forces of the pharaoh, and managed to cross the Sea of Reeds into the desert regions beyond; their divine destiny, as sure and miraculous as a meteor in the night sky, was already leading them on. Moses not only led them through years of hardship but taught them to worship Yahweh, the God destined to bless them and chastise them in their wanderings, until they finally reached the Promised Land. At Sinai they made a covenant with their God and received His commandments. Because the Edomites and Moabites refused them a free passage through their territories, they were forced to follow a roundabout route through Transjordan and so eventually crossed the Jordan at Jericho. By this time Joshua had succeeded Moses, who had died after catching a glimpse of Canaan from a high mountain. Once across the river, the Hebrews conquered such strongholds as Jericho and Lachish, which gave them a strong foothold in the land. Gradually, by the process of assimilation, the Hebrews took over many of the richer districts of what came to be known as Palestine.

In the light of more recent discoveries, especially in archaeology, we can be quite certain that Abraham was living in Harran in northwestern Mesopotamia some time after the reign of Hammurabi.[1] He migrated to the southeast with the Hurrians, who in turn were driven ahead by others pressing down from the north to find a place in the sun. Rather than settle in a definite location, he wandered with his flocks from place to place, living the life of a seminomad in Canaan and the Negeb, a half-desert region south of Palestine. When the Hyksos with their horses and chariots poured down through this country and into Egypt, the descendants of Abraham probably threw in their lot with the newcomers and passed along into the Nile valley. This conclusion seems to fit the chronological evidence at our disposal and also offers an explanation for the change of attitude in Egypt toward the Hebrews. If the latter came into the land with the Hyksos,[2] we can also understand why the Egyptians preserved no record of their departure, for an enemy, especially one who had conquered Egypt, would find no place in their annals. What manner of life the Hebrews led there we are not told, but they evidently were not deprived of their flocks, which they later brought with them across the Sea of Reeds. The pharaoh responsible for their departure is generally thought to be Rameses II, who probably forced the Hebrews into bondage at Tanis, the former delta capital of the Hyksos which, during their occupation, had been known as Avaris. One authority[3] dates the exodus at 1290 B.C. and another[4] claims the Hebrews could not have passed through southern Transjordan before the thirteenth century B.C., which would allow about fifty years for the crossing of the Sea of Reeds and their wanderings in the desert.

Who were the twelve sons of Jacob whose names were attached to the tribes of the Hebrews in Egypt? Nothing outside the Old Testament is known about their personalities, a fact

---

1. T. J. Meek: *Hebrew Origins,* New York, 1936, p. 14.

2. W. F. Albright: *The Archaeology of Palestine and the Bible,* New York, 1935, p. 143.

3. W. F. Albright: *From the Stone Age to Christianity,* Baltimore, 1940, p. 195.

4. N. Glueck: *The Other Side of the Jordan,* New Haven, 1940, p. 146.

which has cast doubts on their existence as individuals. It also appears that only a portion of the Hebrews went into Egypt, a large number remaining behind with the Canaanites in Palestine, which explains, according to one authority,[5] the cultural advance of northern Palestine over Judah; this means that Israel in the north was conquered by the Hebrews and settled some two hundred years before Judah in the south. Later, when the north and south were united under David, the accounts of the invasion of Palestine converted the movements of the Hebrews, for obvious reasons, into a united, contemporaneous undertaking. We note too that some tribes were associated with certain animals: Judah was called a lion, Joseph was a bull, and the Levites were apparently associated with the serpent, all of which was suppressed once the tribes were united under the worship of Yahweh. Until the time of David there seems to have been no common bond in the form of a political organization among the tribes; beyond the compelling force of religious authority, each one went its own independent way, even feuding with one another unless a common enemy threatened them from without. The Hebrew, while he was undoubtedly the most pronounced individualist of the Near East, did not reach the level of either Greek or modern democracy, one important reason being the close association, even dominance at times, of religion over what we should call the secular phases of life. Granted that the priesthood could not become such an incubus on the state as in Egypt or Mesopotamia, democracy, in our sense of the term, could never have tolerated the high-handed dealings of Samuel with Saul or other enemies who crossed his pathway.[6]

The Hebrews, we are told, did not go around the Sea of Reeds, but through it, an episode which has been explained

---

5. T. J. Meek: *op. cit.,* p. 43. He also contends that the Hebrews who went to Egypt were the Levites.

6. Cf. W. A. Irwin in *The Intellectual Adventure of Ancient Man,* Chicago, 1946, p. 354.

in many different ways. The scientist[7] maintains they crossed through the shallows of the modern Red Sea where a strong wind can blow the water away from the sand; the water, returning when the wind ceased, seeped into the sand before it covered the surface and thus may have trapped the army of the pharaoh—a plausible explanation, but why did the Egyptians, who must have known about such a phenomenon, fall such an easy prey to the water-soaked sand? Such explanations of Old Testament miracles, as interesting as they may be to the scientifically curious, tell us little about the religion and viewpoint of the Hebrew.

Some time later the migrants came into the neighborhood of Sinai where a covenant was made between Yahweh and his people, the divinity choosing his people and Moses acting as mouthpiece and intermediator between the two. The event was not only a momentous occasion in the history of the Hebrew nation but a definite milestone in the development of human thought, unique in the relations established between a personal God and his people and unparalleled in the religious experience of the orient. Yahweh pledged himself to stand by his chosen people through all their wanderings and to lead them into the Promised Land, if they would abide by the commandments their God had given them through his servant, Moses. As a leader and commanding personality Moses rose to great heights. He was a molder of religious thought and a guardian of his people, and well it was for this people to remain in the desert for the sake of religious discipline before they were exposed to the gods of Canaan. Henceforth they carried the ark of the covenant in all their wanderings, while Yahweh, as a cloud by day and a pillar of fire by night, watched over them; henceforth Yahweh blessed them again and again and punished them severely for their transgressions, but always he was the one and only God of his chosen people. Any form of idolatry was a grave offense,

---

7. W. O. E. Oesterly & T. H. Robinson: *A History of Israel*, Oxford, 1932, Vol. I, p. 87.

a lesson the Hebrews learned after setting up the image of the golden calf.[8]

Before crossing the Jordan there must have occurred more than one conflict with peoples commanding the approaches to Canaan on the south, most of them unfavorable to the Hebrews. After skirting around Edom and Moab, but before crossing the river, Moses died, and Joshua took over the leadership which henceforth demanded more military strategy and prowess. Whether there were two invasions or only one,[9] whether Yahweh was a single God or merely one among many prior to the exodus, the early development and character of Yahweh seem to be largely the achievement of Moses. The eventual triumph of this God after the invasion may have been due to the temporal victory of Judah, or what one writer[10] calls the absorption of the Levites by the tribe of Judah. Joshua, at any rate, was not responsible for the conquest of all the territory tradition has attached to his name,[11] although excavations at Jericho, Bethel, Ai, and Lachish show obvious signs of destruction, some of which were undoubtedly the work of the Hebrews under his leadership. In Palestine the Hebrews found a land forming a small link of the fertile crescent, fairly uniform in its geographical features, one which had been more fertile in earlier times because of wooded areas along the mountain slopes. Along the east coast of the sea is a low plain rising gradually up to a range of mountains to the east, a range that juts out to the coast at

---

8. T. J. Meek (*op. cit.* p. 139) speaks of Aaron as a bull-worshipper of the tribe of either Joseph or Ephraim, therefore the responsibility for the golden calf must be laid at his door. Meek (p. 43) also claims the invasion of the north antedates that of the south by two hundred years, a fact which explains the cultural advance of the former during the early history of Hebrew occupation. Cf. also W. F. Albright: *From the Stone Age to Christianity*, Baltimore, 1940, p. 211.

9. J. A. Wilson (*The Burden of Egypt*, Chicago, 1951, pp. 255–6) also refers to two invasions, the first in Amarna times, the later one, made up of the tribe of Levi, coming from Egypt.

10. T. J. Meek: *op. cit.*, p. 114.

11. W. F. Albright: *From the Stone Age to Christianity*, Baltimore, 1940, p. 210.

only one point, in the vicinity of Mount Carmel. Further east
we come to what is called the great rift, a depression including
the Jordan valley, which sinks far below sea level at the Dead
Sea,[12] beyond which one passes to the arid tableland of Arabia.
It was a land moderately well supplied with water and thus
suitable for both the shepherd and the farmer, occupations by
no means new to the Hebrew. Apart from their religion and
their language, which was practically the same as later Hebrew,
we know little about the Canaanites. They were of Semitic
origin, of close kin to the invaders, they stood generally on a
higher cultural level, lived in well-walled towns, and presumably
had better weapons.

The Hebrews, on the other hand, had been hardened by
their stay in the desert and united under the banner of Yahweh,
which constituted their greatest assets. They were hardly numerous enough to fight many pitched battles in an open plain;
they must have depended heavily on the element of surprise,
on overwhelming the foe with fright at the first onset. Since they
had scarcely any equipment for a siege, most of the fortified
towns were probably taken by guile,[13] a strategy abetted by
an absence of any kind of organization or federation among the
Canaanites, who were evidently no more alarmed over the
coming of the Hebrews than the Greek cities over the threat of
the Macedonian Philip. The vanguard of the invasion may very
well coincide with the breakdown of the Egyptian empire, as
it is reported in the Amarna letters,[14] and if this is true (archaeology seems to confirm this conclusion), the Hebrews from Egypt
made common cause with other tribes already settled in the
Promised Land. We have to remember that the occupation of
the country at this time was only partial, many of the strongholds,
including Jerusalem, remaining in the hands of the enemy. The

---

12. For a recent interpretation of the destruction of Sodom and Gom-
orrah consult J. Finegan: *Light from the Ancient Past,* Princeton, 1946,
p. 126.

13. Cf. the story of Rahab (Joshua VI:22–25).

14. W. F. Albright: *From the Stone Age to Christianity,* Baltimore,
1940, p. 211.

treatment of captured natives was sometimes ruthless in the way men, women, and children were put to death,[15] a practice which must be judged in the light of contemporary custom. Other sections of the land were attached to the Hebrews by treaty, which means that in time a gradual assimilation took place. With the passing of Joshua new leaders rose from the rank and file of the people, men like Gideon, Abimelech, and Jephthah, to continue the struggle against both the natives and the bordering Moabites and Ammonites, but throughout this period there was no king, no common bond except that of religion, which had set up its sanctuary at Shiloh in the center of occupied territory.

On the heels of the invasion a new menace appeared on the coastal plain in the form of the Philistines, a people which had swept down by land and sea from the north by way of Asia Minor and Crete, had met with a reverse in Egypt at the hands of Rameses III, and were now making a bid for empire in southern Palestine. Because of superior weapons and military tactics they poured over the fertile southern plain, established themselves in its five cities, and then gained control of much of the inland country already occupied by the Hebrews. Up to this time and during much of the Philistine domination the Hebrews had been ruled by military leaders known as judges, men called by Yahweh to lead and govern the people, somewhat like the early Roman *dictator*, when circumstances demanded more than the tribal government could fulfill; but now that an outside enemy threatened their existence in Palestine, they turned their thoughts, however unwillingly, to some form of kingship. The folk tale of Samson[16] tells us something of the loose organization of the Philistines and their treatment of subjects. We know, too, that, except for the privation of weapons, the Hebrews under their domination were given many privileges and considerable freedom of movement. The situation was so humiliating, how-

---

15. *Joshua*, VI:21 & VII:25.
16. *Judges*, XIII:24–XVI:31.

ever, that the Hebrews, always chafing under any form of subjection, continued to struggle until eventually Shiloh was sacked and the ark was captured. This brought them to the nadir of ill fortune because it meant that Yahweh, in allowing himself to be captured, had forsaken their cause. The tribe of Dan, almost exterminated, was forced to look for a new home in the north. At this time of great extremity Samuel, the last of the judges and a man of indomitable will, comes on the stage.

From one of the lesser tribes, that of Benjamin, Samuel diplomatically chose Saul, an otherwise inconspicuous character, to lead his people against the common foe. After his anointment as king,[17] Saul and his son won a number of engagements by shrewd maneuvering and dare-devil adventures and regained control of the hill country. The star of Saul was now at its zenith; his dauntless courage as a commander had raised him to the height of a national hero, although he was a king without a palace or capital. He was the type of ruler most suited to their needs, one who, after the stress of battle was over, would, like Cincinnatus, return to the soil and resume the life of the common citizen. In a short time certain of his actions met with the disapproval of Samuel, and we are told the spirit of the Lord was no longer with him.[18] Why should Samuel suddenly turn against the man of his choice? It is true Saul was gradually losing prestige in favor of the younger David, and Saul was too headstrong to brook the rise of such a rival, but something more important seems to have happened to embitter the former good relationship between Saul and Samuel. It has been suggested that Saul[19] revolted against Yahweh and his prophets, which turned away Samuel, an ardent champion for the cause of the Hebrew God. At any rate, while Saul and David were feuding, the Hebrews lost much of the ground they had gained. Finally, in desperation, Saul consulted the witch of Endor some time after the death of

---

17. I *Samuel*, X:1.
18. I *Samuel*, XVI:14.
19. T. J. Meek: *op. cit.* p. 156.

Samuel to bring the dead man from his grave; very soon thereafter he met his end at Gilboa.

David was the man of the hour in every sense of the term.
Like Saul, he was summoned from the family of a commoner,
in Bethlehem, and by his adventurous daring, his charm of personality, he won over all he contacted to his cause. Whether he
killed Goliath or another giant, he was both the salvation of the
Hebrews against the Philistines and a rock of defense once the
land was free of enemies; he also held his own people in the
north and south under the banner of Yahweh. A soldier, a musician, a poet, and a diplomat, he was able to deal with the older
Saul in a manner which redounded to his own praise, and he
won over the son of his rival to a proverbial friendship; a man
of strong moods, he was big both in his good and evil. In a sense,
he was a symbol of what every Hebrew could aspire to become.
As soon as he was made king, he made every effort to take Jerusalem, where the people established a political center and where
the worship of Yahweh found a secure sanctuary on the captured height, for the new king was definitely interested in laying
a firm religious foundation for his united state. As Napoleon
inspired the federation of the German states, the Philistines had
roused the Hebrews to the advantages of unity, to the centrali-
zation of their kingdom which, even if it was of a comparatively
short duration, gave the Hebrews time and occasion to crystallize
their religious tradition before it was passed on to others. The
new king had little time for the beautification of his capital; he
was kept busy extending the borders of his kingdom, cementing
its bonds within, and settling the differences of his own family.
He was extremely cruel to the Amalekites, the Moabites, and
others; he deliberately planned the death of a man whose wife
eventually became the mother of David's successor; fortunately
for him, there was no one except Yahweh to punish him, yet we
must admit he showed genuine repentance for his misdeeds,
and there were times when he was as indulgent toward others
as to himself. The fact that he never raised himself beyond the
jurisdiction and criticism of religious authority and the prophets
is one good reason for his continued popularity with the people,

but, as we have seen from our study of Egypt and Mesopotamia, this was not a unique situation in the Near East.[20]

Wtih all his foresightedness and diplomacy, David, well aware of his own humble origin, was unable to resist the luxuries, the temptations of the harem, which figured so much in the choosing of his heir. The harem meant intrigues within the family circle; it meant rival divinities brought in by women from foreign lands; it also meant the chosen heir would have trouble with other ambitious applicants to the throne. Moreover, Solomon, the son of David and Bathsheba, was born and nurtured in the palace, in the midst of its luxury, and so came into prominence with far different antecedents from those of his father, Saul, and other Hebrew leaders. Solomon became an international figure by dealing on the diplomatic plane with Egypt, Tyre, and other powers not mentioned by name. The tentacles of his trade routes reached far and wide; he took advantage of his central position on the crossroads between east and west; he made trade agreements with many of his neighbors (the meeting with the queen of Sheba was probably the occasion for such an agreement); he also took pains to develop the natural resources of his own land. Archaeology has uncovered a great number of copper mines on the east side of the Jordan as well as elaborate smelting furnaces at Ezion-geber,[21] a seaport on the Gulf of Aqaba, built up by the king himself. But all this was hardly sufficient to defray the costs of an expensive court, a growing international harem, and a large building program for which he had to levy steadily increasing taxes. Fortunately, his father had left him a kingdom in good shape from a military standpoint. Solomon himself developed quite a reputation for wisdom, while the lavishness of his court life must have dazzled many of his countrymen, and the building of the temple must have been highly

---

20. I do not believe the privilege of the prophets to criticise the monarchy argues in favor of genuine democracy among the Hebrews; excessive individualism, as in modern Germany, may be very damaging to the prospect of democracy in government. Cf. W. O. E. Oesterley and T. H. Robinson: *op. cit.*, Vol. I, p. 228.

21. N. Glueck: *op. cit.*, pp. 89 ff.

flattering to the priests and devotees of Yahweh. But under cover all was not so promising: the foreign women and the strange gods they brought to Jerusalem, the expenses which gradually sapped the resources of the land, the *corvée* imposed on all citizens were endured only as long as the son of David sat upon the throne; his successor, Rehoboam, was too weak to keep the kingdom united.

It had long been recognized that the union of north and south had never been too stable, that an eventual separation was inevitable because of the differences in cultural backgrounds. Furthermore, an independent Hebrew kingdom was made possible only at this time when the empire of Egypt had fallen on evil days and Assyria was not yet strong enough to assert her power in Syria. The northern rulers established their residence at Samaria, their religious centers at Dan and Bethel, and in this new kingdom foreign influences, already obvious in the capital of Solomon, grew more and more prominent.[22] The whole period was one of general attrition, when the two kingdoms, Israel and Judah, were waging exhausting wars with their neighbors, the most powerful of which was Damascus, and with each other. Those kings remaining faithful to the covenant were commended in the Biblical accounts, while those paying tribute to the heathen gods were passed over with little notice; thus, prominent rulers in Israel, e.g., Omri, were hardly recognized. When certain rulers betrayed a moral weakness or gave way to foreigners at court, it was the prophet who stood forth in the name of Yahweh to prick the conscience of the people and defy the temporal ruler; the period boasted such magnetic personalities as Elijah, Elisha, Isaiah, Hosea, and Amos. It was also a time when women like Jezebel and Athaliah played prominent roles in political and religious intrigues. Eventually the Assyrians appeared on the scene, sacked Samaria in 721 B.C., and carried off large numbers to Mesopotamia, replacing them with newcomers from the east in accordance with a policy instituted by Tiglath-Pilezer. Judah

---

22. W. F. Albright: *From the Stone Age to Christianity*, Baltimore, 1940, pp. 229-30.

survived the fall of Assyria, although Sennacherib laid waste many of the cities around Jerusalem before he was obliged to withdraw; in this crisis Isaiah displayed more political insight than the ruler. In the following century it was Jeremiah who attempted to guide the foreign policy of Judah but failed to persuade the pro-Egyptian party to refrain from rebelling against Chaldea; in 587 B.C. Jerusalem fell a sad victim to Nebuchadnezzar, who took a large number of Hebrews back to Babylon.

While any form of foreign domination would have been unpleasant for the Hebrews, their stay in Babylon was not altogether disagreeable. Their king was not put to death but allowed to live in some mild form of confinement. Some of his subjects tilled the soil, some dwelt in the cities where they became wealthy traders, some undoubtedly suffered more extreme forms of slavery. Whatever their condition, however, a general nostalgia pervaded the whole people, urging some to return to their homeland, while others wanted, at least, to see Jerusalem rebuilt and the center of Yahweh's worship established again. The prophets Deutero-Isaiah and Ezekiel took on an attitude different from that of their predecessors: now that this people was undergoing its due punishment at the hands of their own God, there was no further use of chiding; they comforted the people with the messages and visions of a merciful God who would eventually mend their fortunes. About the exiles of the northern kingdom of Israel, now biding their time in Assyria, nothing was reported, but the Hebrews of Babylon seemed charitable enough to hope for a future reunion.[23] In the meantime the population in Palestine was so decimated and disheartened that little resistance could be mustered against invading tribes from Transjordan. Jerusalem had been destroyed, the temple sacked, and the sacred vessels taken to Babylon—she was a lonesome ruin cowering against the barren sky. A political center was set up first at Mizpah, later at Jerusalem under the control of Gedaliah, a Hebrew enjoying the confidence of Nebuchadnezzar. When this viceroy was treacherously slain, a number

---

23. Cf. *Ezekiel,* XXXVI:15 ff.

of Hebrew leaders, fearing reprisals from Babylon, fled to
Egypt. Jeremiah, still a figure to be reckoned with, was forced
to accompany the fugitives. Nothing, however, came of the inci-
dent except Nebuchadnezzar's campaign against Egypt, which
met with little success.

The next event of primary significance for the Hebrews was
the capture of Babylon by Cyrus the Great in 539 B.C. Soon
thereafter a large number of exiles were permitted to return
to Judah[24] in accordance with the lenient policy of the Persians
toward minority groups; but many chose to remain by the waters
of Babylon, content to contribute financially to the undertaking.
In the homeland all was by no means rosy for the returned exiles:
the country was a desolate waste, there were internal differences
to cope with, and the governor of Samaria, which included Jerusalem, opposed the fortification of the city and the rebuilding
of the temple. Under Haggai and Zacharaiah the sacred building
was eventually put up before Nehemiah, and later Ezra, appeared on the scene, armed with royal prerogative from the
court, to grant the people full protection in their undertakings
and to establish Yahwism on a firm basis. The new state achieved
a respectable autonomy under the priesthood, which lasted until
the Seleucids interfered. Greek influence became more and more
pronounced, bringing with it a rift between Sadducees and
Pharisees, because the former were inclined to compromise with
Hellenic ways of thinking.

After the partition of Alexander's empire the Seleucids regarded the Hebrew state as an upstart, insubordinate kingdom,
but they also underestimated its capacity for resistance. Caught
in the midst of a struggle between the Ptolemies and Seleucids
for the possession of Syria, harassed within by a conflict between
those favoring Greek ideals and those who believed they were
supporting the Mosaic tradition, the pious, conservative Hebrews
found themselves pressed against the wall. Once more, in a
contest against great odds, they displayed a stubborn and
vigorous resistance. The Maccabees and their followers took to

24. *Ezra*, I:2–4.

the hills and caves whence they dealt with their enemies much as their forefathers had with the Philistine menace. They depended at first on the element of surprise, on the sudden sortie from under cover; later they were numerous and strong enough to engage large towns or to face an invading force. The fanatical fierceness of their rebellion coupled with the increasing weakness of the Seleucid empire crowned the Maccabees with unlooked-for success, giving the Hebrews an independent state of their own which maintained an unstable position until the coming of the Romans. By dint of a fanatical courage against military opposition, by matching wits against the greatest masters of intrigue, the family of the Maccabees was able to stave off one threat after another.

Family dissension at the court finally invited the interference of the Romans, who found the situation in Syria made to order for the addition of another lucrative province. This meant the end of independence for the Hebrews and brought the overthrow of the Ptolemaic and Seleucid dynasties. Had the Hebrews not constantly chafed under the domination of the Roman eagles and had the Roman generals and governors been more tactful in dealing with Hebrew religious sensibilities, relations between lord and subject might have run as smoothly as during the Persian regime. There was no excuse for Pompey's intrusion in the holy of holies; there was little call for repeated greedy extortion on the part of conniving tax collectors. The Hebrews, on their side, were unable to control the fanatical zealots in their midst, who threw all discretion to the winds in their conviction that Yahweh, wielding the sword of divine retribution, would somehow intervene in their behalf to shake off the yoke of the Roman. Herod, by astute diplomacy, was able to rule precariously over an enlarged kingdom, in spite of the hatred of his own people and the constant intrigues of his family. The tactlessness of such men as Pilate and Florus and the impatience of Hebrew fanaticism finally snapped the thin cord of harmony between the two parties of the state, bringing the hard-fisted Flavians with a strong army before the walls of Jerusalem in 70 A.D. After five months of desperate fighting and rigorous hardship,

the city was completely devastated [25] and the sacred utensils
of the temple were carried off to Rome to enhance the triumphal
procession of Titus. Only a scattered remnant of Hebrews remained in the scarred homeland.

The dispersion of this people, already initiated in 586 B.C.,
now spread over the entire Mediterranean region, but their
greatest contribution to western civilization was yet to achieve
its most crowning success. The spiritual leaven thus brought
to Europe was a by-product of a serious consciousness, whose
value we have not yet learned to appreciate in the measure
of its full significance.

The monotheism of the Hebrew religion, which is one of its
most distinctive features, has no striking analogy in the religion
of her nearest neighbors. The universalizing tendencies of the
Babylonian worshipper [26] are syncretistic in character and tend
only to burden the central divinity with parasitic dependents;
here is nothing of the distinctive "oneness" which, instead of
subordinating, absorbs or obliterates any potential rival. The god
of Akhenaton was too earthy, too pantheistic to furnish much
inspiration for the sublime concept of a single godhead that
stands aloof, for the most part, from his own creation. Neither
of the older civilizations to the east and west produced a divinity
so exclusive of rivalry, so jealous of his prerogative, so aloof
from the earth and man and at the same time so personal in his
relationship to the worshipper. If we turn to Canaan, we can find
analogies in worship but little association on the divine level.
Thanks to the excavations at Ras Shamra we now know something about their pantheon and mythology. The greatest of their
gods is El, his consort Ashirat. Baal, represented as a god of
storm and wind and often called the king of the gods, is the hero
of their ritual drama celebrating the appropriate movements of

---

25. Josephus (*Bellum Judaicum*, VI, 3) gives a lurid account of the
straits of the besieged.

26. W. F. Albright: *From the Stone Age to Christianity*, Baltimore,
1940, pp. 164-5.

the seasonal cycle.[27] This god is slain by Mot, the god of death, who in turn is slain by Anath, by whom Baal is once more revived. The emphasis here laid on fertility is to be expected in an agricultural community, but the worship of such gods, representing the phenomena of the Canaanite's experience, was strongly opposed by the orthodox Hebrew, whose God reveals more of the background of the nomad of the desert.

Before the Hebrews settled down to till the land, they wandered about as clans or tribes under the leadership of a patriarch; this leader was responsible to a god with whom he had established a personal contact. He functioned, then, as a final authority in matters of religion; he was the priest representing his people in the presence of their god. There were doubtless many such gods among the early Semitic nomads of the desert, and Yahweh was almost certainly a descendent of such a tribal divinity, a fact which may account for his personal character. Some are of the conviction that he was originally a mountain god,[28] others think of him as an ancient storm god, but since one aspect is not exclusive of the other, why not call him a storm god dwelling on the mountain (Enlil as a storm god issued forth from the mountain)? The storm god also controls lightning and fire, which he uses to strike terror into the hearts of his subjects, and if Yahweh was such a god, his attributes were carried down to the days of the exodus and thence to the later kingdom of Palestine. Another plausible interpretation makes him primarily a "speaking" god, whose voice spoke from an oracle.[29] Whatever the original nature of Yahweh was to the wandering tribes of the desert, all of which must be based on conjecture, we must be ready to admit that something remarkable happened to this divinity when Moses came into the picture, a fact supported by every line of Hebrew tradition throughout the people's history. Who was this Moses and whence did he come? His name is not

---

27. T. H. Gaster (*Thespis,* New York, 1950, p. 133) has translated this story from the tablets found at Ras Shamra.

28. T. J. Meek: *op. cit.,* p. 95.

29. R. N. Bowman: *Journal of Near Eastern Studies* III, 1944, pp. 1–8.

enough to make him an Egyptian,[30] and his monotheism and all
that goes with it is so different from a possible Egyptian proto-
type that a comparison yields small satisfaction.[31] Whatever his
background, it is certain he was a man of strong personality who
functioned as the leader of the people and a mediator in the
presence of Yahweh, one with more old tribal affinities than
Egyptian associations; hence it may be a matter of some consequence to know something about the man Moses, but it is still
more important to know what happened to the Hebrew god after
the exodus from Egypt. Yahweh's direct antecedent is generally
agreed to be the tribal god of the Kenites (Midianites), the
people from whom Moses chose his wife. Beyond the general
attributes already mentioned we know little that is specific about
him, but we do have a rich tradition about his reformation in
the hands of Moses.[32]

First and foremost, Yahweh became the one and only God
of his people, absorbing all the important prerogatives of other
tribal divinities and including in his supervision all the aspects
of man's experience. He was also jealous enough of his position
to forbid the worship of any other rival; what's more, there was
no family triad, no consort associated with him, although he was
always referred to as a male and his own people were often called,
in a figurative sense, the children of God. It is hardly possible
that, throughout the history of the Hebrews, there was not an
awareness of the existence of other gods beyond their borders,
but Yahweh was certainly the nearest approach to a purely monotheistic divinity in the history of religion. Much of his importance
also lies in his personal nature: he could think and feel, grow
angry and show mercy, reward and chastise, rejoice and grieve
over his people, not merely out of some wayward expression of

---

30. S. Freud (*Moses and Monotheism* (Trans. by Katherine Jones),
New York, 1939, p. 39) calls him an Egyptian who brought Akhenaton's
monotheism to the Hebrews. Freud himself seems to realize that the evidence for his theory is bound together with a number of thin threads.

31. If Moses was a former follower of Akhenaton, what happened to
the divinity of the ruler, of which there is no trace in Hebrew history?

32. Cf. A. Guillaume: *Prophecy and Divination*, New York, 1938, p. 99.

expediency but as an earthly father with intimate ties to his family—all on a sublime level. He was as high as the heavens above, as ubiquitous and pervading as the air one breathes, yet, like a bell tolling over foggy waters, his still, small voice issued from a definite seat of authority with a pointed message to the heart of every man. The Norse Heimdal, perched on a peak of gray eminence, listened suspiciously to the growing of grass and wool as he stood guard against the coming of the giants. As a divine personality and creator of his world Yahweh was able to see and hear, to be aware of anything that transpired far and near, because everything came within the sympathetic sphere of his influence, everything was somehow comprised in the control of his unified interest. It was easier to commune with such a god, to achieve self-identification with his personality than with a more impersonal Egyptian or Mesopotamian divinity, and at the same time his personal awareness of all words and actions made Yahweh at times more frightening in his manifestations.

And here we find the most progressive contribution of the Hebrew to religion: the personal attachment between the worshipper and his god created a moral relationship between the two, a bond such as we might expect from an obedient, respectful son and a father who knows when to punish and condone. Instead of approaching one another in the spirit of expedient exploitation congenial to the deceitful devices of the magician, in lieu of an attitude of mutual distrust, in place of the vague intangibility facing the worshipper of the Chinese heaven, there was a fair exchange between both parties in a spirit of full confidence that the terms of an agreement would be held in honor. The agreement took the form of a contract or covenant.[33] Here Yahweh pledged himself to guide and protect his people as long as they kept his commandments; if they should violate the agreement he would put aside his loving-kindness and deal with them in terms of strict justice. The fact that the Almighty, of his own free will, had chosen the Hebrews as his special people both encouraged their confidence in him and magnified their feeling

---

33. *Exodus*, XXXIV:10.

of self-importance.[34] Man's respect for this being was increased
also because his presence was neither limited to a manifestation
of nature nor was his power restricted to a single natural phenomenon. We read, of course, of the presence of Yahweh in the
pillar of fire and in the cloud, but he was not limited by the
cloud or fire; he could make himself known to the people in a
visible manifestation, but he was never either cloud or fire; he
dominated nature without being identified with its substance.[35]

Man could, then, approach his god in spirit and in truth at
any time, in any place, in accordance with the terms laid down
in the covenant. The approach was made so much easier because
Yahweh transcended nature and at the same time maintained
his domination over nature and its cyclical movements. It enabled
him to speak directly to the human heart without resorting to
any medium of interpretation, without the need of showing the
effects of his power over nature. To maintain respect for such a
lofty concept of divinity must have been difficult in the early
days of Hebrew history, but once the individual was aware of
its pre-eminent value it was most reassuring in times of distress
or persecution; it also required a long process of education to
learn how to measure up to Yahweh's standards. This was the
great task of Moses and his followers.

How, then, did the average Hebrew think of his divinity? It
goes without saying that he pictured him as anthropomorphic,
very much as he was represented by the later Renaissance
painters, as inadequate as such an image may be to express lofty
divine attributes.[36] It is significant that nowhere in the Old
Testament do we find an attempt to describe Yahweh in concrete terms. He speaks to a number of individuals—from a cloud,
out of the whirlwind, in the cool of the day, out of the night—

---

34. It is to the credit of Freud (*op. cit.*, p. 67) that he stresses this
particular point.

35. There was no reason why the spirit of divinity should make any
concessions to the limitations of nature. Cf. H. Frankfort: *Kingship and
the Gods*, Chicago, 1948, p. 6.

36. Cf. J. Muilenburg in *The Interpreter's Bible*, New York, 1952,
Vol. I, p. 302.

the voice comes from everywhere and nowhere, from the spirit to the spirit. The nearest we come to a concrete image is the revelation of God's glory to Moses in Exodus 33:23: "And I will take away mine hand, and thou shalt see my back parts; but my face shall not be seen." Nothing, however, follows in the way of a description of the "parts" of God. The latter could no longer have retained the attribute of holiness for the Hebrew had he appeared as a man wielding a thunderbolt, much less in the guise of a fish or a crocodile.

It was just this general aspect of a single God, so general that men of all stations in life could find self-identification in his presence, as well as his personality that made the Hebrew Yahweh a unique contribution to man's religious striving, a fact which helps us to appreciate why the holy men of God insisted on his aniconic character, forbidding the fashioning of a graven image as a desecration to God's being. An image would only tend to localize Yahweh in time and space, it would tend to detract from him as a responsible personality capable of projecting his presence into night or day or anywhere a worshipper might call on him. Since, then, he was a personality both holy and omnipresent, he was also omniscient. Small wonder man hesitated to circumvent his God by resorting to the expedient devices of magic!

It was not sufficient for an omniscient divinity to know everything that transpired in his universe with equal concern; it was above all necessary to be a knowing personality who would, of his own free will, focus most of his attention upon his people, like a father with a broad awareness of many events and people, who attends to his child with special concern. Without this personal knowledge and concentration on the part of his God the worshipper would tend to lose his identity, like a man floundering in mid-ocean, in such a vast scope of knowing; he wanted to be more than a mere object of common concern in God's broad perspective. As a man was partial in worshipping one God, he expected the latter to return the compliment. Yahweh, as a personality, was also just and merciful, and justice was something more than the Egyptian *ma'at* or the Chinese harmony; it was a moral concept demanding responsibility on the part of both parties entering on a contract. Mercy, also a rarity among early theologies, implies a personal attachment between God the father and his chosen children; man is no longer a slave of divinity but a creature made in the image of God. At this point a question comes to mind: was the Hebrew totally oblivious of the paradoxes involved in reconciling an almighty, omniscient God with the creation of an imperfect man in an imperfect world, of the embarrassing position of a good God fathering an evil world, of the inherent contradiction contained in a God of mercy and justice? So far as literature tells the story, the Hebrew was not concerned with the rational implications and solutions of such problems; Job hurls a few pointed questions at the ramparts of heaven but is quickly squelched by the overwhelming presence of God. In general, the Hebrew was quite willing to leave the solution of these problems to God, who had elected his own people and created the world as it is; instead of asking for a rational explanation he put his faith in a God whose ways were past finding out and who had done all things well.

Those authorities who lay an emphasis on the emergence of monotheism in the age of the prophets and those who stress a gradual development from a primitive polytheism have not, it seems to us, considered the impact of a long period in the desert on the psychology of the individual. There is a sameness about such a landscape which negates the varied phenomena of either a pastoral environment or an agricultural community; the latter is especially conducive to a polytheistic pantheon of nature divinities. The sand of the desert stretches out to the horizon, the one firm line of separation between sky and earth. The broad expanses of space, the empty vistas, added to the silence and loneliness of such a panorama, encourage contemplation; the sameness of so much on all sides would naturally make the infinite a living reality reaching way beyond as well as into experience, even lead one to trust in a single divine force behind all things visible. Added to all this is the bright light of the stars hanging down almost within reach of the distant mountains, the apparently short distance between earth and sky, the divinity who bids his subject, "Be still and know that I am God," manifesting his power most convincingly when he stirs up the wind and sand with blinding devastation. The privation and despair, the solitude and changelessness of the desert demand a powerful divinity who can establish a direct line of communication with his worshippers, unhampered by limitations imposed by other divine spirits.

Once the single divinity was firmly established, once other gods were put aside, we can hardly expect that the temporal power could stand on an equal footing with Yahweh. The government of the Hebrews is generally called a theocracy, one in which God wields the supreme power, the ruler simply carrying out his mandates in the state, which also means that, as the laws of the covenant derived their authority from Yahweh at Sinai, so the ruler received his rights in the state from on high.[37] God spoke directly to the human heart, thereby singling out first, leaders like Moses and Joshua, then to the prophets, and also the kings. There were times, of course, when he spoke to other leaders, like Samuel, who then carried out his injunction, but in each case it was God's voice bypassing natural phenomena to communicate directly with the spirit. This way of choosing a leader directly was, of course, inconsistent with the custom prevalent in the Near East of passing the kingship from father to son, and the adoption of this latter custom by the Hebrews was inevitable once the kingdom was established firmly enough to encourage diplomatic relations with neighboring powers; undoubtedly this change was one reason for the constant friction between the temporal ruler and the prophet. Theoretically, succession should have remained spiritual instead of physical, which means that, in practice, the king should have been chosen by a holy man like Samuel. As feasible as this may have been for the Hebrews, we can hardly regard a domination by the spiritual authority over the temporal ruler, any more than the absolutism

---

37. Cf. G. E. Wright in *The Interpreter's Bible,* New York, 1952, Vol. I, p. 356.

of an independent monarch, as an encouragement to the democratic way of life in a civilized community.

As lofty as such a divinity was, as far as he was removed
from identification with the phenomena of experience, he still
took on varied aspects to answer to occasional needs in the
history of the people. During the period of invasion he was
primarily a God of war and leader of the Hebrews in battle, a
rock of defense, a destroyer of fortifications, a master of strategy;
on occasion he resorted, as in Jericho, to the tactics of the fifth
column. Once the victory was won, a battle hymn was sung in
his honor.[38] After the Promised Land was in the hands of the
invader and national unity had been achieved, Yahweh's war-
like attributes faded into the background. His attachment to a
chosen people made of him, generally speaking, a God of
nationalism, a trait which absorbed his personality more and
more as long as foreign religions or military pressure threatened
to make inroads on his prerogative. To such a God Ezra made
his appeal when he plucked out his beard and tore his raiment
at the sight of certain defections among the people.[39] We see its
influence in the prophet Joel, especially when Hellenic culture
was making so many converts; it continued all the way through
the wars of the Maccabees; though Yahweh himself is not mentioned in the book of Esther, the spirit of nationalism stands
behind the glorification of the Hebrews and the wholesale
slaughter of their enemies. To some degree this was compensated
for by a Yahweh of broad, international sympathies, a God who
included other peoples within the range of his justice and mercy.
Amos was an outstanding example of this more humane attitude;[40] another is found in the book of Jonah, a fanatical nation-
alist who refused to include the Ninevites in the program of
God's salvation until the latter constrained him to preach in their
midst and learn a sound lesson from the gourd vine.

The worship of Yahweh was much more simple than that of

---

38. *Exodus*, XV, 3; *Judges* V, 2.

39. *Ezra*, XII, 13–15.

40. W. A. Irwin in *The Intellectual Adventure of Ancient Man*, Chicago,
1946, p. 226.

other eastern divinities, because ritual, sacrifice, and prayer, although they were a part of the Hebrew service, were not directly concerned with concrete benefits to be derived from the fertility of the soil and therefore not so compelling in their magical cogency. Man was expected to worship a spiritual God in spirit and in truth, a personal divinity who would hear the plea of his subject, regardless of conditions in time and space. A single divinity, omniscient and omnipresent, maintained a close spiritual contact with the petitioner; neither the depths of earth or sea nor even the belly of the whale could escape his divine awareness. Obedience to the commands of God, contained in the apodictic laws, must also be included in Hebrew worship, for they are the kernel of the covenant handed down through Moses on Sinai. Yahweh was both near and far, he could see and hear all, which means that the everyday practice of the individual was under the constant surveillance of his God. For this type of worship there was no absolute need for a priest or special symbols in ritual, and as Yahweh, speaking in a still but insistent voice, was fearful in his retributions and lovable in his mercy, the Hebrew was expected to fear and love him as an all-pervading presence, according to the dictates of his conscience and his merits as a worshipper.

There were also visible tokens to remind man of God's role in the history of his people, tokens that gave concrete testimony to God's presence in all the vicissitudes of fortune. The ark of the covenant, a chest built of acacia wood, was an object of the greatest veneration, dating back to the original promise of God, which explains why it was carried along in the wanderings through the wilderness, why it accompanied them into the battles of the invasion; when it was captured by the Philistines, the Hebrews were especially depressed because, as they believed, the face of God was turned away from them. Nothing parallel to it was known to the Canaanites,[41] hence it must be regarded as a survival of nomadic life. Another object of greater dimensions

----

41. Cf. W. F. Albright: *From the Stone Age to Christianity,* Baltimore, 1940, p. 203.

was the tabernacle, which may originally have been a tent, but according to the description in Exodus 25:10 ff. it was a more elaborate, four-sided structure containing two compartments. Three of the side walls were of wood, the fourth draped with a curtain, the two sections of the interior again divided by a curtain. The outer compartment was reserved for the priests, the inner room being denied to all except the high priest who entered it but once a year. Inside the holy of holies was the ark of the covenant and in the adjoining chamber were the table of the shewbread, the golden candlestick, and the altar of incense; around the outside was a court to which the people in general had access. Difficult as it may seem, the whole tabernacle, we are told, was transported from place to place and eventually into Palestine. This structure containing the ark was accounted especially sacred because here, more frequently than elsewhere, Yahweh's presence was projected into the midst of the people, and his presence could be both comforting in time of distress and awful in its majesty.

Once the Hebrew had gained a foothold across the Jordan a permanent shrine for cult objects was established at Shiloh whence the tabernacle was later removed to the temple of Solomon. After the division of the kingdom two new shrines were set up by Jeroboam I at Bethel and Dan; other subordinate sanctuaries were located at Hebron, Gilgal, Beersheba, and Ophrah. The temple of Solomon was modeled after Syrian prototypes, for the Hebrews had no architectural tradition in their background; but the holy of holies contained no image. This elaborate structure was destroyed by the Chaldeans, and no attempt was made to replace it until the captives returned from Babylon, when another temple was built by Zerubbabel, on a modest scale compared to the glory of Herod's later achievement under Roman patronage.[42] The building of a large, central shrine in the capital city of Jerusalem had one effect on Hebrew religion, namely, a tendency to cast a shadow of state authority

---

42. For the archaeological remains on the site consult J. Finegan: *Light from the Ancient Past,* Princeton, 1946, pp. 243–48.

over that of the priesthood, a threat which contributed to calling forth a strong challenge from the prophets by way of compensation. Though sacrifice and ritual were not stressed as necessary assets in the worship of Yahweh, they were now developed on a more elaborate scale and influenced, to a large extent, by Canaanite customs; the building of the temple also gave room for ritual requirements recorded in the book of Moses but dating from the time of Solomon.

It is very doubtful that sacrifice, especially that of animals, meant as much to the Hebrew as to their contemporaries beyond their borders; it is hard to think of Yahweh on the level with Greek or Mesopotamian gods enjoying the odor of burning fat on the altar. The custom of blood sacrifice, of course, is an old one, common to all the peoples of the neolithic age who earned their living by agriculture, and while the Hebrews learned much about it from the Canaanites, there are also reminiscences of human sacrifice in the Scriptures, e.g., Abraham and Isaac and Jephthah's daughter, a practice going back to an earlier stage of blood-offering. There was a feeling of communion and self-identification with divinity at the sacrificial meal, but as Yahweh was on a higher plane than Zeus or Enlil, so the whole procedure was eventually placed on a higher plane of symbolism.

Between man and God there were two human media, namely, the priest and the prophet, and these too in spite of the emphasis on a direct means of communication between Yahweh and his worshipper. It seems that priests had always been in charge of the worship of Yahweh, but only after the establishment of the sanctuary at Shiloh did the priesthood become synonymous with the Levites. The priest was a holy person consecrated to the service of God, the only man permitted to handle the sacred vessels and to represent the people in the presence of Yahweh; he supervised all the sacrifices and kept the records of the past which included the covenant, the laws, the historical chronicles, and other literature; he is also referred to as a diviner,[43] which

---

43. Cf. J. Muilenburg in *The Interpreter's Bible,* New York, 1952, Vol. I, p. 346.

means he sought to probe into and reveal the will of God, a function undoubtedly going back to primitive magic. Without being as colorful as the prophet, he was still a figure of authority in matters of religion as well as a molder of tradition; he was also more responsible than anyone for the increased emphasis on ritual and ceremony.

The prophet, while often reckoned as opposed to the priesthood, was actually its opponent only during periods when the latter followed secular authority in giving way to the worship of foreign gods. It may very well be that prophets played a role in the religious life of the Canaanites before the coming of the Hebrews,[44] and something of the same element is found in the religious expression of other peoples, e.g., the Dionysiac movement, but the prophet of the Hebrews looms up in much bolder relief because he stands on a high moral plane: he is a seer, an orator, and a guardian of pure religion as it penetrated every aspect of living. The prophet was not merely the sponsor of an occasional emotional catharsis, he reflected the justice and mercy of Yahweh in every thought, word, and deed. In a number of cases he was associated with the miraculous and other trappings of the magician, but the significance of his message lies less in the length and breadth of practical benefits than in the height and grandeur of the good life. Elijah descends upon the priests of Baal like a Titan armed with elemental weapons, his courage in the face of Jezebel's religious incursion is overwhelming, but his merit and integrity stand out in boldest relief when he defends the right of the common man against the monarch Ahab. Amos and Hosea, without the flash of Titanic brilliance, come from the ranks of the lowly to preach a doctrine of social reform. Amos, looking out over an international perspective, berates all the children of Yahweh for excessive indulgence in luxuries to the detriment of the oppressed poorer classes and the neglect of those moral standards which Yahweh laid down as part of the original covenant. Hosea lends his appeal a compelling force

---

44. Cf. W. O. E. Oesterley & T. H. Robinson: *op. cit.*, Vol. I, p. 179.

by drawing on a parallel from his own life with his wayward Gomer; his preaching of a merciful God was powerfully reinforced by his own example. Isaiah, the aristocrat, is a prophet of doom and judgement for those who have abandoned the precepts of Yahweh, for he sees in the advancing Assyrians the instrument of God's awful vengeance. Jeremiah was the poet of the inner man, of a heavy, brooding temperament, expressively portrayed by Michelangelo in the Sistine Chapel; he was also, as subsequent events revealed, a man of penetrating political insight. Although Ezekiel, the visionary, realizes how great is the sin of his people, he brings a message of eventual forgiveness and hope for the future. The most constructive and historically minded is the second Isaiah looking ahead to the new exodus from Babylon, the new covenant of Yahweh with all nations.

The majority of these men preached a religion such as the Hebrews had known in the days of their desert wanderings, a personal relationship with Yahweh uncontaminated with the fertility cults of Canaan. They also lived a seminomadic existence, rushing forth from the desert with the fury of a demon and returning to the solitudes again for communion with Yahweh, for spiritual regeneration; here the silence, the sameness of their surroundings was more conducive to the ecstatic experience. They were not, of course, trying to bring the people back to the desert but to preserve the primacy of a single God's role in history and human affairs, compared to which the cults of the heathen were not only morally degenerate but petty. It is only natural for the reader to ask the following questions: Was the prophet barking up a tree? Were there no followers of these men left in the days of the two kingdoms? Here it would be well to remember that, as in so many modern sermons, the sinner received the greatest publicity while the faithful, few as they may have been in number, were silently taken for granted.

It remains to say something about angels as the ministers of Yahweh. Such beings were mentioned in the older tradition (Genesis 6:1–4) but not organized into hierarchies; in general, the angelic host was regarded as an extension of Yahweh's personality. Once in contact with Canaanites and Hellenic peoples, angels took on an individual and distinctive role, moving about between heaven and earth as the Almighty's heralds. The Persians also influenced the Hebrews by reducing to a concrete basis such concepts as archangel, Satan, and the last judgment.[45] Much the same course of development may be seen in the emergence of the idea of afterlife: the worshipper of Yahweh was generally content to leave his future destiny in the hands of his God; the Hebrew living under Saul or David would have considered Vergil's Hades and Dante's Inferno a form of blasphemy.

Unlike the Egyptian and Mesopotamian languages, Hebrew gave the modern scholar little trouble in deciphering its content because its historical continuity was not broken off in favor of another tongue. Hebrew, like Aramaic, belongs to the Semitic family of languages and is therefore closely related to Akkadian and Arabic. It was not originally used by the Hebrews, to whom Aramaic was native during the nomadic stages of their history, but once settled in Palestine they took over this rather hybrid tongue from the Canaanites and made it their own, a phenomenon we have already witnessed in Sumeria. After the destruction of Jerusalem by the Chaldeans the language of the people, because of imported newcomers from the east, became predominantly Aramaic, but Hebrew remained and still is the language medium of the priestly class and the educated people for two reasons: first, the Scriptures were recorded in that medium, and secondly, literature was the one major art of this people. Their Scriptures contain every category of Near Eastern literature, and that too in greater richness and variety than anything we have found in Egyptian and Mesopotamian writings: the myth of origins, history, the law both casuistic and apodictic, the proverb, the sad song, the hedonistic song, the hymn, the lyric, and fiction. The preaching or oratory of the prophet is more peculiar to the expression of the Hebrew.

---

45. W. F. Albright: *From the Stone Age to Christianity*, Baltimore, 1940, pp. 278–9.

The records contained in their literature from the first book of Moses to the end of Kings II may be called Hebrew history, although we cannot think of it as history in our sense of the term. Much of it is purely legendary, portions have been borrowed from the literature of other peoples, and even the account of David's career, which must have been familiar to the writer, is far from what we should call a scientific treatment. Hebrew history is a compilation by a number of writers who had no respect for our rule against plagiarism and had no laws of copyright to contend with. The Hebrew writer and reader were not as much concerned with the style and personality of the author as with the figures of their subject matter and with the carrying out of God's program in history, for man's relation to God was of a paramount importance, whereas man's relation to events merely served as a by-product in the expression of God's will. Like others who preceded him, the Hebrew had little respect for the foreigner, perhaps because his own writing was predominantly religious and therefore a subjective record of Yahweh's chosen people, but his history was an advance in that it was teleological, it moved on with a definite purpose in view, which meant a broader perspective over the past and future; the emphasis on the cyclical processes of nature made the present more sufficient for the Egyptian and Mesopotamian. The Hebrew's chronological sequence of events is vague and disconcerting to the modern analyst, but the role of God guiding his people through the vicissitudes of time and space is quite clear, and God speaks to his people not so much in terms of man's relation to circumstances as through the inner man.

At the beginning of recorded history Egypt and Babylon had already arrived at such a pinnacle of self-esteem they were able to declare their gods had been created from the rudimentary elements of chaos, and subsequently they had subjected them to the intimidating devices of magic. The Hebrew, by clothing his divinity in greater dignity, where magic could not so easily reach him, also raised himself to a higher level of moral integrity. In the beginning of creation there was chaos, of course, but there was also an omnipotent, eternal God who transcended the limitations of time and space, who was the master of chaos and all its potentialities. In the creation story, events move on to their fulfillment with an awesome finality against a background as severe and revealing as that of Michelangelo on the Sistine ceiling. The overwhelming solemnity of God's word and movement reverberates through the void with a startling momentum—the creation of light, the imposing of limitations, the birth of sun, moon, and stars, the animals, and finally, man. This man is not to be a mere slave of divinity; he is made in the image of Yahweh, which means he is a personality of dignity; he has been granted privileges, given a helpmate, he is the lord of all creatures on earth, the garden is his kingdom; he also has responsibilities to his maker and to other creatures. As an independent character he is given a choice, he has the right to make a decision, and when that decision turns out to be a bad one, he must take the consequences. Above all, he is a personality standing out in bold relief, big in his words and actions whether he is the recipient of God's mercy or the victim of his wrath.

While all events are firmly grounded in experience and so cannot be put down as bald contradictions or distortions, the guiding hand of Yahweh raises them to a level of transcendence where characters move as divine symbols, lending an exalted significance to what otherwise might be a mere matter-of-fact statement or an etiological explanation of tradition or folklore. The story of Cain and Abel is, first of all, representative of the eternal rivalry between the nomad and the man of the soil, versions of which are popular in eastern literature. For the Hebrews it was, specifically, a contest between the settled Baal-worshipping Canaanites and their own people; it might also be regarded as an allegory of the fundamental difference between the contemplative child of the eastern desert and the active apostle of technological progress.[46] The moral overtones, however, foreshadow one of the lessons of the law of Exodus, a lesson which reaches its most articulate expression in St. Paul's "the wages of sin is death." Our writer also leaned heavily on

---

46. The descendants of Cain were great craftsmen (Cf. D. B. MacDonald: *The Hebrew Literary Genius,* Princeton, 1933, p. 112).

foreign sources for the story of the flood, at the same time making it an example of God's inevitable retribution for sin, and therefore, in contrast to the Greek and Babylonian versions, the main character plays a role which has meaning for the whole future history of the Hebrews and their neighbors. There follows then the fantastic tale of the Tower of Babel to account for later differences in tradition, speech, color, etc. The moral turn given here to the ziggurat of Babylon reminds us of the Greek *hybris*, but here we can be sure that a different viewpoint reflects another meaning into the picture—here a personal, wrathful God rather than the limitations of a finite experience is responsible for the punishment meted out to a despised foreigner. There is generally a preference for the nomad over the agriculturalist in these stories, especially in the condemnation of Cain, the cursing of Canaan by Noah, and the Tower of Babel, but the farmer's cause is also brought to the fore in the account of Eden; all this, however, is subordinate to the moral interpretation, which adds both a forcefulness and a personal appeal.

Although a number of writers were occupied, at one time or another, in forging the careers of the patriarchs, the latter stand out in bold, consistent outlines like rough-hewn Titanic rocks jutting out against a primitive landscape. There is a sculpturesque bigness about their personalities—like Moses, they were beyond the good and evil of the common man, cast in the mold of a deity whose spirituality had not yet been clearly defined. As they wandered through the borderland between the desert and the arable earth they talked on intimate terms with their God, wrestled with his angels, and fought ruthlessly with their enemies. Abraham was not above telling a lie, Jacob and Esau quarreled already in the womb, the former resorted to a common form of treachery to best his father-in-law, and the women of their households were by no means charitable toward one another. Whether one accepts these accounts as based on fact or not,[47] it must be granted that the patriarchs represent a

---

47. L. Woolley (*Abraham*, New York, 1936, pp. 51–56) believes firmly that the account of *Genesis* is an accurate reflection of culture among the early Hebrews, as revealed by the spade of the archaeologist.

primitive type of culture we should expect to find on the fringe of greater cultures about 2000 B.C. While one cannot divorce the patriarch entirely from the element of myth, Abraham and Jacob have little in common with mythical figures moving without much motivation across the stage of an impersonal drama; they play their roles as powerful personalities living with their God and, with his aid, working out a design in history which reaches out significantly into the past and future. The dramatic struggles of these divinely inspired characters are the more forceful in that they are purposeful, they move upward from a beginning toward an ultimate fulfillment instead of falling in line with a cyclical pattern which subordinates the past and future to the ever-recurring present. There are times when the writer and his characters seem uncertain about their God and the meaning of their role in his great design, but they are never in doubt about the rightness of his immediate dictates; the writer is also fully aware of the mystery and miracle surrounding the rejection of the older tribal gods in favor of the more spiritual divinity.

With the coming of Joseph the mist rises on a clearer horizon against which the Hebrew and the foreigner stand forth in more human outlines and contrasts, and God, too, by epitomizing the figure of Joseph, reveals his plan with more transparent clarity. The story is a patchwork of history, folklore, and tribal tradition reflecting the mores of wandering shepherds; the background in Egypt, though reliable in detail, has been altered to suit the scheme of the author; the divination is colorful but not too fanciful; the motive of Potiphar's wife, known to us from so many other sources, has been admirably woven into the narrative; the figure of Joseph, whose self-assurance is nauseating, shows no development of character; the story is neither an epic nor a tragedy, yet because of its color and variety of mood, its sensitive humanity, its dramatic crises and contrasts, and its quality of suspense the writer has made it one of the most attractive tales in literature. Joseph is a symbol of the Hebrew nation, the underdog of the east, clinging to a lofty spiritual ideal in its constant battle with the materialism of the heathen. Because God is always with him through thick and thin, Joseph's perfection, though objectionable in itself, tends to justify his role through his humanity toward his brothers and the absence of any malice toward the Egyptians for casting him into prison. One feels that, at the end of the story, there is no reason why Egyptians and Hebrews should not continue to live together in peace in the Nile Valley.

The dramatic struggle breaks out violently again under a pharaoh who did not know Joseph. This time the scene includes two nations pitted against one another in a life and death battle, and again a dynamic personality is the spiritual guide for his persecuted people—Moses was like a towering mountain conversant with the whirlwind of heaven and a refuge for the people at its base. The account of Moses and his contacts with God called forth the most exacting demands from the writer: first he made him a superb leader of his flock, knowing when to chide, to chastise, to destroy, to show pity, resorting to wonders and magic as a matter of indulgence to popular credulity; Moses was not one to exult over Aaron's rod or the brazen serpent. Secondly, Moses had to be a great man of heroic stature, sublime enough to stand in the awful presence of God and superhuman enough to dispute with God in behalf of his charges. He must know how to sway his people by appealing to their most deep-seated emotions, and because of the nature of his appeal and the waywardness of his flock, it had to be repeated *mutatis mutandis*. Likewise Yahweh, in spite of his contacts with the human Moses, must not sacrifice any of his aloofness and grandeur thereby. By surrounding his birth and death with mystery the author has placed Moses apart from the common run of man; by endowing him with the awful wrath and patient mercy of his God he made him as divine as is humanly possible. How striking he has made the contrast between the ways of Yahweh and the heathen gods by arranging the meeting of Moses and his God in juxtaposition to the worship of the golden calf! How far above Aaron is his brother when the former explains his conduct in the absence of Moses! With what terrifying intensity the atmosphere of the covenant has been charged! The elements of nature, in the hands of Yahweh, do not contradict the laws of experience but magnify them in power and sweep; the crossing of the Sea of Reeds may derive from the Egyptian story of the magician who heaps one half of a lake upon the other half to recover the ring of a princess royal, but the behavior of the Biblical waters is not only grounded in the possibilities of experience, it is raised beyond the cleverness of side-show entertainment to the level of breath-taking reality. Likewise, Moses himself follows the pattern of many a mythical hero, but the power of his personality, the historical conviction arising from his acts, transcends anything we find in the career of Herakles, Rama, Siegfried, or Balder.[48]

After the passing of Moses, Yahweh descends from the heights of Sinai to lead his people in the exploits of war, and Joshua becomes his image. The most obvious acts of cruelty, leveling cities to the ground, butchering both man and beast— all is done in the name of the Lord of battle[49] until the Hebrews have gained a firm foothold in Caanan. In the portrayal of Gideon the writer enlists our sympathy, in spite of his military vocation. The calling of Gideon in the midst of threshing, his reliance on the three hundred, the tactful dealing with Ephraim, and above all, his stern refusal of the kingship, paint a picture of moral strength against a background of humble faith and modesty. In the burlesque character of Samson the Hebrews found a figure they were at a loss to understand; at any rate, they had difficulty in trying to fit him into the tradition of their past. The fact that much of his behavior is capricious, even wanton, suggests a strong foreign influence; while his story is too much of a melange from different sources to be put down as a sun myth, the over-all picture of a great, muscular bull in a china shop is reminiscent of Herakles in the Alcestis episode, something of which may have come to the Hebrews through the Phoenician Melkarth.

---

48. F. R. S. Raglan (*The Hero*, London, 1936, pp. 185–6) neglects the importance of his personality in favor of features of his career he shares in common with the mythical hero.

49. Cf. F. James: *Personalities of the Old Testament*, London, 1940, p. 51.

Once we come to Samuel, we move into a period when the temporal side of theocracy comes into clearer view. Whether Samuel's career has too little continuity or he represents the narrow view of the priesthood as a class, the author here is obviously having trouble in enlisting our sympathy for the man we may call either a judge, a prophet, or a priest. The episodes of his life are vivid and startling and they move along rapidly in quick succession without much background or connection. Like some of the later prophets, his presence fills the air with something ominous which lingers in his wake until his death. His boyhood story, devoid of all magic, his service at Shiloh, his loathing for anything wrong or unclean in the sight of Yahweh, his judging of the people impress us with the man's earnest sincerity, his devotion to the cause of the people. The uncompromising voice of the priesthood is evident in his unwillingness to choose a king, but the practical necessity which calls for strong leadership against the Philistines forces his hand. Both Yahweh and Samuel consent to the kingship, but once the king has been chosen, the latter chides the people for their decision.[50] The people repent, whereupon both Yahweh and Samuel turn their faces from Saul to David. The reason for this move has obviously been covered up, but the motive seems to lie in the conflict between one emphasis on control in the hands of the priest and that of a more temporal leadership in a theocratic state.

At any rate, Saul emerges from the conflict as the one figure in the Old Testament who approaches tragic stature, although the writer was hardly conscious of the meaning of tragedy in our sense of the term. At the time of his election he is described as a "goodly man," [51] he is strong enough to rout the Philistines with a small band of men; he is blessed with the favor of God and man—and then he is condemned for a single act of disobedience. To the writer his acceptance and rejection by Yahweh were

---

50. I *Samuel*, XII, 13–25.

51. T. J. Meek (*op. cit.*, p. 156) suggests that Saul revolted against Yahweh and the prophets. If this is true, the courts of David and Solomon must have been a small comfort to the priesthood at a later date.

primary factors; we include his blind envy and persecution of David which alienated popular affection from his cause. Saul wanted to use his own common sense in battle and in the use of its spoils, but Yahweh and the priest Samuel, we are told, demanded unconditional obedience.[52] The inner struggle between the good and evil in Saul's nature, beginning with the popular acclaim for David to the stealing of the sleeping king's spear is nothing less than overpowering; the voice of the innocent David can still reach to the depths of the king's heart, but in the next moment it is lost in the narrow valley of dark shadows. The degradation of his character is finally brought to a climax where the historian describes with consummate skill his visit to the witch of Endor; Saul has sunk so low as to elicit pity from one of his own outcasts. "How are the mighty fallen!"

Both God and man worked together with circumstances to make David the favored child of Hebrew history, and this fact coupled with his natural charm and outstanding ability inevitably raised him to the peak of good fortune. This does not mean that the evil he committed was pushed into the background, for David, like many of his forebears, was outstanding both in his good and evil deeds. To learn that a man who had communed with his God all his days and had had much experience with evil, who had been granted so many blessings and advantages— to learn that this man had intentionally committed murder for the satisfaction of his lust does not tend to ingratiate him in the reader's affections; yet the writer, in recording his repentance, somehow wipes much of the stain from our minds. His personal charm drew a great many men to his banner, men who otherwise never would have been united with Judah; his knowledge of men made him the greatest diplomat of Hebrew history, so much so he was able to dispose of personal enemies (Joab became the scapegoat) without losing face with the people, so that tradition was able to keep David on a pedestal of grandeur. We must acknowledge he was a great leader, warrior, and poet; we feel with him at the loss of Jonathan and Absalom; but we cannot

---

52. I *Samuel*, XV, 22-23.

condone his overfondness for the dynasty, his harem, and the indulgence with which he treated his children, all of which hastened the downfall of the kingdom; we cannot feel for him as for Saul, for after having enjoyed the best things life could offer, he walked into certain pitfalls with eyes wide open. To Hebrew tradition he was the great king and hero, from whom evil might proceed but, like God, he was not essentially evil by nature. In the case of Solomon we find it difficult to penetrate to the personality; the historian is content to contemplate this figure from a distance, removed from the common man by the splendor of his court and his reputation for wisdom. With the coming of the internationalist the personality lost its significance for the historian.

The fact that Hebrew poetry has exerted such a powerful effect, by way of translation, on the people of so many nations, speaks very highly for its superior qualities. Poetry was a common vehicle of tradition from the earliest times, although we can distinguish no example that antedates the period of Moses.[53] Some of the finest of the earliest survivals include the prophecy of Balaam, the triumphal song of Deborah, and David's lament for Saul and Jonathan. Certain poems which met with popular favor must have been sung publicly to the accompaniment of instruments, at times also with dancing and clapping of hands. In the book of Psalms we find subjects ranging through the whole gamut of emotional expression: gratitude, thanksgiving, humility, exultation, praise, trust, sorrow, repentance, all reflecting, in varied tones, the primary attributes of Yahweh, namely, justice and mercy. Because of the great number of recensions and readaptations for special occasions, it is virtually impossible to date a psalm or assign it to an author; again, the work was much more important than the creator who functioned merely as the mouthpiece for divine inspiration. Without resorting to rhyme the poet achieved some very convincing and powerful effects with the aid of rhythm, alliteration, and frequent

---

53. Cf. J. A. Bewer: *The Literature of the Old Testament*, New York, 1933, p. 2.

parallelisms.[54] Once he had conceived a choice image he embraced it with the whole force of his personality and sapped all the flavor of its richness.

The greatest merit of the Psalms lies in the power, the lofty grandeur of the poet's image presented with breath-taking suddenness and terse simplicity. There is no more overwhelming statement of cosmic significance in literature than, "He uttered his voice, the earth melted!" The Hebrew poet was more concerned with the larger aspects of phenomena—the foundations of the earth, the heart of the seas, the bringing forth of the mountains, the valley of the shadow of death, the glory of the heavens—than with the blade of grass, the drop of dew, the thread of gossamer, or the flower in the crannied wall; likewise he was impatient with any form of romantic sentimentality. How insipidly unimportant is mankind divorced from the presence of God! "What is man that Thou art mindful of him?" The reader is hurled very abruptly, by way of contrast, from the heights of heaven to the depths below the earth, from the catastrophe of destruction to the pastoral peace of a shepherd's life, from the awful omnipotence of Yahweh to the utter helplessness of man, from the thunder of wrath to the mildness of tender mercy, from the joys of the righteous to the despair of the wicked. No condition, no exception is permitted in the direct stream of emotion which flows in full-hearted confidence between the worshipper and Yahweh, who has chosen his people for a special destiny, but who chastises them in the same full measure with which he pours out his tender mercy. The ease with which Yahweh expresses himself in terms of Titanic emotions and handles the more awesome phenomena of experience greatly enhances his majesty at the helm of control. Granted the ethics of the psalmist are not always above reproach and the enemy is treated with anything but tolerance, at the same time all men, Hebrews and heathen alike, are " . . . like grass which groweth up in the

---

54. For a discussion of the techniques of Hebrew poetry consult C. A. Dinsmore: *The English Bible as Literature*, New York, 1931, pp. 175 ff. and J. A. Bewer: *op. cit.*, pp. 344 ff.

morning—in the evening it is cut down, and withereth." In spite of any shortcomings we may cite, the Psalms will remain the most universal language for the religious emotions, especially for one who is impressed by the great mysterious power in the universe at large, beyond his ken and control. For the man who disclaims any religious allegiance there is still a large measure of the sublime which, as Longinus says, " . . . imposes its irresistible will upon all of us."

In the case of the prophet, the personality becomes more clear and distinctive to the reader, although the editors did not deem it necessary to abide by any sequence or exact wording in prophetic writing. Because of the nature of the Hebrew state this literature is both patriotically and religiously fanatical; it is at one time oratorical to convey a message of exhortation, it can also be poetical to express the exalted ecstasy[55] of the man uttering the will of God; it is nearly all concerned with the future, the nature of coming punishments and blessings. In general, the prophet felt himself to be the voice of God, justifying the ways of God to man and admonishing the people against too much concern with foreign deities or the lure of strictly temporal power and luxury. They were men of the desert, given to fasting, long periods of meditation and spasmodic preaching, which does not mean their message was devoid of clear thinking, especially among the later examples. The literary value of their utterances derives from the sincerity of their convictions; if God spoke through his servants, the latter could not express themselves in dilemmas and quandaries. They also painted vivid images designed either to frighten the hearer or to transfigure his present state of misery. Like Homer, they were well versed in every aspect of their experience, but the way of bird and beast must be subordinate to a higher purpose; many were statesmen of the first rank, but politics was only a portion of the design God was weaving into the tapestry of history. Standing high on the cloud, their voices were raised to God

---

55. The peculiar character of prophetic ecstasy among the Hebrews is discussed by A. Guillaume (*op. cit.*, pp. 294 ff).

above and reached down to the people below: "Lift up your eyes to the heavens, and look upon the earth beneath." [56]

The sublimity of prophetic literature is indebted to its ethical content, which is much the same as that of the Psalms. The married life of Hosea, the primitive wrath of Isaiah, the questioning of Habakkuk, the apocalyptic of Ezekiel—all point to the same moral teaching so beautifully summed up in the statement ascribed to Micah (6:8): " . . . and what doth the Lord require of thee, but to do justly, and to love mercy, and to walk humbly with thy God?" Like the Psalm writer, the apostle of divine madness is inconsiderate of other peoples; he revels in the most horrible punishment and destruction for the heathen. The book of Jonah, standing out in sharp contrast, reproaches the prophet for his shortcomings; it looks off to a broader horizon where some good may be extracted from the greatest evil. The story, told in simple, narrative style, presents a Hebrew, saturated with his national ethics, looking at the Ninevites like a cat stalking around a bowl of fish. The story of the sea monster, the naïveté of Jonah beneath the gourd vine, strike us as humorous; the foreigner, now included in the mercies of Yahweh, becomes a steppingstone to a new lesson for the Hebrews.

Let the concentrated flow of emotion descend from the sublime and it revels in the sensuous delight of sight, hearing, touch, taste, and smell. The Song of Solomon is no longer regarded as an allegorical poem, an interpretation which prompted its inclusion in the Scriptures; it probably has a historical setting at the beginning of Solomon's reign.[57] The imagery of the similes is uncompromisingly sensuous—we smell the frankincense, myrrh, perfumes, and the flowers of springtime; we taste the juices of rich fruit; we feast our eyes on ebony, gold, ivory, and cedar. The action, such as it is, moves swiftly; each word is not only suggestive of but soaked in sensuous delight. Instead of walking

---

56. *Isaiah*, LI, 6.

57. L. Waterman (*The Song of Songs*, Ann Arbor, 1948, pp. 32–3) identifies the girl with the beautiful nurse of David's old age who, having rejected the suit of Solomon, returns to her lover in the north. Some authorities think of the work as an anthology of love songs.

on the plane of religious aspiration the rose of Sharon speaks of a riot of color, the luscious luxuriance of springtime in the verdant valley, and the flower of youth and love.

With the coming of Greek influence certain Hebrews who had delved into western speculation tried to rationalize the principles of their theology, which had formerly been taken for granted. Such an approach brought them face to face with the relativity of phenomena which cannot be easily reconciled with the personality of a great God ruling over the universe and mankind in terms of a strict moral code. The Preacher, as he was known, was one of these thinkers. Like many a Hebrew writer, he indulges in sweeping generalities, sharply marked contrasts, powerful metaphors, and hasty conclusions, and so we cannot call him a scientific thinker in our sense of the word, but we must admit his sincere effort to search out a theory of life. A mood of scepticism prevails through his writing, a mood which could easily become one of cynical pessimism, had he not been a man of means, had he been a victim of all the injustice he found in the world. Like many a man of the Renaissance he pursued one aspect of life after another with such a passionate eagerness he found nothing but disillusionment instead of satisfaction or security. He tried to explore the meaning of life by the standards of reason and knowledge and found it was a chasing of the wind; he turned to sensual pleasures, and these too he found were transitory and of no permanent satisfaction; in all his efforts he found nothing but toil and vexation. There is no reward for either justice or injustice, for God pays little attention to the merits of men, and each one goes down to the grave as naked as he came into life. Life is an endless round of repetition, of monotonous sameness, futile and vain, in which man too must move along in an endless circle of time. And what is God? No man can discover his nature or purpose in the vanity of his creation, for he has shut himself off from human understanding by a veil no sight or mind can pierce. Hence the sane man will look at goodness and wisdom in terms of their immediate advantages without investing them with any ultimate value or purpose. Ecclesiastes gives us something of the *carpe diem* of the Epicureans as well as the cyclical thought of the Stoics,[58] but his strong desire for certainty can find no self-identification in either one.

An effort to sum up the truth of living in a general statement gave expression to the Proverbs, many of which are assigned to Solomon, while others of equal force and beauty are credited to ben Sira, listed as an author in the apocryphal literature. They deal with every phase of life within the ken of the Hebrew: the administration of justice, the treatment of a neighbor, eating and drinking, relationship with women, business and public life. This type of wisdom, however, cannot be placed in the same category with that of Ecclesiastes; instead of getting down to the level where comparisons are both odious and disconcerting, the writer remains on the height of moral discrimination and rolls up all experience in neat packages of what is right and wrong which, as he believes, must coincide with wisdom and foolishness. The two cardinal precepts of most Near Eastern wisdom, fear and obedience without asking too many questions, motivates the wise man's terse statements. There is no more narrow selfishness in these precepts than in the more sublime heights of prophecy or lyrical poetry; it is simply more obvious when applied to the plane of practice where tangible objects are more within the reach of the grasping hand, whereas all men can reach for divine goodness, mercy, and justice without acquiring a monopoly detrimental to others. Divine wisdom can be understood by the Hebrew in its reflection in a world of practice if he is not too concerned about the object for its own sake, but this same wisdom at its source is inscrutable. The writer achieves his literary effects by parallelisms and contrasts so alluring they charm the reader into forgetting about the possibility of embarrassing comparisons.

In Babylon, we are told, the lawmakers fashioned a code which was largely economic and political, whereas the Hebrew Decalogue was above all moral and religious.[59] Nevertheless, the

---

58. W. F. Albright: *From the Stone Age to Christianity,* Baltimore, 1940, p. 271.

59. T. J. Meek: *op. cit.,* p. 69.

Hebrews, once in Palestine, found it to their advantage to take over from the Canaanites what are known as casuistic laws defining crime and punishment more specifically for the court. As in so many Near Eastern codes, we find the *lex talionis*,[60] but no fine distinctions are made between social classes. Their distinctive contribution, however, was made by the Hebrews in the apodictic laws, stated concisely, categorically, by an absolute, unquestionable authority. First, the name and person of Yahweh are made inviolable by a decree against imagery and taking the name of God in vain. The Hebrew is then told in general but direct commands to remember the sabbath, to honor his parents, neither to steal, murder, commit adultery, nor covet. "Thou shalt not" implied a moral bond between the person of Yahweh and that of the worshipper which the heart understood unequivocally; neither magic nor legal rationalism were strong enough to circumvent such a direct appeal. It also meant that the worshipper was responsible enough to make a moral decision by himself, one which required no hair-splitting interpretation of the law, and one which the conscience would make satisfactory to God and man. Like the covenant, the Decalogue was a decided advance in favor of human dignity.

There are two interesting works of fiction, both replete with oriental dramatic effects, although magic is never resorted to in an effort to sustain interest. The mood of each story, as well as the purpose behind the tale, is quite different. The book of Ruth was written by a man as broad in his sympathies as the author of Jonah, one who objected to the pure race campaign of post-exilic leaders. The characters move along through an Arcadian idyl far from the cry of war and bloodshed, imbued with something of the nostalgic atmosphere of a Poussin landscape. We can say it is too good to be true and at the same time admit it is within the range of human possibility. The characters are capable of making new and important decisions on their own responsibility—decisions which bring forth good fruit because they issue from a good heart—all without theological dictation

---

60. *Exodus*, XXI-XXIII.

or priestly intermediation. The quiet sincerity of Ruth, Naomi, and Boaz, coupled with a telling brevity, drive home the author's point with a convincing effect. If the story of Ruth draws forth the sympathy of the foreigner, the book of Esther is equally successful in alienating him. In spite of its more intricate plot, its court intrigue and luxury, its intense drama, the high moral tone of Hebrew Scripture is wanting; the author, with his strictly nationalistic outlook, paints a picture in which all people and things are subservient means to the glorification of the Hebrew people, so much the more repugnant because they make no recourse to religious justification. A fanatically nationalistic Yahweh in the background is taken for granted, but nobody bothers to ask him a question. Queen Vashti carries off the honors in the admiration of the reader only as a by-product of the writer's conscious purpose.

The most challenging piece of literature in the Old Testament is the book of Job because it penetrates, in the light of reason, to the most fundamental paradox of Hebrew religion, a paradox more patent and therefore more disturbing to the western thinker than to the religious worshipper. The device of the prologue, also used by Goethe and Hardy, diminishes our respect for God and throws more sympathy in the direction of Job, the latter no doubt included in the intention of the author. At first Job is deprived of his family and his possessions, then he suffers the degradation of disease, the justice of which he objects to. His three friends visit him and exhort him to put a bridle on his mouth, to be humble; they argue, at one moment, that suffering is the consequence of sin; then they claim that even if Job is innocent, suffering is sent by the Almighty as a disciplinary measure, as a catharsis. Job, while he admits that God is omnipotent, omniscient, and just, complains that for this very reason God has treated him and other righteous men unfairly, while the wicked seem to prosper in their unrighteousness. In some of the finest poetry of the Scriptures the defiant Job first questions the traditional morality of God's ways and then challenges him to answer the charge. Finally, God, appearing in the whirlwind, overwhelms Job with questions no man has ever been able to answer. Job is cowed into repentance; his last state is even more prosperous than the first.

What happened to Job might very well have been experienced by Ecclesiastes, had he found himself in adverse circumstances. The conflict in his personality was waged between the traditional attitude, emphasizing fear and reverence, and the questioning mind which sought for a reason behind God's mysterious dispensations. This mind was also aware of a fundamental contradiction between an almighty, just God and the evil he allowed to prevail in his universe. Yes, Job would trust his God, but he must also ask questions! Job is not, according to western standards, a tragic character,[61] for such a character in this setting would have run counter to the whole Hebrew tradition and made the case for Yahweh look bad in the end. It is not a philosophical work although it presents a philosophical problem in bold relief; it steps out on the threshold of philosophy, peers curiously into its problems, and then turns back. The writer, undoubtedly brought up with a Hebrew background and exposed to Mesopotamian literature as well as Greek thinking, pointed out the embarrassing character of certain question marks leveled against the old theology, but instead of exploring the implications he ignores them and shows how ridiculously inconsequential is man's reason compared to the magnificence of God, whose ways are far above our ways; at the same time, he inadvertently calls attention to the shortcomings of the old morality championed by the three friends, which turns out to be as futile as man's questioning in the face of God's transcendent justice. The speeches of Job and God contain some of the most exalted and moving poetry in the Scriptures, and Job's complaints might well have served a character in a tragic pattern; in such a pattern, however, the words of God would have lost much of their effect.

To the man who has always lived outside the boundaries

---

61. Cf. H. Cairns, A. Tate, and M. van Doren: *Invitation to Learning*, New York, 1941, pp. 332–39. For a Mesopotamian version of the persecuted Job see S. N. Kramer: *From the Tablets of Sumer*, Indian Hills, 1956, p. 149–51.

of the Christian tradition, who approaches the Old Testament as a source book for psychological study, the story of the Hebrew religious experience will at first present a curious spectacle. He might label it a grand pageant of self-indoctrination or self-deception. Here, he would say to himself, is a people more than convinced of their self-importance, who have objectified their supposed superiority over others in the form of a supernatural being as a means of justifying themselves in their own eyes. Pushed around and bandied about by others for this very reason, they developed a strange but effective resistance against oppression; in fact, they became great through self-commiseration fostered through long periods of suffering; in the meantime their hatred for their enemies tended to raise their God above the divinities of their despised neighbors until he became an exclusive, jealous being, lofty in conception but negative from the standpoint of experience. When they defeated an enemy or rode on the wave of good fortune, they glorified themselves in the name of their God and then conveniently forgot him for a spell. When they fell upon evil days, it was not their enemies who had prevailed against them; no, it was their God who was using their enemies as a means of chastising his beloved people, and as soon as this period of punishment was over, their God would visit the enemy with the most horrible calamities. God was a God of mercy, first of all, for his own people, for they could commit no crime which could not eventually be atoned for; he was a God of justice, as the Hebrew conceived of it, mainly for the poor heathen, for the latter's every blessing was merely a prelude to eventual destruction. In the end this God was destined to lead his people in triumph over all the powers of heaven and earth.

Such an estimate contains a certain amount of truth, but only one side of the picture. It fails to make a profitable comparison with religion as practiced by people on either side of the Hebrews; it overlooks the general subjectivism of early civilizations so necessary for their survival in early days and which has a definite historical value for our thesis. There must have been something unique about a people who, although despised and driven about from pillar to post, persecuted in nearly every corner of the globe in all ages, still handed down a religious legacy to later times, while the gods of others have long been asleep in the dust. Granted that Yahweh was often made responsible for evil effects, that persecutors and persecuted were seldom in the right, the effectiveness of the Hebrew's self-identification with his Yahweh raised him to the highest moral level achieved by man in antiquity; it revealed to man an entirely new concept of divinity. The secret of this advance lies, if anywhere, in the viewpoint of his personality. After a review of the Egyptian and Mesopotamian civilizations we are in a good position to understand what the Hebrew contributed to ethics, to the concept of history, and to monotheism.

The Hebrew never found life so good and pleasant on the finite level that he desired, like the Egyptian, to identify himself with it into eternity, nor was he willing to put up with the uncertainty the Mesopotamian faced on the divine level and the magic the latter resorted to for plugging the gaps of ignorance. Throughout the years spent in the desert or on its borders, watching the great expanse of sky and wasteland, the constant struggles for food and water, the battles with neighboring tribes left him little occasion to grow fond of experience on the surface; he was driven to seek for some compensation within and at the same time he developed a strong resistance against storms, monotony, and privation. It would be too much to say that he was not aware of objects in the concrete and in phenomena, of the role of change in life, for he constantly refers in his poetry to the movements of stars in the heavens, the mountains and their valleys, the roaring of waters, the storm cloud, emphasizing in each case the bigness of their manifestations, the sudden, devastating character of their movements. He was, however, not concerned about such objects and processes of nature for their own sake, but rather as a vehicle for the expression of a higher power above them. The change of seasons in the desert brought no comfort to his mind, no practical benefit he could take pleasure in. It is a rarity to find the Hebrew losing himself in the admiration for "The way of an eagle in the air; the way of a serpent upon a rock, the way of a ship in the midst of the sea . . ." [62] To protect himself against the onslaughts of his experience he built up a stronger subjective reserve than others. The insistence of human desire reached out to an infinite way beyond the disappointments of experience, where it found a divine refuge; nature, as a tool in the hands of the Almighty, became the reflection of his mercy or the scourge of his vengeance. Ultimately, man and God must triumph over finite nature with her disconcerting changes.

Man, then, as a subject made little or no compromise with experience, and that experience included men of other nations who must be content, like the phenomena the Hebrew under-rated, with being a means to the ultimate salvation of the chosen people. The infinite, in the form of God, projected itself into the finite in manifold ways, but the former remained substantially different as well as superior to the latter. Furthermore, the infinite, though identical with a personalized power, remained as it had always been and always would be, almighty and omniscient, without change or variation. The infinite had called the finite into being, i.e., established certain limitations in terms of time and space, and also had the power to annihilate it at some future date. Instead of one running along in harmony with or saturating the other, as in Egypt, instead of reaching up almost despairingly for uncertain help from an unreliable, impersonal realm above, like the Mesopotamian, the Hebrew insisted on the helplessness of the finite in the hands of a purposeful divinity and knew exactly what he could expect, by way of good or evil, from a responsible center of power; it was far more for him than a metaphysical abstraction or an unmoral ogre diffident to the interests of man. It was almost as if the two elements of his viewpoint stood over against one another in marked contrast, each in its own province, which made it easier for man to make a choice between the two. The great figures of Hebrew history, although living in the finite, served as connecting links between man and God and appear so much

---

62. *Proverbs*, XXX, 19.

more monumental as they move along against the background of the infinite. So convinced was the Hebrew of the saving grace inherent in the infinite he could derive little or no rational or scientific value from experience this side of the grave; the effects of an attempt to do so can be seen in the conclusions of Ecclesiastes. The fact that his finite and infinite were so different and one so far above the other invited certain unavoidable paradoxes which, however, gave the Hebrew mind no trouble until he came into contact with Greek thinking.

The Egyptian, as we have seen, sought to align the finite with the infinite by means of the static line, while the Mesopotamian met the challenge of ruthless circumstances with a strong arm. In each case the power of circumstances and the gods deriving from them were fickle, capricious, unmoral, seldom concerned with human welfare, and to compel such wayward forces to operate in his interest man availed himself of the tool of magic. The Hebrew neglected or ignored many of these aspects of his experience and confined the nature of his divinity to the infinite. He then allied himself with this divinity alone and so could afford to snub the finite except insofar as it reflected God's glory, mercy, and wrath. Trust and obey the Lord, and he will control circumstances to the best interests of his people! ". . . for thou art my rock and my fortress." [63] We have also seen that the Egyptian and Mesopotamian made ample use of magic to achieve their ends or to force the object, whether god or man, to comply with the will of the subject. It would be too much to claim that Hebrew life and literature are free from magic, but we can assert it was not admitted within the province of religious teaching and was used only as a last resort, as in the life of Moses and that of Saul. The latter's visit to the witch of Endor violated his own ordinance and brought the king added sorrow. One reason, and the only reason, for avoiding magic in finite experience was the fact that the Hebrew had identified himself with the superior power of a personalized infinite, in whose ability to dominate the finite he had full confidence, and so he

---

63. Psalm LXXI, 3.

could exert some control over experience only indirectly, by
petitioning a righteous God in his behalf; any resort to magic
in Hebrew history meant a weakening of faith in the infinite or
that God had turned his face from man. Another reason why
the Hebrew never employed magic to sway his divinity will be
taken up later.

The value of the Hebrew's contribution to the development
of a balanced viewpoint lies in his special interpretation of the
infinite and its transcendent position above the finite. The Hebrew was not one to probe into the secrets of God's infinite realm
by studying the physical laws of the finite;[64] the consequences
of such a presumption on the part of man are illustrated in the
story of the tower of Babel. The only way to reach the infinite
was through the human heart, the seat of human desire, which
carved out a straight, undeviating connection between the two,
unobstructed by embarrassing question marks or contingencies.
By a very simple process of thinking, the Hebrew concluded that
since the finite was in every way inferior to the infinite, he need
not be concerned about establishing a harmony between God
and nature.[65] Since the heart with its longing for security had
searched out the way to the infinite, it would hardly be content
to deal with it as a mere abstract postulation comparable to
Aristotle's thought of a thought. What was, then, the unique
construction the Hebrew put on the infinite?

For the first time in the history of thought the infinite was
endowed with personality. God took on the reflection of man's
person, which had developed along lines different from that of
the Egyptian and Mesopotamian. It meant that God, endowed
with the power of decision or choice, would not move in accordance with an impersonal, cyclical routine of seasonal events and
that God was not subservient to man's finite needs. It meant
that God was beyond the monotony of a parallelism between the
microcosm and macrocosm; he was capable of initiating a new
course of events if he so desired and could look off to a culmina-

64. W. F. Albright: *From the Stone Age to Christianity*, Baltimore,
1940, p. 25.

65. H. Frankfort: *Kingship and the Gods*, Chicago, 1948, p. 6.

tion when the circle of events in the finite would have to come to an end. He could look back to the beginning and before the beginning of things; he could see off to the end of the finite and beyond, as well as enrich the whole course of the universe with a purpose; while he was moving events in the finite he knew why he was moving them. He was what the Hebrew wanted to become, unimpeded by the limitations of experience. He had put the sun, moon, and stars in their places and ordained their movements in the heavens but remained apart from them; he had made man and placed him in a position of authority over the earth with its birds and animals; he had fitted all things into the pattern of a purposeful design which man, because of his limitations, cannot fathom. As a person he could make a decision and hold himself responsible for such a decision, and because he was infinite in every way, his will knew no obstacles; it was conceived and effected at one and the same time.

But why, we may ask, was this divinity a single God? Why were there not a number of gods, each endowed with a personality? We have already mentioned, as a contributing factor, the wandering in the desert where the sameness of the sandy expanse, the heavens by day and night, as well as the long periods of quiet divorce one from the multifarious nature of horizontal experience.[66] We have seen to what extent the heart expresses itself along a single straight line and with singular concentration, but in Egypt and Mesopotamia this line of concentration opened up lines of communication with a number of aspects of finite experience, and each time attention fastened on one aspect the subject absorbed itself completely to the exclusion of all other interests. The line of attention shifted, of course, as it must in a pluralistic perspective, and a number of possible avenues of communication were formed to give rise to polytheism. If this same line of concentration transcends the finite and attaches itself directly to the infinite, it will find there only one sameness, a single unity undistracted by any other possible aspects. The infinite, by definition, is so much a oneness it

66. Cf. R. Turner: *The Great Cultural Traditions*, New York, 1941, Vol. I, pp. 108–9.

excludes anything more than one. There the Hebrew was able
to construct his monotheism,[67] which he personalized and called
Yahweh. This God was aniconic because, in essence, he was
a denial of the finite, and any concrete image would impair his
unity by suggesting a limitation. Psychologically, he was still
a thinking and feeling unity, which leads Albright[68] to call
him one whose body was hidden in his glory.

Now we can understand the main reason why magic was not
used to bend this God to a conformity with human desire. God
was in no respect related to the impersonal movements of nature,
rather he was a personality with a mind and emotions, with a
sense of justice and mercy, with a definite purpose in view—he
was more like subjective man than any God the world had
known. What man of those days would attempt to practice magic
on himself, and, if so, what manner of magic would he use? We
have seen that magic is a subjective tool for gaining one's ends
in the objective world, either by imitation or contact. God being
an exalted version of the subjective inner man, neither of which
claims any relation to the finite, what can one use for imitation or
contact? What means can one use as a concrete symbol or
analogy in dealing with an aniconic, personal God? In every
case it was God and the inner man against circumstances, which
were so far beneath God and so completely in his control it
would have been utterly ridiculous to use them as a means
against their creator. God saw and knew all things, including
man's desires and needs even as he conceived of them in his
mind, and he could bend circumstances to fill man's needs far
more easily than man could deal with them for any purpose.
It would be an insult to God's authority and omniscience, an
attempt to bypass his prerogative, if man should use magic on
his objective world rather than make a direct, personal appeal
to his God. To influence impersonal, limited divinities who had
no special concern for man, who controlled only one aspect of

67. E. Cassirer (*Language and Myth* (Trans. By Suzanne K. Langer),
New York, 1946, pp. 76–77) has offered the most sensible explanation for
Hebrew monotheism.

68. *From the Stone Age to Christianity*, Baltimore, 1940, p. 201.

finite experience, by means of magic was permissible, especially
since they were unethical enough to practice it on each other,
but to sway an all-seeing, all-knowing and responsible personality
like Yahweh by magic was out of the question. Moreover, the
confidence man placed in such a tool implies that the object of
magic is no more than a means to man's subjective end, and the
object thereby loses its dignity; Yahweh could only be treated
as an end in himself. To use such a device to achieve an end
in circumstances might be justified if God were not in full control of the helm, but the Hebrew never caught the Lord of
creation off his guard.

Job also registers a strong protest against the sacrosanct
procedure of magic: when his friends assert that his sufferings
are a visitation of divine justice for his misdeeds of the past,
they are lending their full support to the unerring connection
between a definite cause and a definite effect—a necessary feature
in the thinking of the primitive magician. The other insists that
the connection, although molded by divine ordinance, ought to
be subject to the awareness and criticism of both cause and
effect which, in the Hebrew covenant, were personal factors;
man should be granted more dignity if the relation between the
two was to be balanced and fair. Job, as a person, expected a
personal God not only to create such a sequence between two
events, or between himself as a subject and man as an object,
but to make it function for their mutual benefit in a program
of righteousness.

God was, then, an object of dignity and commanded the
greatest respect of man as a subject, a fact which brought forth
for the first time a balanced subject-object relationship, one
whose connecting link remained constant as long as man looked
up to God with trust and obeyed his injunctions. Man was a
changeable creature in a changeable world, hence his part in
maintaining a connection with God was not always reliable,
whereas God could always be relied upon to do his part. This
subject-object relationship had no analogies in experience, where
both subject and object were imperfect, prone to change, requiring constant patchwork, where one set of relationships may

outlive its usefulness and then give way to others; hence it contributed nothing to a scientific point of view, it added nothing to a comparative sense of values, because the Hebrew kept it somewhat removed from the contingencies of the finite. It was strictly vertical instead of horizontal in its orientation. It implied a certain standard governing good and evil, and insofar as such a standard is not grounded in experience, the subject-object relationship of the contract between Yahweh and his people was largely subjective in its exclusiveness, although we must concede the advance contained in the balance of the two factors. This relationship did, however, exert some influence on the problems of experience because the contract was a moral one, and morality has a direct bearing on human action. On the other hand, the application of moral principles inspired by the contract was rather arbitrary in character, because they, coming down from above, were less concerned about the object itself than for the inviolability of the principle, and thus contributed more to the subject's moral character than to the object per se; with all the objections we can find in the contract from a scientific point of view, the Hebrew still made a decided moral improvement over the peoples who resorted to magic at every unfavorable turn of events.

And in what respect was moral character improved? It meant the Hebrew learned to be morally responsible, first to God, then to himself; foreigners and other objects were of secondary importance. As subjective as the projection of the self into divinity might be, once the divinity was firmly established as an object, his dignity was maintained, and that, too, by an imperfect subject. Two parties concluded a compact according to which God agreed to bring prosperity to his chosen people and lead them to a great destiny, while man was expected to fear and obey his God. Even though man, living as a finite creature in a finite world, was bound to violate it on occasion, it was of the greatest importance that man knew when he broke the terms, then repented, and made himself right with his God. The covenant, the greatest monument to the Hebrew's moral advance, endured throughout the people's history, its terms were obeyed wherever man harkened to the voice of the heart within, whereas the use of magic on the part of either party would, by its expediency and its lack of respect for the personal object, have voided the contract. Man was reminded over and over again how Yahweh had brought him up out of Egypt, through the Sea of Reeds, had guided him through the wilderness and into the Promised Land—to keep the subject-object relationship of the covenant in a good state of balance. God gave his commands to man at Sinai, telling him what was expected of a God-fearing subject—the terms of the contract were always valid for the man who walked in the paths of righteousness, for the man who sincerely repented of his misdeeds, for God was constant in his word, however man might stray.

Sorrow can be explained, from one standpoint, as a compensation or defense thrown up by human desire against the violent and unexpected upsets of experience. In the countries of the east, where desire is so concentrated, where absorption in the object is so complete, sadness and tears are more a part of life than in the west. For the Hebrew, sorrow was not merely a compensation for an unexpected upset in the finite but a sign of repentance for moral shortcomings, the real causes for the upsets which had induced God to visit man with punishment. The sackcloth and ashes and the wailing wall of the Hebrew are manifestations of much greater sorrow than the wistful, at times nostalgic, sadness of the Hindu. The wider gap of separation between the finite and infinite accounts for much of this mood in the minor key as well as a deeper consciousness of sin; the exalted position of God, his aloofness from phenomena, made the transgression of his ordinance so much more an aberration and hence the more reprehensible. "Who shall ascend into the hill of the Lord? or who shall stand in his holy place? He that hath clean hands and a pure heart . . ."[69] The transgression was a moral violation of an agreement with a personal God. It must also be borne in mind that the Hebrew did not think of the mere contact with material things as a sin (there was nothing of the

---

69. Psalm XXIV, 3–4.

Puritan about him), rather, any moral defection involved in such
a contact constituted the offense. The prophets objected to the
luxury of the rich because of the social injustice, the moral
depravity of conditions they saw around them. No one thought
of the great possessions of Job as a moral tarnish on his
character.[70]

For the same reason the Hebrew never became an ascetic
in our sense of the word. We read of men who denied themselves
the comforts and conveniences of the good life, who fasted and
meditated in the desert, but not from any distaste for material
things; in their concentration on higher things they were indifferent to material comforts without despising them. We must admit,
however, that the separation of the finite from the infinite and
the example of their holy men were inducements to asceticism,
especially after the Stoics made it popular. The same separation
helped to desecrate any association of God with a concrete
image; the plastic arts were entirely neglected in favor of literature. Likewise the Hebrew made little attempt, unlike the Mesopotamian, to improve the practical conveniences of everyday
living; he borrowed much of his language, astronomy, and
casuistic laws.

So much reliance was laid on a personalized infinity that any
order in the finite had to be dependent on the moral order dictated by God, although any parallel relationship between the
two, as in China, was neither mentioned nor implied. The regu-
lation of the movements of the universe resulting in the prosperity of man was reckoned to be in direct proportion to right
living, which means that personal responsibility to his divinity
was highly important to make God's plan effective in man's
behalf. Human personality was also triumphant as never before
or afterward in the east; it was, in the Hebrew's opinion, a
reflection of God's person, both bound together by the moral
bonds of the covenant. And why did man look to the terms of
the covenant? Not to obtain any immediate glory through his
own efforts, but in response to a still, small voice within, which

---

70. In the last verse of the concluding chapter of Jonah "much cattle"
is not reckoned against the account of the Ninevites.

acknowledged God and his righteousness as the arbiter of all his thinking and doing; he gave God the glory, who in turn could be relied on to give him the advantage over enemies and other obstacles. "My covenant will I not break, nor alter the thing which is gone out of my lips." [71] The complete self-identification with divinity produced a personality of exaggerated self-importance in much the same way as that of the late Middle Ages and Renaissance was brought forth on another plane by a similar identification with Christ. The difference between the two can be seen in the way the Hebrew God dispensed with all the theological trappings the God of the Middle Ages carried in his wake.

In the first place, the Hebrew personality imposed the moral law, which came originally from God, on all phenomenal events, and although the Hebrew was willing to admit their bearing on his life, God was after all the first cause, all effects coming somehow within the range of his control, while causes and effects which flit over the surface of experience were important only as they reveal the workings of the moral law. The personality of the late Middle Ages and Renaissance reached out into the various aspects of experience on a horizontal plane and applied the same enthusiasm it had formerly expressed to achieve self-identification with God, which resulted in a gross distortion of the finite. Above all, the person sought for the perfection, the certainty of the infinite in an imperfect world: instead of chemistry he rushed to alchemy, in place of astronomy he preferred astrology and the music of the spheres; mathematics was a steppingstone to the squaring of the circle, physics was a ladder to perpetual motion. Once he discovered the first cause operating behind each segment of experience, its connection with the subordinate effects was expected to reveal itself like an open book. The Hebrew personality believed in a God who was omnipresent and omniscient, he was in a mysterious way consistent with the infinite with which he was identified; man had no way of discovering the ways of God through finite experience nor did he, as a rule, feel any need for searching them out. "For my thoughts

---

71. Psalm LXXXIX, 34.

are not your thoughts, neither are your ways my ways, saith the Lord. For as the heavens are higher than the earth, so are my ways higher than your ways, and my thoughts than your thoughts." [72]

Likewise, the Hebrew was loath to project the order of finite experience into the province of God's sway. The Christian personality made bold to people heaven with a hierarchy of angels; he even created an aristocracy in hell and probed into afterlife and the last judgment. This the Hebrew would have labeled presumptuous blasphemy. The personality of both periods, based on a complete self-identification with divinity, bred an inflated sense of self-importance which confesses humility before God but, for the outsider, rose to the highest mountain of self-conceit.

This attitude of subjective importance, sanctioned by religion, was no encouragement to a broad historical perspective. We learn about Egyptians, Assyrians, and others in the immediate neighborhood only insofar as they played a minor role or served as a means to an end in the history of the chosen people. We have already noted a balanced subject-object relation between God and man which contributed toward making the Hebrew responsible to himself and to others of his own people, but it contributed nothing to the study of science or philosophy for which he seemed to have no need; it did little for his dealings with people beyond his borders. It is true that moral responsibility means much in forwarding the cause of democracy, but God, as well as the interpreters of his word, was so nationalistic in his bias, so arbitrary in dealing with human affairs that this type of government had little chance to grow on a horizontal plane. When the monarchy was established, every man was still equal in the sight of God without gaining the same status on earth. David and Solomon were quick to fall into the temptations of oriental autocracy. A concept of tragedy likewise had no chance to develop, as we have observed in the careers of Job and Joseph. The Mesopotamian, who was rather uncertain about

---

72. *Isaiah*, LV, 8–9.

the infinite, had strong intimations of the tragic meaning of experience, but where a strong personal God showed boundless mercy toward the worshipper in a mood of repentance, such an outlook was at its lowest ebb. Humor, too, was almost out of the question. The Hebrew's high degree of self-importance seldom became sufficiently conscious of its imperfections to give way to a good-natured laugh at its own expense. If personal superiority received any kind of a jolt it was considered a chastisement from heaven, and on such occasions the subjective tear was far more comforting than humor.

Where God made his presence known to men like Moses and Job he came with thunder and lightning, a shaking of the earth, or in a whirlwind. To the righteous he could speak with a still voice, but to his enemies he was a scourge, and when the Hebrew thought of his God, he conceived of him as clothed in power which could express itself with startling or comforting immediacy in all places. His complete dependence on a personalized infinite made the fear of the Lord, more than elsewhere in the east, the beginning of wisdom. Knowledge was, then, a matter of revelation more dictatorial and uncompromising because it came from a single God directly to man in terms of a moral code everyone could understand, and the world as we know it in experience lay before this God as a clear mirror reflecting his power, his majesty, and his will. God was certain about the world he had created, and man was certain about his God's attributes, so why should he be so concerned about knowledge derived from phenomena? He learned what was necessary for the needs of daily life and left the fundamental laws of the universe to an omniscient deity. A view of this nature made it easier for a teleological theory to achieve a complete triumph over contingencies in the finite, to transcend the impersonal, uncertain, cyclical movement of changing seasons.

The same concentration of emotion[73] the Hebrew applied to the worship of a single God he also carried over into other fields of expression. This can be seen especially in his poetry. The con-

---

73. T. J. Meek: *op. cit.* p. 184.

stant use of repetition and parallelism describes the enthusiasm of the writer more clearly than the concept in his mind, a concept he tries to color and make clear from a number of angles, by various images which contribute much by way of aesthetic value; for comprehensive understanding they leave much to be desired. It stands to reason that a comparative scale of values had little chance against such emotional concentration, and the healthy question mark could not compete with the certainty bred from self-identification with a perfect divinity.

God was the first and only great cause that had not only created and set the world in motion, he would also continue to watch over it to the end of time. He encompassed the finite to such an extent he could mentally anticipate the destiny toward which he was directing his world and people. The manifold effects emanating from the first cause came down to prophets and teachers as general truths with an air of finality intolerant of exceptions; whatever opposed such a statement, handed down by revelation, could be presented by sharp and exclusive contrasts, all of which afford a colorful effect and, in the hands of a zealous interpreter, leave little room for argument. To make such a truth, drawn down from the infinite, clear to another, analogy or allegory must be used to illustrate the universal as it can best be reflected in the particular. In the absence of reasoned argument there was little occasion to develop the abstract idea for purposes of scientific thought.

It was the personality of a single God that maintained the connection between the infinite and finite, so opposed to one another, and God demanded that man conform to the moral law if he wished to remain in touch with the infinite; the Hebrew saw no need of dealing directly with the finite by imposing the static line or an impress of power to preserve order. His connection with God assured man of the efficacy of the moral order which in turn would keep all else in order. Where a single and a jealous God controls his world with such a powerful hand, it is out of the question for an earthly ruler to assume the garb of divinity; politics must remain subordinate to religion and the moral law. Moreover, the priestly class never achieved the position of power reached by the same class in Egypt, for the priest, like the king, was open to the sharp criticism of the prophet, in fact of anyone who communed in secret with his righteous God; nor could the priest lay any claim to the control of a cycle of the seasons as elsewhere in the east.

The Hebrew was the first to make a sharp distinction between the finite and the infinite, to personalize his divinity, and to make the worshipper responsible directly to himself and to his God. For these three contributions the western world is deeply indebted to him, both in its religion and its thinking. That the sharp cleavage between God and the world would involve the later thinker in hopeless paradoxes was not a matter of concern to the Hebrew who left the laws of the universe undisturbed in the lap of God. The Hebrew's achievement in ethics is nothing less than astounding, and it might have been more fruitful had it spread its influence abroad beyond the direct connecting link between God and man, along the horizontal plane of experience.

THE HINDU

MANY OF THE ARTERIES of cultural expression converging upon the West in ancient times can be traced back to the Far East, especially to Mother India where so many traditions in religion, philosophy, and music were germinated. As often as she is misunderstood and misinterpreted, as much as she is abused and castigated, she has remained the centripetal point of attraction for many things spiritual from the days of Pythagoras and the Orphics to the present day; she has leavened the lump of intellectualism with a constant reminder of the needs of the inner man; she is the center of a great mystic circle radiating countless challenges to the reason and phenomenalism of the west—in more ways than one, India is the East! From the cold, bleak ranges of the Himalayas in the north to the hot, sultry plains and plateaus of the south, her geography includes a variety of climates, flora, and fauna, and one of the most dense populations of the earth. Her two great rivers, the Indus and the Ganges, and their tributaries, bring down water and silt aplenty from the mountains to the hot plains, in fact a large percentage of the land is fertile enough to support a very large population. Famines have been known to bring starvation and distress, but when the monsoons bring their rainfall, the peasant can reap two harvests and his cattle thrive on rapidly growing vegetation. In this colorful land the extremes of the tropics stand out in sharp contrast and at the same time give way to one another in rapid succession. Light and darkness, growth and decay, birth and death move through the pageantry of life like shooting rockets, leaving only a transitory impression in their wake; the constant play of opposites and contrasts on the surface is baffling to the thinker trying to pry into the underlying design of the cosmos. Perhaps this feature of his life has led the Hindu to seek reality somewhere beneath the sparkling but disturbing arabesque of appearances.

We know now, from recent excavations, that an advanced civilization flourished in the Indus valley as far back as the early third millenium, one which is as old and perhaps older than the cities of Sumer with whom the peoples of the Indus valley maintained contacts. Mohenjo-Daro was inhabited by people who had a well-developed system of writing, had mastered the arts of construction, were meticulous about sanitation in public and at home, and had learned how to harness the resources of the Indus. The writing was phonetic, not alphabetic, by no means as advanced as cuneiform, but the surviving remains furnish sufficient evidence to stamp it as pre-Aryan; likewise the appearance of the mother goddess in imagery tends to place this people in a distinctive category. Their facial features, dominated by large eyes with half-closed lids, are common to no other known early civilization. Their wealth was derived, in the first place, from agriculture, producing a number of cereals and dates from a very rich soil and a climate much different in ancient times; they domesticated the humped bull or zebu, the buffalo, the elephant, the camel, the sheep, the pig, and the fowl; the Aryan horse was not used. For weapons and utensils they availed themselves of copper, tin, and lead and were acquainted with gold and bronze, the last of which is a rarity in later Indian civilization. The second major source of wealth was trade, for which the Indus was a great asset as an outlet for goods passing out to Mesopotamia and elsewhere—goods which took the form of various articles produced at home: among weapons of war they fashioned axes, daggers, spears, and maces, but, strangely enough, no defensive armor. On the wheel they made red, black, polychrome, and glazed pottery. They also had garments of wool and cotton, barley and wheat for cereals, and a wealth of personal adornments.

Religion presents a perplexing problem to one who is familiar with Egypt, Mesopotamia, and the Hebrews. There are figures of a fertility or mother goddess; stones in the form of baetyls and lingas were invested with religious significance; there are indications, as in Crete, of aniconic worship and anthropomorphic gods; they paid great respect to animals as well as composite monsters; yet, with all these tokens of religious worship, we cannot assert they had either a temple dedicated to divinity or any set place for a cult.[1] One male figure has been called a priest, but beyond this identification, specious as it is, there is no definite sign of an organized priesthood. Food stored in jars and buried with the dead points to a belief in survival after death; other aspects mark their religion as the forerunner of subsequent developments among the later Hindus. We might think of their religion as a primitive pantheism or an enlightened animism, which might explain the fact that not a single building was set aside, as far as archaeology can reveal, for religious purposes. The art of construction is one of their outstanding accomplishments. For materials they used brick of a fine quality, gypsum, limestone, and alabaster, but for roofing they apparently relied on wood, both for public buildings and houses, which had two stories, a central courtyard, doorways, an occasional window, and brick floors much more substantial than in the houses we have observed elsewhere; roofs were flat and only the corbeled arch was known. Because careful provision was made for bathrooms, drains, and rubbish disposal, indicating an emphasis on cleanliness of body and living quarters, the largest and most remarkable building in the city was a bathhouse in which we find the bath itself in the center of a large quadrangle surrounded by a fenestrated wall and galleries, all of which show signs of careful construction. Where other peoples built a temple for the worship of a patron divinity, Mohenjo-Daro devoted its best resources to a bathhouse. Is there the slightest possibility of associating such a structure with religion?

Images of bronze and stone were found, but none of any great size, another feature suggesting a parallel with the Minoans. These figures all reveal a fairly good knowledge of anatomical proportions, good modeling, and, in some cases, a soft

---

1. Sir John Marshall: *Mohenjo-Daro and the Indus Civilization*, London, 1931, I, p. 48. For much of our information about this city we are indebted to this authority.

treatment of contours, especially the bronze figure suggesting a dancing girl, a most challenging piece of art from so early a period; there are also a number of heads which may be portraits without revealing the vocation of the subject. There are a great number of animal figures such as the rhinoceros, the buffalo, the bull, the monkey, the goat, and the bear as well as symbolic forms which seem to have a religious or magical significance. The artist was also acquainted with faience and intaglio engraving. Much, of course, remains to be learned about this civilization and its connections with others in the East, but of one thing we may be certain: it contained a number of germs which developed more fully in later Hindu times, as different as they may seem, on the surface, from what we know about the India of the *Vedas*.[2]

Aside from the fact that the Hindus had no Herodotus, they were not sufficiently interested in their past to produce a Manetho or Berosus, which compels the modern investigator to rely on archaeology, neglected inscriptions, religious literature, and the records of outsiders who came into occasional contact with India. From the *Vedas* comes most of our information about the Aryans who, some time in the fifteenth century, were on the move in Europe and southern Asia and eventually made their way into the Indian peninsula. Here they pushed back a dark-skinned people known as Dravidians or Dasyus, so repugnant to the invaders they gradually developed a caste system to draw a strict line of demarcation between the Aryan and the native. This system, sanctioned by religion, included the priestly class, the warriors, the peasants, and the slaves; the mere presence of a member of the class of outcasts was regarded as impure. The Aryans were great horsemen, and the use of the horse on the field of battle gave them a great advantage over their adversaries. The literature of the *Vedas*, composed of hymns as well as more prosaic passages, exalts the warrior to a high social level similar to that of the hero in the *Iliad*, all of which is a natural ideal for a people invading a strange, new land. Although there is no clear doctrine of life after death, the ideal of the hymns implies

---

2. Sir John Marshall: *ibid.*, pls. III, VII, and XXIb.

that the good warrior, in the next world, made his abode with
the gods in happiness, while the coward fell into a bottomless
pit.[3]

Like their cousins in Greece, the Aryans in India worshipped
male gods, for the most part, that had established their sway
over sky and air. The chief members of their pantheon included
Varuna, the great god of the sky; Indra, presiding over the rain
clouds and thundering regions of the air; Rudra, the god of the
forests; Agni, the lord of fire; and Mitra, the sun; the earth
goddess, so important to the agricultural natives, played a subordinate role. The later triad of Hindu religion, the doctrine of
transmigration, and the philosophical speculations of the *Upanishads* were latent, without any obvious influence and slumbering
until time and climate would have a more telling effect on the
invader.

The historical element in the *Vedas,* going back no farther
than 1200 B.C., deals chiefly with the conflict between two tribes
or groups, the Purus and the Panchalas, a reflection of the
struggle between the natives and the Aryan newcomers. As the
gods of the Aryans were predominantly male, so the father was
the final authority in the family, the owner of its property, the
arbiter of its destiny, and therefore boys were preferred to girls.
Government, resembling that of the Homeric epics, was vested
in a monarchy whose king, although hereditary, was somewhat
limited by the voices of the elders and the people as a whole.
The king's functions were largely military and judicial in nature,
duties which continued to be associated with the ruler throughout Indian history. Because of the emphasis on the tribe or clan
among the Aryans the people lived in villages, where the king
or raja was able to supervise all activities personally. In the
absence of a system of coinage, all trade was carried on by barter
for which the cow was the unit of value. At first they gained their
livelihood by grazing their flocks and herds as well as by hunting,
but agriculture became increasingly popular as they learned
more about it from the natives. So far as we know, they made

---

3. Cf. H. G. Rawlinson: *India: A Short Cultural History,* London, 1937,
p. 32

no use of writing, which means that all tradition, law, and literature were handed down orally and retained by memory. Unlike their descendants, they had no scruples about eating meat. For diversion they indulged in horse racing, hunting, and gambling, the latter with so much abandon the loser was often forced into slavery as a consequence. As they continued to spread over the peninsula, except for the southern section, we become aware of a greater consciousness of caste distinction, a greater respect for animal life, and a tendency toward monism in religion, and it is tempting to think that these aspects of Indian culture were already present prior to the coming of the Aryans, who merely suppressed them for a time.[4]

By the time of the Magadhan dynasty, the village, in certain localities, was giving way to the large city, the expanding domain of the single ruler demanded dependence on a viceroy and officials, the peasant became a landowner, and castes more rigid. The *Brahmanas,* which we shall consider again later, were compiled some time after 800 B.C. The sixth century brought with it the *Upanishads,* containing the philosophical speculations on religion and metaphysics, also the two sectarian movements, namely, Buddhism and Jainism, for many a man in those days was inclined to protest against the increased ritual demands of the priesthood in favor of meditation, asceticism, or wandering in the forests to achieve salvation in his own way. Buddha, who was a member of the upper classes, saw how vain, inconsistent, and full of suffering life around him had become and consequently left his family and wealth behind to seek for some kind of release. Neither he nor Mahavira, the leader of the Jains, led a crusade against the Brahmins as a class of people or their way of life, but they objected to their doctrine, their emphasis on formal sacrifice; in general, Buddha adopted a tolerant attitude toward the priesthood without receiving the same treatment in return. There was also some friction between the Buddhists and Jains, who carried their self-discipline to the point of severe asceticism which Buddha had abandoned as a futile extreme.

---

4. On this subject cf. *The Cambridge Ancient History,* New York, 1922, I, p. 144.

Historically, Buddha was a man of tremendous political influence at home and abroad, for a number of powerful rulers became his followers, but the common man, always a lover of religion in more concrete manifestations, had neither the leisure nor the understanding to follow such a doctrine, in spite of the democracy it opposed to the system of caste. Buddha made a strong appeal on the surface of India's religion before his doctrine passed to foreign lands, where it submitted to a compromise its founder would hardly have recognized as Buddhism.

The period of Greek penetration into the Punjab gives the historian one sound point of departure for Indian chronology. Alexander marched into Asia Minor and met the Persians at Granicus in 334 B.C., then defeated them a second time about a year later at Issus. After conquering Egypt and Phoenicia he made his way eastward through Bactria until he arrived at the Indus, where Porus and his army were waiting on the other bank. It was 326 B.C. when he defeated the Indian prince. He was finally halted by a rebellion of his own troops, after which he returned to Babylon and died in 323 B.C., leaving his eastern conquests to Seleucus, who eventually met with defeat at the hands of Chandragupta and then submitted to a compromise. Subsequently the Greek princes adjacent to India asserted their independence, and once the Mauryan empire disintegrated, Menander penetrated much farther into the heart of India than Alexander.[5] Megasthenes, the ambassador of Seleucus at the court of Chandragupta, furnishes ample evidence for the difficulties the West was meeting in coming to congenial terms with the East, even when he was most positive in his interpretations; he made enough interesting observations on India to tickle the curiosity of the Greek and furnish us with information of cultural value, but he made only a passing impression on the Hindu. He was, for the most part, an accurate reporter, although the caste system caused him some confusion; he distinguishes seven in all: philosophers, farmers, traders and artisans, herdsmen, overseers, soldiers, and councilors. Aside from art, it is hard to trace

5. R. C. Majumdar, H. C. Raychanduri, and Kalikinkar Datta: *An Advanced History of India*, London, 1946, p. 114.

any lasting influence brought to bear on the Hindus by the coming of the Greeks, unless it was an awareness of the need for political consolidation, which the Mauryas effected soon after the exit of Alexander.

Chandragupta, the lowborn empire builder, began his reign in 324 B.C. and within a few years, by putting into practice the military knowledge acquired in his youth, he molded a good share of northern India into a large kingdom. We know he was a capable organizer and military leader, one who set the pattern for many a ruler who followed him. The empire was divided into provinces which in turn were made up of smaller divisions of territory, including a certain number of free cities. Caste rules were rather strict during his reign but somewhat difficult to control, for a foreign element invaded the ranks of soldiers who thereby lost their former high rating in the eyes of the people. The peasants were exempt from military service; the hunters kept the land free of wild beasts; slavery, now an established institution, included: unfortunate gamblers, the lowest caste, and prisoners of war, but we must remember that most of them could purchase their freedom. The person of the king was not exclusively divine, or let us say the spark of divinity in his personality burned no brighter than in the best of his subjects, for in the diadem of Hindu divinity all jewels, both large and small, display an equal brilliance, a feature that offers an interesting comparison with rulers of the Near East already considered. Chandragupta was carefully guarded in all his activities, because assassins were always waiting for an opportunity to displace royalty in India.[6] He led his troops on the field of battle, he presided as judge in his courts, and in general acted in the best interests of his people, but he also felt privileged to spy on them. The support for his vast administrative system and for his huge army came from a tax on the produce of the land and, to a more limited degree, from trade now thriving with the Greeks in the West.

---

6. The fact that Chandragupta was a usurper, I believe, had very little to do with it. Cf. W. H. Moreland and A. C. Chatterjee: *A Short History of India*, London, 1936, p. 50.

Asoka, the most well known of the holy rulers of India, began his reign in 274 B.C. very much like his predecessors. He suppressed all opposition and then set out to enlarge his kingdom, but suddenly the course of his life was radically changed after viewing the slaughter his first great battle had occasioned. He became a convinced Buddhist in word and by example and he did all in his power to glorify the name of Buddha by setting up shrines, by despatching missionaries beyond his frontiers, by concentrating on philanthropical enterprises, by stressing toleration and nonviolence toward all creatures. So much glory has been gathered around the head of Asoka it is hard to know how effective his experiment was among the people as a whole, but we may be reasonably certain no one took advantage of his preoccupation with religion to cause a major upset in the kingdom. He was practical enough to avoid the mistakes of Akhenaton; he was colorful enough to build up a glorious tradition around his personality.[7]

Soon after the birth of Christ, the Greeks of northwest India were hard pressed by the Sakas or Scythians who had been pushed forward by others behind them. Something more than a century later the Kushans, coming from the same direction, supplanted the Sakas and extended their sway much farther into the heart of the peninsula. A heavy shadow surrounds the figure of Kanishka, their outstanding ruler, but two facts emerge in rather clear outline: he must have been a man of some military ability to build up a kingdom from such a heterogeneous group of people; he was also a figure of consequence in religion, not only because of his support of the Mahayana doctrine of Buddhism, which was especially palatable to foreigners, but also for the mark he left on its sculpture and architecture. The unity of the kingdom was evidently maintained by the force of his personality, for soon after his death the usual disintegration covered his footprints in the sands of time. Like so many swift conquerors from the north, the Kushans adopted Hindu culture as their own and soon lost their identity.

---

7. For some interesting comments on the character of Asoka consult E. Hawkridge: *Indian Kings and Gods,* New York, 1935, pp. 104–116.

When Hindu leaders once more asserted themselves over a broad area in the fourth century A.D. India found herself flourishing in what is called the classical age of her history. The monarchs of the Gupta period who established themselves at the old capital of Pataliputra would hardly be known were it not for epigraphical evidence, their coinage, and the commentaries of a Chinese pilgrim. Princes like Samudra Gupta and Chandragupta II were two of the most capable men India has ever produced, men who by their own example encouraged the development of the whole man in the Hindu sense of the term. In their marriages contracted with other ruling houses and their dealings with neighboring powers they showed themselves masters of diplomacy; while they did not, as Asoka, actively campaign for a certain sect, they included religion in their program of reviving the old Indian culture; their conquests afield marked them as military leaders; they were poets and musicians and encouraged the arts in a kingdom embracing most of northern India. The paintings in the Ajanta caves, more than anything else, reflect something of the *joie de vivre*, the color and wealth, manners and refinement among the upper classes in an age that flourished as luxuriously as the vegetation of Ceylon—and passed away as quickly. Sanscrit, the classical medium of those who knew, achieved its greatest popularity as a vehicle of literary expression. Kalidasa, the greatest name in Indian letters, composed his poetry and dramas under the patronage of a monarch who granted financial support to literary talents.

The account of the Chinese pilgrim, Fa-Hsien, is especially interesting because he noted aspects of Indian life the native would have passed over as too obvious and matter-of-fact. The persevering traveler had come from a distant region of China, had traversed river, mountain, and desert before he was welcomed in India, where he hoped to find some precious Buddhistic manuscripts for his people at home. He found people living in great prosperity without resorting to the vices that frequently go with it. It seemed that the Hindus of this time had extracted all the fine points from the teachings of Buddhists and Brahmins alike and were taking advantage of all the aesthetic values created by the writers and artists of previous periods. He found palaces, temples, and monasteries aplenty; he saw both Brahmins and Buddhists thriving in a tolerant atmosphere; he was especially pleased with the house where medical care and charity were dispensed without cost; people were generally benevolent,[8] and criminal cases were treated with leniency; they refrained from killing living creatures and abstained from strong drink, onions, and garlic. Whatever we may put down to exaggeration in his account, it is still obvious that India under the Guptas saw the finest flowering of the universal brotherhood of man, triumphing over all sectarian differences which have so often wrought havoc in man's everyday living. To the doubting Thomas we can only reply that tolerance, in general, was as basic in Hindu thought as sin in Medieval theology. The Chinese pilgrim wrote down his impressions, found his manuscripts, and then made his way back home by way of Ceylon and the sea.

During the fifth century the Huns, following the usual route of the invader, knocked hard at the gates of India but were repulsed. A century or more later they met with success, spreading carnage and slaughter in all directions in the most harrowing disaster India had as yet known. The barbarian hordes were finally checked by Yasodharman at Mandasor. In 606 A.D. a new king, Harsha by name, established himself at Kenauj, a city centrally located in northern India on one of the tributaries of the Ganges.[9]

Our information about this monarch also comes from inscriptions, the literary records of Bana, and another Chinese pilgrim, Huien Tsang, whose stay in India follows a pattern somewhat similar to the visit of his predecessor. Harsha, the youngest son of a house which had fallen on evil days, avenged all the wrongs of his family before uniting north India into a compact kingdom

---

8. Not all Hindu monarchs found it necessary to maintain a military regime to collect money from a subject by terrorizing him. Cf. R. Turner: *The Great Cultural Traditions,* New York, 1941, II, p. 750.

9. For information on the selection of Harsha and the difficulties that stood in his way consult R. C. Majumdar, H. C. Raychanduri and K. Datta: *op. cit.,* pp. 155–57.

again. Once more we are told the people were law-abiding in a land where the king reaped so much wealth from royal lands and from commerce he found it unnecessary to levy additional taxes. Like all potentates of his kind he maintained a huge fighting force divided into infantry, cavalry, chariots, and elephants; he established relations with the Chinese court, although he cherished no high regard for the Chinese people. Some time after ascending the throne he embraced Mahayana Buddhism, perhaps because the practice of magic had been popular with his family and congenial to his temperament. If he was not intolerant toward the Brahmins and sects of his time he did his utmost to defend the doctrine of his choice and used his Chinese visitor, who cherished similar convictions on another plane, as a means for his ends. He presided over a large assembly of learned men representing the two main divisions of the Buddhists, the Mahayana faith championed by the visitor from China; the arguments of the latter, as might be expected, completely confounded the defenders of the Hinayana persuasion. If there was one practice that made him an outstanding monarch, it was his way, like that of Frederick the Great, of touring the main provinces and thus dispensing with intermediate ministers.[10] He was an autocrat to the core, sensational in his love of display, charitable with the property of his people, but a hard worker and in some respects, very responsible to himself.

With the passing of Harsha the northern kingdom was split up into a number of smaller units, constantly at odds with each other, the more important including the Palas of Bengal, the Pratiharas in Kenauj, the Chalukayas in the Bombay country, none of which were strong enough to cope with a foreign invasion. After the end of the Gupta period the king was regarded as more divine, an incarnation of Vishnu, the preserver. Because of the foreign element it was becoming increasingly difficult to maintain caste distinctions. Women succeeded in raising themselves to a higher status; at least we hear more about queens than formerly. These features, however, had little to do with the

10. J. Allen, T. W. Haig, and H. H. Dodwell: *The Cambridge Shorter History of India,* New York, 1934, p. 108.

gradual political debilitation, which made India a fatted calf for the fanatical digestion of the Turkish Muslims pouring in from the west in the twelfth century.

With the Muslims we are not directly concerned, except insofar as they stood at variance with the Hindus, whose religious outlook was so diametrically opposed they found themselves in a bitter conflict with Islam on many issues.[11] Not even the chivalry of the Rajputs, unfortunately without much unity, was a match for the fierce, frenzied attack of the Muslims, who at first gave the Hindus a choice between death and conversion to Islam; later the terms were apparently more lenient. The invading rulers were greedy for wealth and display, suspicious of any possible rival, relentless in exacting punishment, and although they campaigned theoretically for the glory of Islam, actually they carried on in their own interest, owning but a nominal connection with the Caliphate. The common people were left more or less in peace as long as they paid their taxes and minded their business. While the newcomers held sway in Delhi, the Mongols made repeated raids into the Sultanate, and at the close of the thirteenth century were encamped outside the walls of the capital; suddenly, for no accountable reason, they broke camp and left. In 1398 they returned under Tamerlane, sacked Delhi, murdered countless people, and thus broke up an already weakened Muslim empire. Tamerlane departed soon after his devastating raid.

On the ruins of this empire a Hindu revival centered around the city and kingdom of Vijayanagar, whose fabulous wealth and splendor reads like a Spaniard's dream of El Dorado. It flourished from the fourteenth to the sixteenth centuries in southern India. Report has it that the walls were sixty miles in circumference, reaching out into mountains and valleys; within the walls were huge and sumptuously carved temples and palaces where kings ruled in the most lavish pageantry India had ever known. The Brahmins reigned supreme over the religious life of the people. Travelers who visited this city of extravagance

---

11. The reason for this difference will be discussed when we take up the religion of the Hindus.

expand on the jeweled wealth of the people, the riotous but colorful festivals with their accompanying sacrifices, the music, the dancing, the processions. Women rose to positions of rank at court and the rite of Sati was a common occurrence. The city maintained contacts with many foreign powers by trade which brought more wealth to its coffers than at any other time in India's history, while the kings, men of some taste in their own right, patronized a revival of music, art, and literature. The army was a most formidable force, including large numbers of elephants, but by no means mobile enough to stand up against the Muslim cavalry, although the walls of the city offered a safe retreat until the decisive Muslim victory at Talikata in 1565. Soon thereafter the fabulous splendor of the city was a colorful mirage floating over a desolate wasteland.

The Muslims surged back into power in the north, after Babur overpowered the Rajputs in 1527, under the so-called Moghul rulers. Among a number of powerful personalities who reigned in accord with the usual political formula of the East, Akbar stands head and shoulders above all sultans. Having shaken himself free of the intrigues of the harem in 1562, he proceeded to fortify his position by military conquests on all sides, and then, whether because of his early experience with his family, his epileptic seizures, or the awareness of a yawning abyss within, he became a solitary searcher after divine truth; at times his quest led him into paths of ecstatic mysticism, on other occasions he sought the secret of the universe in debate, in questioning theological authorities on every faith. He invited Christians, among others, to his court, treated them kindly, listened attentively to their attempts to convert him—all to no avail; he could not understand how God had become flesh or how three persons could exist in one. If he failed to satisfy his own yearning by such experiments in religion, he did achieve a tolerant outlook which extended freedom of worship to all sects. He also tried to do away with the feudal noblemen and thus establish a closer relation between ruler and subject. In spite of rumblings of heresy among Muslims, he set up an eclectic faith and creed and made himself the supreme arbiter in all matters of religion by issuing the so-called Infallibility Decree. His ultimate impatience with uncertainty led him to adopt an artificial dogma by which he hoped to preserve his own dignity and all that was best in every religion. Akbar was a great military leader, a good administrator, a keen student of human nature, and the most progressive thinker the Muslims produced in India. But, in spite of all his ability and assets, his restless mind gave his soul more torture than rest!

The Portuguese, coming to India about 1510, captured Goa from the Muslims, a port they used as a trading post over a long period. In the course of subsequent years the Europeans came with their armies and missionaries, their traders seeking gems and spices, until the English, under Lord Clive, succeeded in rendering all India subject to the crown.

For the student of the West the religion of India presents a number of perplexing problems: with his eyes focused on the phenomena of a pluralistic experience and a mind equipped for and readied to deal with the finite, he looks at what the Hindu calls religion only to find that at one stage of its history it is polytheistic, again it may be predominantly pantheistic, and at another time it may even appear monotheistic, all of which the Hindu considers normal and consistent with the nature of his universe. The Hindu can also, for reasons we shall discuss later, attach any of these attributes to his own religious experience without violating the integrity of his thinking. Why should the Indian be too concerned about our analyses, our categories, our consistencies, and what we call contradictions as long as his experience can be genuine in any of these classifications? We like to draw a distinction between philosophy and religion which becomes dangerous, if not disastrous, in the cultural expression of the East; we feel it necessary to distinguish between secular thought and religious revelation or inspiration, but the Hindu can no more exclude thought from religion than he can enclose a sensation in a vacuum. Whether we learn to understand his viewpoint or not, we must admit he is more at one with his experience than others, or, let us say, he has no need of a complex system of thought to achieve self-identification with what he calls reality.

The religion of the Aryans, reflected in the *Rig-Veda,* is that of a people who were first shepherds and herdsmen and, in the second place, tillers of the soil; there are repeated references to cows, to roaring and charging bulls, to the green of the grass, and the rain that nourishes the pastures. Their gods, like those of their kinsmen of Persia, Greece, and Rome, are in some way akin to light as seen in the sky, the sun, the dawn, an emphasis on luminosity we should expect of a people from the north, where a lighted sky was more rare and hence more precious than in the south. Their pantheon was patterned after the family or clan; the gods conformed to a large family organization with the male element, especially the father, in a dominant role. The moral tone of their worship is also that of the clan: those gods who benefited the group became the most powerful and glorious, received the most devout prayers and sacrifices, and dwelt in the light, while the gods and demons identified with adversity eventually had to go down to defeat, condemned to pass their time in darkness. Because war was the preoccupation of an invading people, their gods also had to respond to the battle cry and rejoice in the victories and spoils of their subjects. Polytheism, better than any other term, expresses the reverence of the Aryan toward nature and his experience, for in this period the gods evidently stood out in bolder, more personal outlines than in later Hindu history; yet we must be cautious in applying such a term to their divinities without qualifications, for as soon as the Hindu seems to move in one direction where we can pin him down categorically, we become aware of a new and different development under cover of a phenomenal manifestation, ready to be cast off like a snake's dead skin. On the surface polytheism appeared almost crystalized, but the functions and provinces of the gods overlapped to such a degree their individuality gradually became a mirage whose eventual transparency revealed something very different below the surface.

The universe was divided into three sections: heaven, midair, and the earth, each of which was presided over by a major divinity attended by a group of others, totaling a number of thirty-three; those of heaven were higher in rank than the rest. Varuna, the supreme god of heaven, encompassed the earth and fertilized her with his rain. As the god of the sky he was omniscient, keeping a watchful eye over the movements of the cosmos as well as the deeds of men, which means he was both an ethical monitor and a cosmic ruler. The eternal order which found expression both in the change of seasons and the moral life of man was known as rita,[12] a concept which shows a general similarity to the *ma'at* of the Egyptian. As the moral arbiter of the universe, Varuna was responsible for the punishment of wrong, frequently taking the form of drought or disease, and also for forgiveness dispensed to the sinner who had truly repented in his heart. Varuna was, then, a god of justice and mercy. At the peak of his power he was apparently making a strong bid for monotheistic exclusiveness, when he was strangely and embarrassingly demoted to the supervision of lakes and pools.

Indra, the most anthropomorphic god of the pantheon, was the most popular divinity of the period because he was an advocate of action, a practical, blustering, and ruthless god of war, trampling his enemies underfoot and rewarding his followers with the spoils of battle. He owed much of his prominence to the struggles of the invaders against the dark-skinned natives. Like many of the heroes of Aryan peoples, he became the great benefactor of mankind by slaying the great dragon, a tradition antedating the invasion of India. In prehistoric times the dragon Vritra was no doubt the ice of winter holding the warm rains of spring in check, but in a tropical climate it became the drought destined to be wiped out by the rain clouds. Before going into battle Indra consumed large quantities of soma, a drink whose effect increased the energy and courage of the military man and which was also sublimated to the divine level as a dispenser of health and immortality. Armed with his favorite weapon, the lightning bolt, accompanied by the Maruts,

---

12. In Egypt the control of cosmic law was in the hands of the pharaoh. For further comments on the subject consult H. D. Griswold: *The Religion of the Rig-Veda*, London, 1923, p. 107.

his boisterous companions of war, he set forth against the enemies of man, usually thought of as demons, who were repeatedly hurled into a deep abyss of darkness. Like most monarchs, after a rich victory he generously divided his plunder with his friends.

Usas, the goddess of the dawn, was a paragon of feminine elegance—she removed the black robe of night and drove away the specters of darkness. Prithivi, the earth mother, was a silent, patient, passive, and long-suffering model for every respectable matron of an Aryan family. As Indra was the favorite of the warrior caste, Agni, the god of fire, became the special patron of the priests, a god represented by the sun in heaven, the lightning in midair, and the fire on the altar of sacrifice. The artist depicted him as a red man with three flaming heads, three legs, seven arms, and riding on a ram. Fire, like soma, originally came down from heaven to the earth, whence it was continually passing upward to the gods by way of burnt offerings, a profitable exchange which somehow gave both man and god a mutual pat on the back. Other deities include the twin Aswins or the divine physicians; Tvastar, the patron of artisans; Pushan, the shepherd god; Vishnu, the guardian of paradise; and Rudra, the storm god of destruction who became the later Siva; the latter two assumed much more important roles in a later period. The popularity of cremation and the doctrine of heaven and hell argue for a belief in immortality but do not fit in with the later concepts of transmigration and karma; enough, however, is suggested to prepare us for the change realized in the later *Upanishads*. It is interesting to observe that in the later Vedic period sacrifice looms up as the all-important tool of the priesthood;[13] it not only compels the gods to comply with man's bidding but by sheer force of its magic gives the gods power to carry out their duties in the interest of man.

Some time about 1000 B.C. a great change[13a] manifested itself in the religious outlook of India, in which both the climate

13. M. Hiriyanna: *Outlines of Indian Philosophy*, London, 1932, p. 36.
13a. G. Misch (*The Dawn of Philosophy*, London, 1950, pp. 79 ff.) has made a noble effort to trace its development in the thought and literature of the foregoing period.

and contacts with native peoples no doubt played a role. Once there was no longer a need for constant warfare, once the Aryans had settled down in their new home, the rapid growth and decay of life and vegetation in a tropical climate must have impressed them with the vanity of so much they formerly valued in experience. As lethargy gradually dulled the edge of positive energy, a certain degree of pessimism appeared as a vanguard to a more negative view of life.[14] Furthermore, the priesthood had laid so much stress on sacrifice and ritual that many thinkers were encouraged to re-evaluate reality for themselves in terms of what we call religion and philosophy. The result was the great body of speculation embodied in the *Upanishads* which was brought to light between 800 and 600 B.C.

The Hindu thinker was resolved to find a permanent reality behind the constant change of his world, something all-sufficient in itself which would maintain its own consistency and also explain the multifarious appearances of everyday experience. He concluded that reality is a unity, permanent, eternal, and not to be observed by sensation; this unity which can only be penetrated by introspection the Hindu called Brahman. Brahman was the ultimate source of the world outside; in other words, it extended itself into all living creatures and concrete objects where it was known as Atman. Inasmuch as reality was basically one and the same, the two, Brahman and Atman, were of the same nature; in this way the thinker avoided the contradiction in calling the Atman particular and finite over against the universal and infinite Brahman, thereby separating them into two different entities. In so doing, however, he made it more difficult to explain the manifestation of difference in the realm of sensation. At any rate, we are told to accept the following statement as axiomatic: Brahman is that which creates the world, it sustains it, and eventually reabsorbs it. A large share of the thinking of the *Upanishads* and much of that following their compilation is made up of variations on this prevailing theme. If we ask the Hindu to tell us about Brahman in and by

14. Cf. S. Konow and P. Tuxen: *The Religions of India*, Copenhagen, 1949, pp. 86–87.

itself, like Parmenides writing on being, he descibes it in terms of negatives; if we seek to know why an all-sufficient Brahman should desire to extend itself or, for that matter, should desire at all, we are given analogies instead of reasons.[15] Plato was likewise at a loss to explain why perfection in the world of ideas should be patient with the imperfections of shadows, and Plotinus found it impossible to state why the "one" should be moved to emanate.

In the *Upanishads* a number of speculations are made about the relation of Brahman to the world, the important difference depending on whether Brahman is immanent in the world or transcends the world. When a student asks how one can learn to know Brahman, he is told that from one standpoint it is like any universal in relation to its manifestation in form, e.g., the block of marble to anything carved from it (what does this mean if we assume Brahman and Atman to be basically of the same nature?); or he is flatly told it cannot be known at all from a psychological standpoint. The Atman, or soul, once extended from the Brahman into the world, forgets it is one with ultimate reality, but is endowed with the ability to transcend the conscious state which informs the soul only of the finite world. How can the soul become aware of its true nature and obtain release from the bondage of the world? Because the Hindu has long known how inadequate words are in exploring reality, the student is first of all urged to maintain silence. There are a number of states through which one may pass: the waking state, the dream state, that of dreamless sleep, and the *Turiya* state, the most mystic and exalted of all and hence impossible to describe. Actively, the student must achieve a detachment from the world, listen to a master, reflect on what has been imparted, and meditate on the unity behind the plurality and difference on the surface of things. Once the highest state is reached and all distinction between subject and object has been removed, the soul has crossed the razor's edge to self-realization, self-identification with Brahman and selflessness. Success in this great

15. Cf. F. H. Ross: *The Meaning of Life in Hinduism and Buddhism*, London, 1952, p. 26.

adventure of the spirit is also conditioned by the state of moral purity of the aspirant; kindness toward all living creatures implies a realization of his oneness with the universe and a willingness to renounce the world of appearances as values per se.

And what consideration is given to matter in this scheme? Is it merely a deceptive mirage known to the Hindu as *maya*? We are told that organic bodies, as opposed to inorganic bodies, can contain transmigrating souls. The former include those born from the egg, those born from the seed, and those coming up from the soil. Evil, far from being synonymous with matter, is rather the result of poor choice and a lack of moral perception and good judgment on the part of the agent. Evil results from his failure to see unity at the root of all difference, and the effort to be apart from the unity of things is responsible for desire and frustration of desire, calamity, sadness, and sorrow. One life, however, is not sufficient, as Kant also agreed, for a full realization of the meaning of life, hence there must be transmigration of the soul from one life to another. Karma implies that the present life, in which the agent is endowed with free will, gives one an opportunity to prepare for the lives to come when Dharma, the universal law of the universe, determines what rewards or punishments are to follow in the future. Eventual self-conquest will release the soul from such a cycle of necessity. Man is, in a large sense, the master of his own fate and once he finds himself in adverse fortune, he must blame the choice he has made instead of fate or a god in heaven beyond. And what, we may ask, has happened to the old gods of the Vedic pantheon? They are no more than divine manifestations in experience, as much a part of Brahman as Atman, and thus they too have bartered their initiative, their individuality, their apartness for a corporate share in the universal Brahman.

A number of interpretations and variations on the fundamental doctrines taught in the *Upanishads* are either found in the work itself or were developed as an aftermath. Bhakti, often called loving devotion for a single, personal deity, is more social in character in contrast to Yoga, an intellectual discipline applied by the disciple alone, a method of attaining release by solitary contemplation. Samkara taught that the individual obtains deliverance once he realizes his identity with the whole world, when he learns that the transmigration of souls is only an illusion. Here we should remember that an illusion, to the Hindu, assumes a kind of reality to consciousness, a reality that grows very dim in its particulars as the Atman approaches self-realization. Samkhaya bases his teaching on two principles, that of energy and that of matter. The various properties of matter, e.g., light, energy, and weight, are reflected in the souls where they assume conscious reality. This illusory connection between the soul and matter convinces the soul of the genuine character of its feeling, acting, and suffering until the soul achieves release, when it becomes aware of the fundamental difference between itself and its former illusion in consciousness.[16] We must be careful here not to confuse the spiritual experience of self-identification with any form of exalted pleasure learned in experience, for where there is pleasure of this nature, pain is not far distant;[17] Brahman has nothing in common with the heaven of many Christians and Muslims. As strange as it may seem, there is also a school of materialists who advocated the middle road in sensual indulgence and dismissed all spiritual reality as illusion.

The teachings of the *Upanishads* are the earliest attempt on the part of civilized man to explore the relation of the world to divinity on a spiritual level; what's more, it has stood the test of centuries during which it has produced concrete results among the Hindus, whereas no one in the West has been as successful, along a similar pathway, as Meister Eckhart. As adequate as the exploration has turned out to be for the Hindu mind, the effort to make it convincing, in rational terms, to the western mind is no more effective than the attempt of Narcissus to grasp his own image in the pool.

---

16. For further elaboration of this and other teachings based on the *Upanishads* the reader is referred to Theos Bernard: *Philosophical Foundations of India,* London, 1945, pp. 23 ff.

17. F. H. Ross: *op. cit.,* pp. 37–39.

The lower classes of people, who were unable to grasp the significance of philosophical religion, went on worshipping more personal gods, but a decided change came over the whole pantheon. Trimurti, the great trinity of Hinduism, must have been pretty well established in popular favor by the time the Greeks invaded India in the late fourth century B.C. Brahma is simply a personalized form of Brahman, the creator of the universe and all it contains, the prime mover, the being whose nature defies all description. The *Puranas* and the two great epics, our main sources on the trinity, speak of Vishnu as the preserver, probably because he took over the sun from Varuna, and as the most human of the great ones. Whenever humanity was threatened by some great calamity, it was Vishnu who appeared at the eleventh hour in one of his avatars to save the day; such an avatar might take the form of an animal like the fish or tortoise or even the heroic figures of Krishna and Rama. Buddha was also said to be one of his manifestations. Vishnu's interest in humanity, his way of championing the dying in the face of death, and the colorful tales woven about his avatars have made him the most popular of the triad. All things are born, are preserved, and prosper for a time before they are destroyed, whereupon the process begins once more. Siva, the lord of time and death, the patron of robbers and ghosts, closes the cycle of change on the surface of nature; but if Siva is the symbol of death, he also stands for resurrection, for one cannot be without the other. Ganesa, the son of Siva, rose from the ranks of demons to a great popularity because, to the average Hindu, he is a symbol of success and prosperity, a bon vivant, a jolly good toper crowned with the ungainly but shrewd head of the elephant.[18]

There are two important movements, sometimes classed as heretical, which rejected the *Vedas* and at the same time rose to a position of great importance in the Indian world, namely, Jainism and Buddhism. The chief historical propounder of the first was Mahavira, born about 540 B.C. into a family belonging

---

18. A. Getty (*Ganesa*, Oxford, 1936) has made a careful study of the god's career in history and art.

to the ruling class. After giving up his family for a life of asceticism, he spent much of his time teaching and organizing his order. There are, according to his doctrine, two important principles in the universe: spirit and matter (jiva and ajiva) and, unlike most Hindu teachings, as much attention is devoted to the one as to the other. The obvious reason is the fact that one is so compactly joined to the other the ascetic must know as much about matter as spirit to effect a release. Man's personality, like the world in general, is dual in character: it is made up of spirit and matter, and the object of Jainistic discipline is to remove the latter from the soul. Since the two principles are genuine, the same degree of reality must be attached to both permanence and change. Spirit is the life principle, extended into an infinite number of entities, eternal and the same throughout; matter, also eternal, is made up of countless atoms very much like those of Democritus, except for the spiritual element contained in each one; they are subject to the usual changes of the world but they also contain something permanent as well. Another aspect of reality is its relative character; it may be regarded from a number of viewpoints, and each viewpoint uncovers a partial truth, hence reality cannot be absolutely this or that; in other words, every statement about it must be conditional. Another reason for its relativism is the complex nature of reality in which nothing is isolated.

Since right knowledge is an important factor in the eventual release from Karma, the Jainist apologist has devoted much time and energy to the construction of an effective epistemology. When the disciple has removed every trace of Karma that permeates every bit of the soul as water saturates ice, the soul arrives at the state of pure knowledge or kevala. This goal, presupposing right faith, right knowledge, right conduct, forbids injury to living beings, falsehood, theft, and ownership of property; it demands celibacy and a renunciation of the world; for the layman these restrictions were somewhat modified. Suicide is justified only if the body is too weak to help the spirit on its way to release.[19] Because they do not believe in a god

---

19. N. Tatia: *Studies in Jaina Philosophy, Banaras,* 1951, p. 20.

who created the world, the Jainists were sometimes called atheistic; but how can such a charge be leveled against a doctrine which postulates a divine principle? To their credit we must explain that they have built up a moral parallelism[20] in Hindu philosophy, one which dispenses with the old embarrassing question involving creation on the part of a perfect being. They realized how inconsistent it is for a being of such a nature to desire anything beyond itself, and so man is raised to a higher level of dignity; since both matter and spirit are eternal, one can never hope to annihilate the other; the spirit must always be on the *qui vive* to anticipate the evil demon lurking around the corner.

Moreover, the binding connection between these two great principles calls for a much more rigorous discipline to obtain a release, a factor which, we may suggest, has tended to confine Jainism to India where such an asceticism could more easily find disciples.

Buddha, the founder of the second sect, was born about the middle of the sixth century B.C., likewise of a noble family, Gautama by name. After his marriage and the birth of a son the young man was seriously impressed by certain examples of suffering he saw, whereupon he decided to leave home and family to search for a solution to what, for him, was life's greatest problem. His first effort was by way of asceticism, in which he failed; a more moderate discipline eventually brought release, or nirvana, beneath the bo tree. Henceforth he spent his time teaching and preaching, attracting a great number of followers until he died at an advanced age. When we consider how radically different, in many ways, his teaching is from that of the Brahmins and how difficult it must have been for the common people to understand it, we are left with the fact of his personality, whose charm and persuasiveness must have been most telling, even if we discount much of what we read as legend. Soon after his death his ashes were kept in various stupas which became shrines or centers of attraction for pil-

---

20. In one sense, it is like the two attributes of God in the system of Spinoza.

grims. In a sense, this was a disadvantage for the movement, for when his followers raised their leader to a high level of divinity, they were yielding to an all too human tendency which contradicted his doctrine and played into the hands of the Brahmins.

As it was the awareness of suffering that brought Buddha to a turning point in his life, so the problem of suffering acted as a point of departure for his whole theory. His preoccupation, at the outset, with human misery and pain has led some critics to label him pessimistic, but these categorical labels, as we have pointed out, are as dangerous in Hindu philosophy as segregation in the organism; to the Buddhist the doctrine contains as much, if not more, optimism. Let us also state at the outset that we are interested primarily in the original thought core of Buddhism, and since the authorities are not too sure about this core,[21] we shall confine ourselves to a general statement.

On the surface Buddha's doctrine may appear to be a radical departure from the *Upanishads,* for he lays no stress on Brahman and its connection or identity with the Atman.[22] This is due both to the pragmatic nature of his teaching and the substitution of nirvana for Brahman. The central purpose of his teaching is the removal of human suffering from human experience, a theme to which, to the impatience of the theorist, he returns again and again. He realizes that man's pain and misery are bound up with desires for this and that which, when attained, bring, in the place of satisfaction, only more desire and misery in their wake; desire, as has been said, is sad, it is voracious and knows no limitations. Who desires, we may ask, and what is the nature of a subject that desires? What is the nature of the object desired? What is the connection set up between them that makes desire so demanding? The self, as the subject on the surface of experience, desires things beyond itself to main-

---

21. The difficulties are explained by E. Conze: *Buddhism,* New York, 1951, p. 27.

22. E. J. Thomas: *The History of Buddhist Thought,* New York, 1951, p. 96.

tain its apartness, to render itself greater than other selves or things, and this, to the Hindu thinker, has usually been reckoned as the major reason for evil. But what is this self? Buddha finds it has no substantial, focal center but is rather a conglomerate of conscious states we call the mind or consciousness. And what is the desired object? Merely a conglomerate of attributes without a common center, and these attributes include the Aristotelian universal and particular. This point is illustrated by his famous question about the chariot: if this object is neither the pole, the wheel, nor the axle, what is the chariot? We have, then, a subject composed of sensation, perception, reflection, etc., and an object masquerading as a collection of attributes, but actually there is neither a subject nor an object; we merely cling to suffering by feeling, perception, willing, and reason.[23] Such a construction on human thought, for the European, would have resulted in hopeless chaos and relativism similar to what the Sophists threatened in Greek thought, but for the Buddhist, who was turning his back on the role of thought in experience, such an annihilation of subject and object may have been negative in character but not at all disastrous for the further unfolding of his theory.

What, then, is the connection between the sum total of conscious states and the sum total of attributes held together by desire? Here Buddha resorts to cause and effect for an explanation, but if cause and effect are rigid and necessary, there is no way by which man, by free will, can alter the inevitable sequence of events which carries him along in a deterministic universe. But this necessary sequence Buddha denies. The effectiveness of an effect is governed not so much by an arbitrarily operating cause beyond the reach of choice as by contingencies in circumstances; there one can find plenty of sufficient, Leibnizian reasons for an effect which are within the province of man's control, and thus the effect may be changed by man himself. By altering these conditions man becomes the master of his fate. A desire for narcotics or intoxicants may very well be due to an illness of the body; once this is removed, the otherwise

23. F. H. Ross: *op. cit.*, p. 86.

usual chain between cause and effect breaks down. Buddha does not elaborate by erecting a mountain of theory to support his contention, for such a theory, he asserts, merely creates more desire to defend it and so would tend to defeat his original purpose. He keeps his main thesis in the foreground often to the sacrifice of satisfaction demanded by the analytical thinker; this thesis calls for the destruction of suffering in man's experience and the choice of a substitute at the expense of desire.

Having eliminated fatalism from the sphere of human striving, Buddha returns to the nature of things which he finds so transient they are worth little in the scale of values. In terms of time the subject and object are made still more undependable. Like a Hegelian he postulates being and nonbeing as extremes to characterize substance, but, as we have seen, the mind and the object can fit into neither one of these categories; they are neither permanent entities nor, on the other hand, can attributes and consciousness be called nonexistent. Hence he strikes a medium by declaring everything to be in a state of becoming which is approximate to the flux and flow of Heraclitus.[24] One conscious state, however, preserves a recollection of former states in a modified form, which means we can be held morally responsible for the past. The origin of suffering, then, lies in ignorance. Why desire something which has no permanence? Remove ignorance and contingent circumstances, and the world with all its desirable effects seems to fade on the horizon. In this way Buddha explains the four-fold truth: the nature of suffering, the origin of suffering, the removal of suffering, and the last sums up the practical method of effecting such a removal by right views, right intentions, right speech, right conduct, right livelihood, right effort, right thought, and right concentration.

In the practice of the above rules Buddha left much to individual discretion except for the general admonition to follow the middle of the road; monks, of course were held to stricter

---

24. I believe it would be more correct to say Heraclitus taught at about the same time as Buddha, not a generation or two later, as claimed by M. Hiriyanna (*op. cit.,* p. 142).

account than the ordinary layman; suicide, in contrast to the Jains, was forbidden.[25] He gave no quarter to the priests, their ritual and sacrifice, for every man was able to work out his own salvation. If by following the eight prescribed rules, the self and objects fade away, what happens to karma? If there is no self, no object for the man endowed with right knowledge, what manner of survival can he experience? That depends on your state of knowledge, Buddha would say—or your state of ignorance. If ignorance still prevails, karma will carry one around the wheel of existence again and again; from another standpoint there is, because of the fluid nature of things, a kind of rebirth with every passing moment; ethically, survival is the passing on of character[26] from one life to another, one generation to another, one day to another. Much the same holds true of nirvana, the final goal of the disciple following the eight rules. To the outside observer and critic this state may appear as self-annihilation, a blotting out of all experience, but to the man who has followed the prescribed discipline it means a calm, cool selflessness; ethically, it is freedom from desire; metaphysically, it means removal from the flux and flow of becoming and decay, the resolution of all opposites (a *coincidentia oppositiorum*), a spiritual release and freedom. The modern critic of the West then asks: is nirvana equal to God? On this point Buddha was evasive, but certainly one who realizes the spiritual character of his teaching will not put him down as an atheist. It was much more important for him to shed a practical influence of tolerance, of generosity, after the nirvana of selflessness has been attained.

Later in the history of the movement we hear of the Hinayana and Mahayana schools of Buddhism; the latter developed the doctrine of the bodhisattva, the transfer of merit on the part of a saintly figure, and the creation of a heaven or paradise. After 500 A.D. it deteriorated in India into Tantric Buddhism which, like Neo-Platonism in the hands of Jamblichus, lost itself in the mazes of subjective magic.

---

25. E. J. Thomas: *op. cit.*, p. 17.

26. This is practically the same as the "action" in the *Brihadaranyaka Upanishad*, III, 2.

Just a word about Sakti, the popular religion which clings closely to nature and therefore is frequently misunderstood by the outsider. It centers around the great mother as the consort of Siva, and like the manifestations of nature she can inspire terror, at other times she is full of mercy and tenderness. As a fertility goddess she demands blood sacrifice; she has much in common with the great Cybele of Phrygia and Ishtar of Mesopotamia. Her roots go back to neolithic times and evidence of her worship may be seen at Mohenjo-Daro; thenceforth it lies dormant, like similar cults of earth divinities in Greece, and rises into the foreground again whenever popular demand cries out for something more immediate and tangible than the more metaphysical cults can furnish. The European must be careful here as elsewhere in Hindu religion to pass final judgment, not on the visible aspects of the cult, but on the sum total of such aspects, for what the Hindu creates in his religion is a whole containing a number of potentialities which hardly admit of separate analysis. There is nothing Puritanical in his worship because there is no apartness of good and evil in the tangible effects of life for either the Hindu's mind or religion.

The age of the Vedic hymns is even more difficult to fathom than the time of the Aryan invasion, because so much of this literature was handed down orally from one generation to another before it was finally recorded and, furthermore, certain incidents mentioned are part and parcel of all primitive mythology. The first achievement of Indra,[27] the slaying of the dragon on the mountain where he holds back the waters, is a common motive so many primitive peoples have included in their traditions in neolithic times. Eventually the whole work, as we have it, was recorded in what is known as the Vedic language,[28] the precursor of Sanscrit as the classical medium for literature. Although early writing materials included wood, palm leaves, gold and silver plate, all the important works of litera-

---

27. Hymn I, 22.
28. For more information about the language consult M. Winternitz: *A History of Indian Literature,* Calcutta, 1927, I, pp. 40 ff.

ture can now be found on paper which was brought into India
by the Muslims. All the hymns of the Vedas were regarded as
revelation, handed down by the gods, and hence there must
have been a certain reverence attached to the word, a view
which was no doubt changed with the coming of the *Upanishads*. The hymns were regarded as the exclusive property of
the priests who had composed them and recited them at the
appropriate sacrifices.

In this body of literature there is a strong feeling for the
presence of nature, its benign and destructive influence on the
life of man; nature in such a role is not found later on in
Hindu writings. Many of these manifestations, e.g., the clouds,
the lightning, the rushing waters, the consuming fire, are
respected for their power which benefits their worshippers and
casts down their enemies. We are inclined to think here of the
Hebrew and his view of nature, but in this case Yahweh is not
a part of nature, while Indra and his associates are one with
their manifestations. At the same time the writer, when he
praises the splendor of the dawn[29] or begs Pushan to lead his
subjects into rich meadows,[30] is not interested in aesthetic values
for their own sake. While he may have delighted in the rosy
tints of morning clouds and the lush green of the grass, he
wished first to flatter the gods and also to express, by way of
sensuous description, the significance of such phenomena for
the enjoyment of his living; green grass meant as much for his
flocks as the rainbow after the storm for the sailor. Moreover,
the effect produced is one of bigness and power necessary to
overcome powerful foes and to reap a rich harvest. Vishnu
takes huge strides, Varuna sees everything, Indra drinks huge
quantities of soma, the storm and lightning are overwhelming—
nothing was done with a half-hearted effort.

Any impression of beauty or power the reader may experience is somewhat diminished with the realization that the hymns
are saturated with magic, that most of this volume of literature
was composed as a matter of expediency. The gods must be

---

29. Hymn V, 80.
30. Hymn I, 43.

magnified to a high degree to overcome so many foes, to bring such great benefits to their worshippers, but they become great only by the grace and good will of man. The latter is willing to grant them a certain measure of praise and sacrifice, he will even condescend to beg for mercy and ask for forgiveness, but the gods must obey the subjective will of man if they wish to share in the fruits of victory. What god would not care to enjoy what man enjoys? Yes, Varuna has his laws which must be obeyed and will be obeyed as long as he realizes that right is on the side of his worshipping clients. This great mass of hymns is the overflowing of a spirit confident that subjective power, controlling the forces of nature, is the key to all the blessings of the earth. When they fight, they expect to be met by force; when they worship, they call on divinities of power; they stake their all in all on the battlefield and the gaming board[31] on one desperate, mighty thrust to gain the spoils of victory. Like the primitive Germans, their emotions were uncompromising, their moods heavy, giving quarter first to a full expression of powerful energy, after which they could be fair, kind, and condescending. Constant warfare naturally tended to foster such an attitude; once the pressure of the enemy abated, the climate and ease of a new way of living soon debilitated the mainspring of superabundant energy.

This, of course, was all a part of a sincere, spontaneous expression on the part of the primitive Aryan without any afterthought of unfair expediency, and once we realize this, we can appreciate his exalted attempt to paint the warrior's image on the clouds and sky, to invite the gods to sit with men on the green grass, to marshall the forces of heaven and earth for the heroic struggle, to take a full draft of the best life had to offer before giving up the game. In some of these verses, in which there is no rhyme but a great variety of meter, there is something of the innocence of the child reaching out for the moon and stars, expecting the ear of the universe to hearken to his plea; in some there are intimations of a higher morality, a more universal god—concepts which were to bear more fruit later on;

---

31. Cf. Tacitus: *Germania,* 34.

occasionally there are poems embellished with sensitive imagery and dramatic contrast, by-products of a more serious purpose in the mind of the poet; there are also a great number of sacrificial recitations droning their way from the beginning to the end of a priestly formula. We should be very thankful to have at our disposal such an impressive collection of literary material which hardly a culture can point to in its formative, childhood days.

The *Atharvaveda,* from the later Vedic period, is a collection of spells, incantations, and benedictions, most of which can be included under the heading of magic, having little or no literary value. We mention it here because it marks the period when the priesthood was attempting to standardize religion in its own interests, when the power of the "word" became the exclusive property of the Brahmins. Had they been successful over a greater period of time, India, like Egypt, might have fallen a victim to a rigid conservatism, and this type of permanence, like the machine in full control, can be most enervating. The Brahmins sought to achieve the same degree of control through the sacrifice; all men must sacrifice, just as the gods sacrifice, to achieve a position of merit, and the Brahmins, who knew when, what, and how to sacrifice, were extolled as divinities to whom presents were due. The one redeeming element is the narrative which, although employed as a means to an end, has a certain intrinsic charm. In the flood story of Manu and the fish we find something of the communion of man with the animal spirit, a kind of animism the Hindu has always cherished in his viewpoint. It is also interesting to observe how Manu and the fish, as well as Hariscandra and Varuna, in the tale of Sunahsepa, deal with each other in terms of a *do ut des* bargain, a primitive and pragmatic construction on the golden rule. Aside from the fact that the tale of Sunahsepa explains the substitution of animals for humans in sacrifice and that other stories point to parallels in Mesopotamia and Greece, the charming simplicity of this narrative style harks back to an early period for its composition, much earlier than that of the *Brahmanas.* The allegory of speech and mind and the stories of creation belong, of course, to a later time. The first two narratives mentioned above are merely an intimation of the wealth of tales the early Aryan must have composed and which might have survived in greater numbers had it not been for the predominance of the priest and his undue emphasis on sacrifice.

From the continuity of subject matter running from the *Vedas* to the *Upanishads* one might suppose there is no radical departure in the themes of the latter—we find the same gods mentioned, a large residue of magic, something of the same analogies drawn, but the emphasis and viewpoint are rapidly changing. The thinker is abandoning the gods as separate manifestations of phenomena in favor of facing up squarely to what he finds beneath the surface of things and not so clearly apparent to the senses; above all, he is probing for a reality within himself and its connection with a related reality behind the appearances of his outside world. "Upanishad" means a pupil sitting near a teacher, sometimes loosely rendered as "teachings"; at any rate, the presentation is one of demonstration or instruction, the student at times present to take part in a dialogue. The subject is not held up to the light of reason and argument, because such terms as Atman and Brahman cannot be understood in this way. The teacher cannot compare it adequately with anything outside itself, for there is really nothing outside of it to shed any light on its true nature. Still he gropes from one phenomenal aspect to another, he moves constantly from the outer to the inner world by way of analogy and back again until, by a flash of insight, the student becomes aware of the significance of reality. The method appears to be rather hit and miss, the teacher seems to be floundering for the right approach, but when awareness dawns, it reveals the whole truth in a sudden emanation of light; one cannot know a part of such a reality without knowing the whole at the same time.

There is, then, every reason why the writer should seem vague or fumbling in his style, why his work should be lacking in system or organization. Where there is no definite dividing line between the microcosm and macrocosm, between a term, e.g., "self," used in a particular or universal sense, both writer and reader are destined to have difficulties. To describe creation at the hands of an omnipotent, personal god, from the body of Tiamat, or simply from chaos, may seem a ridiculous fancy to the apostle of reason, but the starting point is at least comparatively tangible; to explain it as issuing from an invisible aggregate of potentialities is much more difficult. Again, the attempt to describe Brahman in terms of what is not calls for a tortuous search for analogies which, at best, give but a faint glimmer of its nature without defining it in the western sense. Once the reader has removed from his mind all trace of "otherness" in the consideration of reality, he is ready to follow the writer and can appreciate his problems. The reader must likewise realize that words are much more figurative or symbolic than in western thought where "come," "go," "depart," and "develop" imply some kind of direction in time and space, whereas the Hindu is merely trying to explain the potentialities of a being that is beyond movement in terms of experience, and so he is at a loss to describe clearly the relationship between the two aspects of being.

Moreover, it is evident that these men who grappled with the problems of being belong to an early stage of Hindu culture before the epics were composed. A long period of meditation must be taken for granted before a man found it possible to explain Brahman in its fullest realization by the analogy of a man in deep sleep.[32] Equally fascinating is the metaphorical language of the *Chandogya Upanishad*, especially the reference to the honey from a variety of trees,[33] the salt dissolved in water,[34] the tree[35]—all efforts to clarify the nature of reality as a unity reaching out into the particular. There are also foreshadowings of devices used in Greek philosophy: the Atman as the bridge[36] or the connecting link between the two worlds

---

32. *Brihadaranyaka Upanishad*, II, I and IV, 3.
33. VI, 8.
34. VI, 12.
35. VI, 12.
36. *Chandogya Upanishad*, VIII, 4.

points ahead to the bridge of Plotinus between the universal and individual souls; the individual soul in the chariot[37] is convincingly like that used by Plato in the *Phaedrus*.[38] Reading these discourses is like gazing into a large, revolving crystal; the eyes are concentrated in the same direction, directed to the study of the same subject, but the images presenting themselves in the revolving glass are manifold and varied, according to the caprice of circumstances playing about between subject and object; the task of the teacher is to demonstrate how each one of these images is merely a token of the more unified but invisible reality lying in the heart of the crystal. One can read the *Upanishads* over and over without learning what the ultimate reality is, but with each reading there will come a richer awareness of a significance which the East and West, each in its own way, are striving for. The writer uses both prose and verse as media which work no hardship for the interested reader who is hardly conscious of any transition from one to the other; this varied medium is a welcome contrast to the monotonous didactic meter of Alexander Pope.

Several treatises on the subject of law have come down to us, one of which is the *Dharmasastra* with its emphasis on rules of conduct for the castes and the duties of the family head; they include the so-called laws of Manu, supposedly going back to the mythical survivor of the flood. In addition to the code itself we find, in the first book of *Manu*, an account of creation, while the final book includes a summary of Hindu philosophy and religion, directions for ultimate happiness, and the penalties certain wrongdoers may expect in another transmigration. The code takes for granted that the institution of caste is divinely ordained and established beyond a doubt; this means that it shows an aristocratic preference for the highest caste, especially if it is composed of men of learning, but a decided burden, by way of ceremony, is laid on their shoulders. There are features that hark back to the *Vedas*: the brave kings who meet their end in battle will find happiness after death; a prince is expected

37. *Katha Upanishad*, III.
38. 246.

to kill his enemies.[39] There is also considerable magic and emphasis on sacrifice: to comfort the slayer of the sacrificial animal it is decreed that the hapless creature shall attain to an exalted birth in the next transmigration. Superstitions also crop up here and there: intercourse on even nights will result in male offspring, on odd nights in female issue.

It is tempting to compare such a code with that of Hammurabi. The divinity of the ruler, even of the Brahmin, is taken for granted,[40] a fact which, as we shall see, is by no means as important in India as it might be elsewhere. In court procedure the king assumed a very important role as presiding judge. The code makes provisions for property and business contracts, although the Hindus were not as property conscious as the Mesopotamians and very little concerned about commerce. There is also a strong feeling for the *lex talionis;* however, it seems to be applied most strictly to the lowest caste. There are, as we might expect, fines for putting animals to death, both large and small. Much emphasis is laid on hospitality, on the respect of a student for his guru, condemnation of gambling, avoiding incest, and the bearing of present conduct on the next life. While the husband is told to honor his spouse, the wife's will is not to be trusted;[41] she must look up to her husband, regardless of his character, as to a god;[42] other references to women indicate that the Hindu put no more faith in the female than Machiavelli in human nature. We may note with interest that punishment is regarded as justice,[43] while various forms of penance are also recognized, but there is evidently no way by which a sinner could be washed white as snow in an ocean of mercy through the medium of faith. As in Mesopotamia, physicians were penalized for unsuccessful operations. There were also a number of other legal systems, some more concerned with trade.

39. VII, 89.
40. VII, 9; and XI, 85.
41. V, 148.
42. V, 154.
43. VII, 18.

There are works on political science, on the art of making love, on medicine, music, grammar, architecture, and subjects dealing with other phases of secular life, which we have no time to consider in a general review of literature.

The pantheism of Hindu literature, like that of his religion, reveals itself in various guises, all genuine manifestations of the spirit within. First we saw the Hindu as a singer of hymns, then the lord of magic and sacrifice, later the prober into metaphysical reality, as the man of practical insight, and now the writer of epic poetry. All branches of literature, all types of subject matter, as they follow on the heels of each other, have something of the cumulative effect of a great ocean wave; all potentialities, all motives are present as the wave rolls along, one after another standing out in bolder relief on the surface of concrete experience. The epic, while it stands out as a heroic tale of adventure, also contains in its makeup something of the *Vedas*, the *Brahmanas*, the *Upanishads*, and the laws, and looks forward to other subjects of the future. It is a case of all for one and one for all; apartness is less evident here than in the cultural expression of other peoples we have considered. Furthermore, the spiritual energy which goes into the creation of these works knows little abatement; the merit of a certain work may be questionable in our eyes, but the continuous flow of creative power that was poured into such literature as the epic is still astounding. The *Mahabharata*, written in the heroic couplet called the sloka, is longer than the combined epic poems of any other Aryan people. As is the case with the Homeric works, the authorship is unknown; the work was steadily swelled by accretions, but the additional padding of later poets apparently did not affect the general merit of the writing. Unlike Homer's creations, however, the *Mahabharata* has a definite beginning and an end, whether one marks it at the culmination of the great war or at the ascension of the Pandu heroes, and the narrative continues in a regular sequence of events in time without the backflashes of the *Odyssey* and the *Aeneid*.

The epic opens with a delightful tale of the love of the Ganges river goddess for a mortal king, an interference of divinity in human affairs which brings many trials and woes in its wake for mortals. The descendants of this strange union are the Kurus and the Pandus, cousins who divide a single kingdom but who are constantly enemies because the Kurus cannot brook the obvious superiority of their cousins. Fundamentally, the war which follows is a contest between virtue and vice, the latter finding all manner of devices to thwart the righteous. The Kurus, envious of the Pandus, seek to deprive them of their birthright by enticing their leader into an unfair game of dice. The Pandu king, Yudhisthira, unable to resist the fatal fascination of the game, loses all his possessions, his kingdom, his wife, and pawns his brothers and himself into slavery. It is finally agreed to send the Pandus into a thirteen-year exile, at the end of which they return to reclaim their share of the kingdom. When this claim is denied, a great war between the two parties and their allies ensues in which, among a mass of slain on each side, the Kurus meet their end. The main part of the epic ends with the coronation and horse sacrifice of Yudhisthira, who, according to a later addition, finally leads his family into paradise.

The war has no doubt a historical kernel going back to a period soon after the Aryans settled in northern India, and the theme of the epic preserves much of the spirit of the invasion of the early days. The main characters are of truly heroic stature, at times shining forth as incarnate divinities and at times giving way to deep human emotions in very human situations, but this does not mean they are close parallels to the Homeric leaders. The great mass of men who fight behind them are nameless hordes, a fit background against which the heroes fight their duels. Many of the leaders like Arjuna, Karna, and Bhima bring recollections of Homer, but Bhishma, sacrificed like an innocent lamb on the altar of virtue, is in a class by himself; Krishna too, while he is as ingenious as Odysseus, is too much a divinity to make the reader humanly comfortable in his company (this need not, of course, trouble the Hindu reader). Although the eventual fate of the Kurus is known in advance and proclaimed before the battle, the heat of their passionate hatred, their insolent pride, makes no concession to the inevitable; Duryodhana, a scoundrel to the very end, died a happy death after learning of the treacherous slaughter engineered by one of his own men.[44] Whether noble or ignoble, Kuru or Pandu, each character is consistently true to his type, each one projects himself into speech and action with all the force of his personality up to the very climax when Arjuna and Karna engage in their Titanic struggle, both equal in strength and bravery, so that an unfortunate circumstance must intervene in favor of the former. The heroes of Homer must all descend to the dark halls of Hades; in this respect the Indian hero enjoys a happier lot, for even if the ascent to heaven is not the original ending of the epic, it was generally understood that all warriors reap a happy harvest in the life to come, a fact which rarifies the tragic atmosphere in which the hero moves. The style is simple, the similes are sparing but naturally spontaneous, the epithets well chosen, and the phenomena of nature reflect the glory that should surround demigods and their deeds on earth.

Apart from the didactic material inserted by the priesthood, the somewhat irrelevant material offers a welcome variation in a long epic: one of the finest examples is the narrative of Savitri, the Hindu Alcestis, whose love for her husband prevailed against death. The most impressive interlude is not a story but a song, the *Bhagavad-Gita*, composed in eighteen cantos. Arjuna, the bulwark of the Pandus, hesitates to fight the great battle when he sees so many of his friends and kin on the opposite side, whereupon Krishna succeeds in overcoming all his doubts: the duty of the warrior is to fight without any regard for the consequences.[45] True being cannot be killed; death merely hastens the decay of the body. Krishna explains why and when he came to birth,[46] summarizes a number of Hindu teachings (which argues for the later date of this insertion), urges his charge to

44. X, 545.
45. Cf. Emerson's *Brahma*:
> If the red slayer think he slays,
> Or if the slain think he is slain,
> They know not well the subtle ways
> I keep, and pass, and turn again.

46. IV, 5–8.

be indifferent to pain and pleasure in life, lays before him a doctrine of devotion dedicated to doing (*bakti*) without the interference of personal desire. The *Bhaghavad-Gita*, an evident but happy afterthought, is the most poetical, the most appealingly philosophical exhortation in Hindu literature.

The *Ramayana*, compared to its companion epic, is more peaceful and idyllic. Less lengthy, more compact, it is a tale supposedly composed by Valmiki, an ancient sage, about the hero Rama who ascends the epic stage as another avatar of Vishnu. After a boyhood of great promise and his marriage with the fair Sita, he is exiled to the forest at the instigation of a conniving queen who wishes to see her own son displace Rama as heir to the throne. Husband, wife, and a faithful brother leave for the forest where Sita is stolen by an evil king, Ravana, but later rescued with the aid of Hanuman, the leader of an army of simians. Eventually the couple is reunited and returns home in triumph. For the westerner this epic lacks the lofty theme of the *Mahabharata*, the suspicions of Rama affecting Sita are obnoxious, the effort to exalt a character to a level of purity without the tragic flaw hardly enhances his humanity, and too much reliance is laid on magic; however, what it lacks in sublime measures it makes up for, in part, by the tender touches of human relationship and the quiet atmosphere of forest and countryside. Such are the epics that were recited by bards (*sutas*) at the courts of early kings; such are the poems which have contributed more than any other agency to a common bond of cultural unity among the millions of people in India.

Storytelling is an art which is more at home in the East than elsewhere. In Indian lore there seems to be an inexhaustible storehouse of tales and romances, some told solely for entertainment, others designed to bring home a lesson. Such a collection is the so-called *Ocean of Streams of Story*. Here one finds tales of sheer cleverness in which magic plays the stellar role, stories illustrating the fickleness of women, others deriding the eternal fool, and some designed to teach practical lessons in everyday wisdom. Another mélange of tales is contained in the *Panchatantra*, in which prose and verse are intermingled, the latter generally used to point up some manner of lesson, wise or otherwise. Here we read of the weaver who, to gain a princess for his bride, feigned he was a Vishnu riding a mechanical Garuda; in this guise he won the sympathy of the god himself and so won not only his bride but turned back a whole army of invaders. A Brahmin carrying a fat goat for sacrifice, is accosted by three rogues successively who tell him he is carrying anything but a goat, and after learning the goat was now a dog, then a calf, and finally a donkey, he concluded the goat was possessed and left it behind for the three hungry rogues. Many of the fables include only characters from the animal world. In the collection of *Jambhaladatta* we find the famous tale about the transposed heads.[47] Many of these stories and fables of the Hindus passed into the West and back again, and because of the number of variations on the same theme it is sometimes difficult to trace the origin of the story in the East. Who can say, for example, where the parable of the prodigal son, found in Buddhistic and Christian lore, was first recited? The Hindus—and this we may be sure of—retained their primitive fondness for the animal fable longer than other peoples.

The Hindu had evidently built up a long tradition for playwriting before Kalidasa appeared in the age of the Guptas. Undoubtedly drama in India, as elsewhere, goes back to the ritual associated with imitative magic of primitive times, as the dialogues of the *Vedas* seem to testify. The development of the stage and play from the more primitive forms is completely lost to us, but most of the themes were derived from the heroic age, some actually taken from the epics. Did the Greeks exert any influence on the development of the Hindu stage as they did in the field of sculpture? If there was any influence, it may have come from Menander, the idol of the fourth century Greeks, in the form of certain types of character and the plot rooted in a social background.[48] This does not mean, however,

---

47. M. B. Emeneau: *Jambhaladatta's Version of the Vetalapancavinsati,* New Haven, 1934, pp. 59–65.

48. Kalidasa makes mention of the Greeks (B. S. Upadhyaya: *India in Kalidasa,* Allahabad, 1947, p. 264).

that the Greek drama of the fourth century B.C. had anything
to do with the Hindu's rejection of tragedy; the reason for the
exclusiveness of comedy is much more fundamental and will
be taken up later. The play was primarily designed for the
courts of kings where the language, the source material, and
the motives would be readily understood. In the plays which
have come down to us the plots have been well constructed and
furnished with a happy quality of expectancy, although there
are times when, to a modern, the action seems to linger unneces-
sarily; this may be due, in part, to an emotional stress which we
cannot fully appreciate, and perhaps also to the meager stage
furnishings. Moreover, as in much of Hindu literature, the playwright uses alternate passages in prose and verse, a device
which from our viewpoint must have caused some embarrassing delays in the action. Each play has a benediction,
usually addressed to Siva, a prologue, an epilogue, and sometimes interludes.

The oldest extant plays are those of Asvaghosha, three in
fragmentary condition, dealing with the personality and teaching of Buddha. He was a contemporary of Kanishka, flourishing
in the late first century A.D. The first play which has come down
to us in complete form is the *Little Clay Cart,* a long piece of
work in ten acts, of unknown authorship. The plot is somewhat
involved but unfolds itself very clearly; the main theme is one
of love conquering with the aid of virtue over vice, although,
strange to say, the leading lady is a beautiful courtesan, the
hero a married man, and their affair excites no jealousy in the
wife. For the modern reader the lyrics, regardless of their questionable contribution to the stage production, are hardly an
enhancement to the story, and the ending is altogether too
drawn out to be effective on the modern stage. The work
of Bhasa shows a great resourcefulness of invention and variety
of theme, even if most of his thirteen plots are based on stories
of earlier literature. One noteworthy example is *The Minister's
Vow,* which holds the attention of the reader without bringing
the two chief characters on the stage. In *The Vision of Vasava-
datta* the queen who gives her name to the title must have

made an unusually strong appeal to the Hindu audience. *The Broken Thighs,* another theme from the epic cycle, has been referred to as a play portraying the tragedy of one of its chief characters,[49] but in a broad sense the play is not at all a tragedy.

The foremost Hindu playwright is reckoned, by common consent, to be Kalidasa, the greatest literary figure of the Gupta era. As in the case of so many notables, his life is almost a blank except for a few legends to impress us with his popularity. The *Shakuntala* is an outstanding achievement which calls forceful attention to Kalidasa's pre-eminence as a poet of nature, his sensitive understanding of human emotions, and his ability to bridge the gap between the human and divine levels in the last act without sacrificing human appeal. On the other hand, the modern would find the development somewhat slow in the first half of the play, and the madness or amnesia of the king demands a strain on the credulity of the audience. The plot of the *Malavika,* centering around a lost princess in disguise among the palace maids, is a close parallel to a New Comedy device in fourth-century Greece. Poetic charm and genial good humor characterize the *Urvashi,* his third play, which makes us realize, more than elsewhere, how much more effective such a piece could be with musical accompaniment; the resolution at the end is a little difficult for one familiar with the same theme in the epic. *The Dynasty of Raghu,* an epic poem covering the saga of Rama's family, is an ambitious undertaking, far too ambitious, for not all the poet's brilliant figures of speech or his versatile powers of description can compensate for the dull repetition involved in a series of royal biographies. *The Birth of the War-God* brings out the poet's abilities to much greater advantage. Along with the romance of Siva the subject matter includes the more tempestuous moods of nature, the clash of Titans in battle, the potentialities of Brahma, the creator, all of which is handled with convincing ease. Kumara's struggle with Taraka, however, rings in our ears like that of Marduk

---

49. A. C. Woolner and L. Sarup: *Thirteen Trivandrum Plays Attributed to Bhasa,* London, 1931, II, p. 41.

with Tiamat. There are times when the subject matter of Kalidasa is unsuited to his muse, but as a lyrical singer of love and its moods reflected in nature he never seems to have exhausted his resources.

The most favored, and perhaps deservedly so, of lyric poems is the *Gita-Govinda* of Jayadeva of Bengal. The variety of meter, for which the musical score must have added great charm, the sensuous and at the same time airy character of its language, and the popularity of Krishna have made the poem a paragon in its class. And what is the meaning the poet wished to convey?[50] If there must be a significance, it lies obviously on the surface: Krishna simply follows the course of every wayward soul as best he can in the bondage of the senses until he sees the light and attains to a higher knowledge. Bhartrihari is another poet, dating from the first century B.C., who deserves mention here. His style is terse and compact, his language direct, sometimes barbed, all of which may be a reflection of his experience. In many of the works of such poets we find their songs of beauty were tinted with a plaintive sadness, perhaps because one extreme has a way of foreshadowing its opposite; in the back of the poet's mind there lurks a suspicion that heaven is not to be found at the bottom of nature's cup of nectar.

Greek and Chinese records inform us of the great buildings in Pataliputra, but since most of them were of wood, little of the construction of Bindusara and Asoka has survived. From excavations it can be seen that the Mauryans were strongly impressed with the pillared halls, such as we know in Persepolis, and one of their wooden halls was furnished with sandstone columns provided with acanthus ornaments on the capitals.[51] This does not mean, however, that all the motives and styles of

50. The critics have strained themselves to discover some subtle or profound meaning in its lines. Cf. H. H. Gowen: *A History of Indian Literature,* New York, 1931, p. 421.

51. A. K. Coomaraswamy: *History of Indian and Indonesian Art,* London, 1927, p. 19.

art at this time were borrowed *in toto* from the West; it does mean that, at a time when architectural material was changing from wood to stone, the Mauryans saw fit to use this pillared support for the interior of a large hall. Little can be said of pre-Mauryan architecture except in regard to decorative patterns which seem to have affinities with a number of civilizations in the West. The most concrete remains from the Mauryan period itself are the sandstone monolithic pillars of Asoka with large capitals of lions resting on inverted lotuses; the best example is to be found at Sarnath. These pillars, most of which were put up to carry the edicts of the emperor, were of similar workmanship to those found in the pillared hall—all highly polished, another feature pointing to Persian influence. The Mauryan rulers also concerned themselves with caves cut out of the native rock, the most interesting being that known as Lomasa Rishi, whose façade reveals how the chaitya of wood looked at an early period.[52]

Two symbols worshipped in primitive Indian religion have survived in Buddhist art, namely the stupa, a mound in the shape of a hemisphere, and the chaitya, a sacred tree or grove of trees.[53] The best examples of the former are the stupas of Bharhut and Sanchi. The stupa consists usually of a huge dome-shaped mound of brick and rubble, exposed to the sky, set up as a shrine for the relics of Buddha or another great teacher. Above the mound is a structure from which there rises a mast weighed down by several concentric circular extensions, diminishing in size as they approach the summit. Below the mound and surrounding it is a series of terraces providing room for an ambulatory and an opening to the space below approached by stairs. The whole is encircled by a railing or fence which is furnished with four elaborately decorated gateways. The remains of the Bharhut example are now in the Calcutta Museum, but the Sanchi stupa is fairly well preserved on its original site. Both were erected not long before the Christian era. The sculptures,

---

52. Nihar-Ranjan Ray: *Maurya and Sunga Art,* University of Calcutta, 1945, p. 58.

53. Nihar-Ranjan Ray: *op. cit.,* p. 3.

concentrated on the four gateways, relate certain outstanding events in the legendary life of Buddha.

The elaboration of the second primitive symbol is realized in the form of the Buddhist church or chaitya, the best example being that at Karli. The façade, which has two levels, shows traces of earlier work in wood; the upper level has a large horseshoe-shaped window anticipating the contour of the ceiling inside. The lower section is decorated with sculptured figures, sometimes designated as donors, standing between the doorways on the same level with a number of Buddhas. The sides of the porch, extended out before the façade, are sculptured out in the form of several stories, the lowest supported by elephants. The interior is divided into a nave and side aisles by two rows of huge columns surmounted by well-shaped capitals and groups of sculptured figures, above which is an intervening space below the level where the ceiling begins. The wooden ribs then rise and soar across the upper expanse to give a singularly dynamic effect and, contrasting strangely with the ponderous columns below, are joined to the stone roofing above, a rare survival of the combined media in the same structure. At the far end is the stupa, raised up rather high above the floor level, and around the stupa the aisles continue into an ambulatory.

The temple was laid out in accord with the cosmic symbolism developed by the priests. The earth, they claimed, was round when considered as a growing or moving entity, but fixed by its marriage with heaven because it is fastened to the latter at four points, thus forming a square enclosing a circle. Since the temple was meant to be a kind of microcosm of the universe and the architect a diminutive Visvakarman, the prescribed shape of the temple is the square, which may be regarded as the symbol of the universe in its aspect of order.[54] Since all the early examples of temples, constructed in wood, have disappeared, it is next to impossible to study origins in this field, but we can be reasonably sure that the Hindu temple, in its simplest

54. For a more exhaustive treatment of this symbolism consult S. Kramrisch: *The Hindu Temple,* University of Calcutta, 1946, I, pp. 10 ff.

version, is a rectangular structure, and all variations depend on the form or arrangement of additional members making up the temple complex. There is a flat-roofed temple with a porch and a pillared hall surrounding the central shrine; there is the temple equipped with a tower of vertical, curvilinear ribbings, more common in the north; the tower prevalent in the south rises up almost on a perpendicular line to the dome, its abruptly sloping sides broken up by separate stories. These types as well as the earlier chaitya temple were all popular during the Gupta period when Buddhism was declining at the expense of a Brahmanistic revival.

One of the most remarkable temples of the Middle Ages is the Kailasa shrine at Ellora. Here the excavator has not carved his way into the rock on a horizontal line but from above downward; in fact, the whole structure was carved inside and outside from the solid mass of stone. The interior of the building must have been dug out through the doors and windows. The temple, two stories in height, is fronted on each side by a square, freestanding pillar rising up well over a hundred feet, a feature reminiscent of the Mayan Temple of the Warriors. Even as it stands today the structure gives an impression of primeval solidarity, whose piles are sunk deep in the foundations of the earth. The shrine, of the usual square shape, is dedicated to Siva, whose figure appears in the temple sculptures. In the interior there are bridges, one leading from the upper story into the porch, as well as a stairway leading down from the porch to the court, one of the most novel devices in any architecture. The interior also contains a central aisle and broadside aisles culminating in a porch on two sides of the temple. The west porch with its great, ponderous roof, its short, stocky columns, and prominent cornices emphasizes both the horizontal line and the solid, earthy character of the building. The overhanging roof and cornice as well as the sculpture in high relief contribute much to a baroque effect, although the important structural lines are clearly visible. The temple is called Kailasa from the sacred mount, the dwelling place of Siva.

The finest representative of the northern or Nagara temple

is the Lingaraja of Bhuvanesvara, one of the most impressive of
its kind in India. Its most striking feature is the sikhara, containing the sanctuary with its ascending, vertical ribbings which,
as the sunlight plays on their surface, give the impression of
water rippling over cascades. The impression gains forcefulness
by the fact that a narrow ribbing alternates with a broader one
all the way around the sikhara, both held in place by the crowning dome. It has been suggested that such a roof traces its
origin to the bamboo framework on processional cars.[55] The
horizontal indentations put a check on the soaring vertical line
without destroying its flowing effect, especially when one sees
it from a moderate distance. At the same time the westerner is
aware of the turning inward of the vertical lines and the dome
putting a limit to their soaring, thus producing an effect much
different from the Gothic tower. The sikhara has at least one
internal chamber which can be reached by a staircase.[56] It is also
interesting to observe that the sikhara itself is reproduced in a
miniature series, one above the other, as part of the decorative
pattern on the narrow line of ribbing of the tower. The mandapa
appears much more squatty in contrast, an effect due partly to
the heavier horizontal indentations dividing it into two stories.
Without the greater number of lesser temples surrounding it,
this shrine would be still more imposing.

The temple at Madura, though much of it was built as late
as the seventeenth century, is a fine example of the southern or
Dravidian type. The temple proper or vimana, built on the
usual rectangular plan, is by itself an imposing structure, perhaps because of its pyramidal roof, although the larger buildings
of the complex tend to dwarf it. Outside the vimana is a large
rectangular enclosure on the borders of which stand the gopuras
or gateways guarding the temple area like sentinels, and in the
intervening space we find pillared halls decked out in sculpture,
and a tank of water for ritual purposes. Looking at one of the

55. V. A. Smith: *A History of Fine Art in India and Ceylon*, Oxford,
1911, p. 25, fig. 7; A. Coomeraswamy (*op. cit.*, p. 97) suggests the roof-
slab of the primitive dolmen as the inspiration for the flat-roofed temple.
56. S. Kramrisch: *op. cit.*, I, p. 148.

four large gopuras we notice something hardly surprising in
Indian architectural design, but which would appear monstrous
in western art. In the first place, how strangely this pyramid
contrasts with the great work of Khufu of Egypt! It ascends more
abruptly than the latter, a fact which prompts us to ask: why
the emphasis on the vertical, if so many obstacles are put in the
way of its culmination? The crowning feature of the tower
tends to offset the steep ascent, and the division into horizontal
stories whose central section projects from the surface tends
to defeat the purpose of the vertical line even more than in the
northern type of temple. Added to this, the whole surface is
literally covered with a mass of columns and sculptured figures
executed in high relief, as if the sculptor was horror-stricken
at the sight of an empty space. It is almost incredible that the
strong light of India can absorb all this detail into the general
scheme of the tower,[57] a problem which gave the Hindu no
concern at all. Without taking the general viewpoint of the
Hindu into consideration, and before we realize how different
the East is from the West, it is difficult to understand why the
Hindu artist created something so contradictory to what we
should call architectural common sense.

When Buddhism declined in India, it migrated to the south,
to Ceylon, and to Java where we find one of the most stupendous
of all architectural monuments, the Stupa of Borobudur. The lowest terrace, laid out in the shape of a square, is 497 feet on each
side. The monument holds 504 large images of Buddha, 1300
panels of sculptured reliefs, 72 stupas, excepting the large one
on the summit which is 52 feet in diameter.[58] The whole colossus
which looms up on a site commanding a view over the surrounding countryside constitutes a hill laid over with stone in
the form of a square at its base. From the foundation six terraces
rise up, each one having a double projection on each side of
its square, to the point where the stupas appear in their circles;
again we find the circle under the control of the square, a

---

57. Cf. S. Kramrisch: *op. cit.*, I, p. 220.
58. These figures were obtained from J. P. Vogel's paper in *The Influences of Indian Art,* London, 1925, pp. 55 ff.

principle already expressed in the ground plan of the early
Hindu temple. The square terraces are furnished with ambula-
tories, statues of Buddha, decorative panels, and are connected
with each other by four stairways leading to the gateways
placed at the middle of each side. The upper three circular
terraces are decidedly plain in contrast to the lower part of
the monument, a fact which has led some authorities to believe
a stupa was not in the original plan, but because of signs of
weakness appearing in the foundation in the course of construction, they claim, the burden of the upper terraces was made
lighter than the first plan had prescribed. It has also been
pointed out that the panels describing Buddha's life come to a
halt with his first sermon.[59] The statues of Buddha presented in
different poses and with various gestures, the quiet mood of the
reliefs and the unadorned upper terraces all contribute to create
an atmosphere of repose for the whole monument, and what
could be more appropriate for a shrine of Buddha? The edifice
was built in the latter half of the eighth century A.D. from a
stone called andesite, a gray volcanic formation which enhances
the impression of strength in the mammoth structure.

An entirely different mood pervades another colossus, the
Angkor Wat in Cambodia. The whole area is surrounded by a
broad and deep moat which can be crossed by a bridge, on the
west side, leading to the main gateway. There are four entrances
leading to the temple itself. Outside the main entrance is a
raised roadway running from a raised platform to the gateway
at the moat, from which the spectator commands a sweeping
view of the temple and three conelike towers jutting out above.
Within the temple are galleries and courts raised on terraces,
some richly decorated with sculptured reliefs. The central court,
at the greatest height, contains five sikharas, pyramidal in shape
and raised on a high base; the sikharas are connected by galleries
and can be reached from below by stairways. The reliefs in

---

59. This is an interesting observation of A. Coomeraswamy (*op. cit.*,
p. 205). On the other hand, if these panels had been continued along three
or four terraces, what kind of a Buddhist temple could have found room on
the summit?

sculpture, whose subject matter is drawn from the two epics and Hindu mythology, are full of vigor and action and so present a marked contrast to the work of Borobudur. We now know that this temple was constructed in the twelfth century and dedicated to Vishnu.

It is tempting, in view of the remains we find, to think of sculpture as the major art of India, but this assumption can be true only in a restricted sense. In many cases it is difficult to know, where the structures are carved from solid rock or cut away from the walls of caves, just where architecture leaves off and sculpture begins; and in many another temple the Hindu artist reveals he is no advocate of a strict separation of the arts. One thing is certain: all Indian sculpture and much architecture are religious in character, an attribute which tends to break down the limitations of each individual art. Hindu sculpture is also more emotional than formal; instead of looking for the order and symmetry of the Parthenon pediments, we should try to place every figure into its proper emotional setting, to determine what role it plays in a drama of natural religion. And much of what we prefer to call grotesque, overdone in Hindu sculpture is merely due to the inadequate forms the artist found in his experience, inadequate in the sense that they could not contain the boundless spiritual energy he sought to express. He used any medium within reach, he carved vast compositions from the native rock, and for a westerner the attempt to measure the effort and skill that went into the carvings of a Dravidian temple is a futile task. Of the sculptor's identity we hear little or nothing; personality suggests too much apartness to play a role in their spiritual program.

For the models of the earliest sculpture we look not only to wood, as in architecture, but also to ivory and metal work for analogies in technique.[60] Asoka, whose reign marks the first development of stone as a medium, must have summoned a number of artists from Persia for his polished pillars, but in the Bharhut Stupa there are figures recalling technique in wood,

---

60. W. Cohn: *Indische Plastik*, Berlin, 1922, p. 7.

which were probably executed by Indian artists with the Vedic traditions still fresh in mind. Something of the same rhythm and ease of movement, the same delight in motion for its own sake, is found here as in later Hindu work, but in the single figures there is more truth to nature, a more conscious awareness, an eye that looks off into a given field of space and limbs that bespeak some concern with anatomy. Such figures are an afterglow of early Aryan ideals of positive actions which experience a decided transformation with the composition of the *Upanishads.* The Sanchi sculptures move farther away from wood technique but preserve a docile naturalism, unsurpassed in Indian art, notably in the animals united in adoration before the presence of Buddha. The simple devotion of these creatures, the spiritual harmony pervading the composition, is enough to compensate for shortcomings in perspective. The female figure of the east gate, the so-called dryad, has surrendered herself to the natural abandon of rhythmical movement; from the standpoint of our experience she exemplifies a kind of *dolce far niente,* but in the context of the whole gate she reflects something of the spiritual joy that permeates all its living creatures. To see how different she is from the figures of the Bharhut Stupa, we must compare her with the donors of that monument.[61] The figure of Buddha is represented, not in human form, but by way of symbols such as the stupa, the throne, his footsteps, the sacred tree, or the wheel.

The Gandhara school probably reached its highest peak of achievement under Kanishka. It has long been recognized that the Hindu sculptor of the northwest was open to Greek influence at this time, but this influence is largely on the surface beneath which the Indian viewpoint still asserts itself. The reliefs, e.g., the Jatakas in Boston, are somewhat reminiscent of early Christian examples not only by reason of style but because of the quaint narrative way of recording events. The ponderous figures, weighted down with heavy accessories, move about with an awkward sophistication. The single head or figure is not involved

---

61. A. Coomaraswamy: *op. cit.,* pl. XII, 44.

in the same difficulty as the relief where figures, otherwise accustomed to move in harmony with an inner law, now find themselves to be individuals coping with other individuals in different areas of time and space. The mere precision of eyelids, brows, ears, and lips, like those of the Lemnian Athena, is no great hindrance to a motionless, introspective Buddha. On the other hand, the Buddha of the Sravasti miracle in Lahore is uncomfortably hemmed in by a multitude of demanding figures, and at the same time the inner control of the seated figure is not at all convincing. For one who has grown accustomed to the Hindu viewpoint in art, the Gandhara figures can be, at best, a disagreeable distraction.

By the time the Guptas had built up their empire, the Greek vogue had completely disappeared; like Alexander's fusion of the Greek and Persian civilizations, it was no more than a superficial gloss. The Sarnath Buddha had been praised as the finest image of the reformer in Indian art. The Gupta first rendered drapery clinging to the body like a thin, moist garment, then made it so transparent it is scarcely in evidence; he also emphasized the curve of the eyebrow.[62] The completely placid features of the face from which every token of expression has been removed, the absence of any anatomical detail, the posture entirely relaxed but not inert, the simple harmony of smoothly rounded curves make the Sarnath Buddha an outstanding example of the passive, introspective type. The temple at Deogarh furnishes an excellent example in relief: Vishnu coming to the rescue of the elephant king caught in the coils of the serpent. The western critic may point to a number of flaws in the composition of the group, but one all-important element, not so common in the European tradition, he might overlook, namely, the common bond of sympathy uniting all creatures great and small, animal and human in a union of the spirit against the harmful, the evil. Here is an excellent example of what is referred to in art criticism as empathy. At this point we might ask why the Hindu

---

62. R. Grousset: *The Civilization of the East* (Trans. by C. A. Phillips), II, New York, 1931, p. 139.

artist developed such a distinctive style under the Guptas; perhaps the answer lies in the fact that India was now cut off from the West by the Parthians and, after the fall of the Han dynasty, also lost her connections with China. The southern peninsula had an opportunity to bring her own latent powers to the surface, untrammeled by any foreign influence.

The moving figure of Siva taxes the patience of the modern to the limit because he takes no trouble to understand his cosmic significance. We shall cite two examples of his activity: first, the relief in the Dumarlena Cave at Ellora, where the divinity appears as Bhairava, in his most terrible aspect. A powerful figure with eight hands, each of which holds some vestige of destruction carried out, in a mood of righteous anger, against a giant disguised as an elephant; in two of his hands he grasps the distended skin of the beast. But why so many hands jutting out in all directions? The artist was not concerned about the normal aspects of experience as long as he could find an expressive outlet for the overpowering energy of the god; manifestations of experience must somehow make an exception for such a demanding spiritual force. Another example is the well-known bronze of the dancing Siva (Nataraja) in Madras. Anyone will admit it is a masterpiece in the bronze technique, but the subject matter usually arouses a shudder of revulsion. What religious significance can be attached to a sensuous ogre with four arms dancing on the helpless body of an infant? Siva is the god of the transitory aspects of life, the god of destruction and death and therefore of regeneration, also the spirit that transcends sensuous desire, the good and the evil, that dances within the circle of cosmic fire on a symbol of evil. The western observer is revolted by the sensuous face, the mad frenzy of a beast dancing in an orgy of lustful self-indulgence, and we must admit that Siva constitutes the popular version of spiritual expression, a survival of pre-Aryan religion. On the other hand, the Hindu insists that the Atman also comes into contact with the lower levels of experience, like Krishna in the *Gita-Govinda,* which serve as a point of departure to a level where a higher religious self-realization can be appreciated. In this sense, the Hindu would agree that whatever is, is right. And we must admit, regardless of the bias of our tradition, that the artist has succeeded admirably in projecting such a difficult concept into a concrete medium.

The most ambitious undertaking of an Indian artist was the carving of the *Descent of the Ganga* from the rock at Mamallapuram, a composition thirty yards in length. As a result of the penance of King Bhagiratha and the generous aid of Siva, the divine stream of the Ganges finally came down to the earth where all living creatures could purge themselves in its waters. The subject has always been a popular one in the mythology of the epic period, and the river has always been a focal point of religious enthusiasm. The composition includes as much in its scope as the Parthenon frieze, and its center of interest, the descending Ganga, is as prominent as the priest holding the robe of Athena over the east doorway of the Greek temple, but the means by which unity is achieved in such vast panoramas is very different. The liquid blessing descends on a vertical line, in the cleft of the rock, supported by hybrid creatures whose upper torsos and heads are those of females, the lower parts serpents equipped with coils, meant to function as springs to ease the shock of contact with the horizontal. On either side all manner of figures are ranged, paying homage to the benefactress of the earth: Bhagiratha standing on one leg, his hands joined over his head; a seated ascetic bows his head in all humility; the four-armed Siva, holding a club, as well as other gods, spirits, and animals lost in adoration; a cat is so overwhelmed she pays no attention to the mice at her feet; an early model of the Dravidian temple containing an image of Siva stands next to the ascetic. The arrangement of figures we should call careless; little attention is paid to perspective or details of anatomy; size in proportion to the area of the composition is not a major concern, and the composition seems to overflow into endless space without any reference to a possible frame; while some figures are at rest, others are moving at a whirlwind speed; but the quiet devotion of the ascetic, the mute but obvious respect of the huge elephant, the spontaneous outburst of joy in the upper right quarter is highly impressive for the spectator. Each figure is more or less unconcerned about his neighbor; like many Romanesque and Gothic compositions, each character is absorbed in his own emotional experience, his own kind of spiritual regeneration which is more than an Aristotelean catharsis and strong enough to hold the whole composition together. This unity cannot be observed on the surface; the spectator must feel his way into it and identify himself with the spirit behind the scenes. The breadth of such an undertaking and the natural background of solid rock have much the same breathtaking effect as the Borglum portraits on Mt. Rushmore.

The Buddhism of Borobudur is the Mahayana type which, in response to popular demand, had deified the reformer, created an elaborate and picturesque theology, and then spread abroad outside India. The Buddhas in the niches of the great Javanese stupa must be interpreted in the light of this teaching. It has been difficult, however, to distinguish the different types of Buddha because of their similarity, although some differences can be recognized between the preaching and meditating figures by the gestures of the hands. The Hindu artist was bound by the same rules for poses, gestures, and symbols as the medieval craftsman of Europe, and the spectator had to be familiar with such information. The Javanese Buddhas have become very limp, drapery is barely indicated, the lines of the faces, less sharply drawn, have taken on a filmy *morbidezza;* the two or three concentric lines below the neck are like silent ripples rolling over the surface of a placid pool. There is nothing here to disturb the quiet introspection that permeates the body and which apparently finds no limitation on the exterior.

The reliefs relating the story of Buddha are the nearest approach to the picturesque we can find in Indian art. The figures, serenely peaceful, without any anatomical detail, move with a quiet respect through a divine pantomime as though evil were merely a fortuitous contingency and the consummation of each episode could be controlled from the outset. Each figure, including the Buddha, reaches to about the same height and remains on the same plane; the trees, animals, and buildings are given such a size as not to interfere with the narrative;[63]

---

63. W. Cohn (*op. cit.*, p. 84) calls this a kind of isocephalism.

the vegetation seems to have been drawn from local areas. The proportionate size of accessories to the human figure keeps them within the category of decoration and makes them worthy contributors to the all-important narrative element.[64] It can readily be seen that each relief is not executed on a separate slab of stone.[65] It is also remarkable that, in spite of the number of artists who must have shared in the sculpture, not a one sought to advertise his technical skill to the disadvantage of another. The sculptor displays a simple devotion toward his work and at the same time suppresses his own personality.

The subject matter has been drawn from the Jatakas, the previous births, Buddha's life as a prince at court, and his religious experiences up to the first sermon. In spite of the even flow of figures and landscape in very much the same mood, the close observer can sense an interesting variety in the grouping, in the way the artist brings his main character into the foreground of attention. The specialized skill of the sculptor, however, has everywhere been subordinated to the effect of the whole. The naturalism of the vegetation carries us back to the early Buddhistic stupas; the buildings are ornate without infringing on the rights of the figures, dress is refined but sparingly indicated, water is represented by wavy lines; every character, every animal seems to know instinctively what role he has to play.

Do these figures have any solid bones in their bodies? Are they not like those of Botticelli, which the slightest breeze might topple to the ground? In Hindu art, where movement or any exertion in time and space is a drawback to the introspective life, this defect is not as serious as in western art. In addition to a lack of perspective, there is also an occasional example of awkward foreshortening, all of which is likewise less serious in a highly spiritualized art. The whole panorama of reliefs sug-

---

64. Reliefs and statues, as in Greece, were painted, but nearly all traces of color have disappeared.

65. The reliefs were executed after the blocks had been put in place, as can be seen from an unfinished example (K. With: *Java*, Hagen, 1920, pl. 24).

gests an atmosphere of opulence; it is a world in which everything happens as it ought to, where the hardships on the road to salvation have been purged of ugliness and evil, like the work of Fra Angelico and the Middle Ages of Ruskin, and where the rigid formality of primitive ritual has been overlaid with the fluid ease of a picturesque idyl.

In Cambodia we find some interesting and well-modeled figures of Buddha. One example in particular[66] is executed with a highly polished surface, with such clarity it seems to bring eternity into the immediate moment. The faces, though superbly done, have received undue emphasis in the wrong direction: the expression is not one that approximates selflessness as well as the Sarnath Buddha, nor does it come close to the state of dreamless sleep, a western criticism which need not reflect much discredit on the sculptor in question. The reliefs of Angkor Wat include a number of well-known scenes from the *Ramayana,* the war between the gods and giants, the churning of the sea, and representations of heaven and hell. These reliefs are much lower than most Indian work, some of them resembling incised drawings. The dancers all display considerable dynamic energy but, from our standpoint, they are cramped; again we must recall that the Hindu is less conscious of the demands of space. The churning of the sea is a masterpiece of rhythmic movement, but the battle of the gods and giants, the figures heaped up to the top border of the frieze, is a galaxy of movement for the sake of movement. In this series one can study the difference between the eastern and western interpretations of movement which in turn reflect two different viewpoints. As one can readily see, the emphasis here is on positive action, in the Hindu sense, rather than on the introspective serenity of Borobudur, and this particular emphasis calls obvious attention to the awkward feet of female figures, turned to the right in something of the Egyptian fashion, while the bodies face the observer.

For a number of reasons only a comparatively small amount of Indian painting has survived, and what we have is preserved

66. V. Goloubeff in *The Influence of Indian Art,* London, 1925, fig. IV.

because of its out-of-the-way location. The best examples we can cite are the Buddhistic murals of the Ajanta caves. They can hardly be called fresco painting any more than the tomb murals of Egypt because the binding medium is more that of the tempera technique; this does not mean, of course, that the Hindu never practised genuine fresco painting. The Hindu artist evidently had a limited palette of colors, but he knew how to make the most of it. Again we must reckon with a long tradition in this art before the creations of Ajanta; again we must not look for anything like clear symmetry, perspective, and all we think is necessary to place an object in the western context of time and space; once more the observer finds himself surrounded by the opulence of the upper classes. It should also be understood that each color, generally speaking, was symbolic: white for purity and water, blue for the firmament, green for animals, and black for space. The line, especially when defining figures, is subtle and contributes most to the rhythm of form and movement, but the rich coloring is even more striking; in its original condition it probably added more to the atmosphere of the composition than the line. Like the Borobudur reliefs, the narrative element is predominant, and many of the paintings are permeated with a similar feeling of devotion; many are also intimate scenes of court life endowed with similar qualities of richness and refinement.

The Hindus were as much concerned as any group of people both with the search for some kind of permanence beyond the reach of finite change and the interpretation of their world of experience in terms of something more ordered and reliable than what the realm of sensation offered them. At the time of the invasion the Aryan bade fair promise of effecting a compromise between the finite and infinite along lines similar to those of the Hebrews or Mesopotamians already considered. He worshipped and sacrificed to powerful cosmic gods dwelling in a region far from human affairs but not so powerful or distant they could not be controlled by the long arm of magic. Such a control assumed a number of guises, the most powerful being the sacrifice and the service associated with it. An emphasis was laid on action, on hunting and fighting, traits also reflected in their gods, which implies an effort to create a more dependable world in terms of time and space relations—all action, in a sense, is aimed at complementing the shortcomings of the finite, at introducing into the latter something of the lasting sameness of the infinite. The Aryan was even somewhat delighted with the varied manifestations of experience for their own sake, not merely for their symbolic value, especially those which favored his material prosperity: the green grass, the running water of a stream, the dark storm cloud. A compromise along these lines never developed into a definite viewpoint because within a comparatively short time a new attitude was born, one of the most unique in the history of viewpoints. Soon after the fighting was over and the Aryans settled down, they must have been impressed with the rapid growth and decay of vegetation, the oppressive heat of a tropical climate so different from the invigorating change of seasons in the north. With these impressions must also have come a temporary wave of pessimism.[67] The new viewpoint emerged in definite outline with the writing of the *Upanishads.*

It is significant that no radical reformer like Zoroaster or Akhenaton was associated with the change which took place both on the intellectual and popular levels, a fact which indicates its need was generally patent to all classes, however they may have looked at the universe from their respective positions in life. The lack of a savior or reformer also tells us that the individual felt himself in such close contact with the reality of the infinite he could save or reform himself without the aid of a special representative of divinity. There is also the possibility of influence issuing from the conquered Dravidians, evidence of which survives in artifacts, but the extent of this influence cannot be fathomed. The resulting change in viewpoint has remained fairly constant since that time. Buddhism and Jainism cannot be considered revolts as much as variations on the same

---

67. S. Konow and P. Tuxen: *op. cit.,* pp. 86–87.

underlying interpretation of reality; they did not involve a change from polytheism to pantheism but a change in how one can identify himself with reality. Regardless of the difference of this viewpoint from our own, one cannot say it has not been fruitful in cultural expression; it has even passed on many valuable suggestions to the West. The European, as often as he has gone to India, has come away either condemning the Hindus as distorted and depraved, or misunderstanding completely the orientation of their thinking. Prof. Sheldon[68] refers to the Buddhist as viscerotonic in temperament because of what he sees as an emphasis on relaxation, comfort, toleration, etc. We can only say that if Buddha had been born in the West, he might have had a tendency toward viscerotonia, but what Sheldon has observed on the surface are but negligible by-products of something much more fundamental and common to both Buddhists and other Hindus. This is only a sample of the misinterpretations of their viewpoint, some of which imply that the whole Hindu way of life is an education in self-deception and therefore the art and literature of this people represent the distortions of a misdirected mind.

To bring this viewpoint into bold relief it is necessary to keep it in constant juxtaposition to that of the West. The main difference between the two lies in the fact that, for the westerner, the infinite toward which he directs so much of his striving is somewhere in the far beyond, but the Hindu finds this same infinite within himself. To emphasize this difference and keep it before our attention, we shall have to repeat this statement from time to time, for it is this location of the infinite in reference to the finite that spells the difference we sense so readily in Hindu religion, art, and attitude toward the powers that be. Is the Hindu construction on the infinite tantamount to what we think of as god? In a sense, the answer is in the affirmative, if we do not think of the divine as a personal power in the Hebrew sense of the term. We must remember that when the Hindu gave up his Aryan polytheism he exchanged it, not for a mono-

---

68. *The Varieties of Temperament,* New York, 1944, p. 256.

theism, but for a religion largely pantheistic, and this type of divine presence can neither be compressed into a person nor pushed out of the reach of the worshipper. This pantheism implied the presence of divinity within every living creature, Hindu and non-Hindu, which explains why no attempt was made to bind the distant infinite to the finite by means of a divine monarch. Brahman has projected itself into finite experience in the form of the Atman, in fact, concrete experience, including every human being, is only a manifestation of the divine in the finite world, of the one into the forms of the many; divinity is not in the here and now in the form of a shadowy reflection or lost soul, it is here and everywhere, now and always. Why should the Hindu emphasize the divinity in the ruler?[69] Whether his statement to this effect is a survival of Aryan tradition or a product of later pantheism makes no difference: since all living creatures partake of divinity, the ruler has no exclusive prerogative in this respect.

We must not forget, then, that the divine element of the cosmos is living within every man, animal, and plant, that these same creatures have their being somewhere on the periphery of true being responsible for their creation, a being which also manifests itself in experience in terms of recurrent phases of a cyclic process. The soul, however we may think of it, and the individual, in his context of society and government, cannot be considered as something distinctively apart from the fundamental reality of the universe and therefore does not go beyond itself to seek for self-identification with that divine reality as the westerner has done throughout his history; the soul has never strayed away from its maker, the individual has always been part and parcel of a divinely ordained social organization which is a manifestation of divinity itself. It cannot be emphasized too strongly that the part, while it manifests its separateness on the surface of experience, is overshadowed, in the Hindu viewpoint, by the unity of reality, or Brahman, to which it is inseparably joined.

---

69. *Laws of Manu*, VII, 9.

Brahman being the central core of divinity, to use a figure of speech, and projecting itself into the Atman and the world outside, is at the same time one with the world. If this is true, it cannot be claimed that the realm of experience is unreal;[70] one may call it deceptive or illusory but such an attribute in no way annihilates it. There are, as we have seen, a great number of schools of Hindu philosophy, all of which take for granted some basic connection between Brahman and the Atman, the unity within and the diversity without. The Hindu, with the reality of infinity tucked away within, can see how varied the world of pluralism can appear to different people, how each thinker can put a different construction on the connection between the one and the many, and therefore he can see how each theory or theology, beneath the surface, is basically true,[71] and at the same time that no single theory or theology is exclusively true because the truth of Brahman cannot be summed up in a concept or series of concepts[72]—each one is grounded in the truth and has possibilities for truth in the illusory finite. If the finite is definitely connected with Brahman we have the right to ask, of what does evil consist? Evil may be called a potential property of desire that reaches out greedily for something it can extract from experience for its own enjoyment, a craving for something exclusive for the pleasure of an organism that thereby endeavors to set itself apart from the unity of the universe by acquiring something more or better than other creatures. Evil is a kind of apartness, whether regarded subjectively or objectively. Good consists of a kind of sharing of all things, spiritual and physical—life, possessions, and values with other creatures, all with an eye toward the underlying unity of all things in Brahman. The evil of desire turns us toward the separateness of plurality, goodness orientates us with the fundamental truth of reality.

How does man, born in the realm of finite appearance, turn his face away from the evil of desire toward a more complete

---

70. M. Hiriyanna: *op. cit.*, p. 62.

71. F. H. Ross: *op. cit.*, p. 22.

72. F. H. Ross: *ibid.* p. 30.

identification with the infinite? To appreciate the uniqueness of Hindu self-realization we must first recall how western tradition has dealt with the same problem. The religious heritage of the West goes back, in a spiritual sense, to the compromise the Hebrew made between the finite and the infinite, between man and his God in the form of a moral compact; Yahweh and man each agreed to cooperate toward an end which would be of advantage to each party. A great deal of theology was later superimposed on this compact. Among the Greeks, Plotinus employed his ladder of emanation to connect the two extremes of unity and plurality and presented man with two means, ecstasy and a life of virtue, to achieve self-identification with god. For the common man of the Mediterranean world the moral compact of the Hebrews held no promise because he was outside the chosen people; he also had difficulty in understanding the wandering reason and terminology of the Neo-Platonist. The figure of Christ was substituted for the ladder and carried the whole western world in its wake along the road to salvation. Christ, the incarnation of God, was the most effective connection between the finite and infinite western man ever devised; belief in Christ became the prerequisite for salvation. Then Augustine bolstered it with his doctrine of the fall of man and the dispensation of grace, and eventually the church well-nigh took the place of Christ as a mediator between God and his lost children. The lonely and frequently suspected mystic is the only one who could dispense with all the support of the church and theology in bringing about an inner reconciliation with his divinity.

In the light of what we have said about the close connection in India between divinity that resides within and man and his experience, we can see that the Hindu was in need of no ladder reaching up through time and space to the infinite, no rationalized theology to reach upward and outward to a distant god. Since Brahman was within, it was the Hindu's business to look inward, and since he was already joined to divinity, he stood in no need of a savior to intercede on his behalf. It meant that he must concentrate on the inner man to effect a more complete identification with Brahman, and the farther he penetrated in his search the more different he found his approach to reality necessarily was from the approach to experience, hence his search became not only a process of introspection but also a renunciation of all associations with experience; this also meant an interdict on desire. He also realized he was on his own in his quest for salvation, for the decision, the initiative, the renunciation were all in his power. The close proximity of the finite to fundamental reality, the location of the infinite within the cosmic circle of appearances, the omission of a mediator between the two opposites, and the necessity of looking inward instead of beyond to find the roots of reality is responsible for the wide gap in viewpoints between India and the West. The difference also comes out in their attitudes toward perfection which, in terms of the spirit, is frowned upon by neither East nor West; as a manifestation on the surface of experience, it is approached much more closely in the East where the godlike Rama, Sita, Arjuna, and several dramatic characters of Kalidasa are held in high respect; an approach to perfection in the West, where most values are based on delightful imperfections, can become, in the course of time, somewhat offensive.

Western man has also inherited from the Greek a concern for the part the Hindu has never appreciated. This fragment of finite experience, in the Greek tradition, had no support from a fundamental reality either within, as we find it in the Hindu viewpoint, or in the beyond where it became a personal divinity for the Hebrew. Such a fragment had to strive for improvement within a framework of time and space limitations and gave birth to the ideal of progress so important to modern man; it was, however, beyond the understanding of the Hindu harboring the kernel of perfection within reach of human control.

Western man is an isolated fragment torn from his original moorings, and therefore reaches out in terms of thought and action to make up for his deficiencies; he must move about in time and space to change his own location, to move other things to his advantage, he must worship his God in deed to come a little nearer to the divinity out beyond himself. We may also say the positive character of his actions contributes something

to his security, economic or otherwise, for the very desire to
move on the part of a living creature is a confession, from the
western view, of insufficiency. Instead of relying on positive
action the Hindu resorts to a passive state to achieve permanence, and because of the greater degree of variation in his
environment his longing for stability is so much the stronger.[73]
A man who gives himself up to introspection, like anyone who
meditates or the cow that ruminates, is thwarted by an active
body. When he gives way to motion, much of what he does is
in response to an inner urge unimpeded by any restricting in-
hibition and without too much concern for the distant future or
a remote end in space. Theology has no great significance for
one who need not look into the far beyond for the fulfillment
of an exalted purpose. The movements expressed by the Hindu
artist and dancer illustrate well the difference in motivation between the East and West. Aside from the motion necessary for
the satisfaction of immediate needs, the Hindu thinks of the
physical as a means by which the divine carries out its program
in the cycle of natural existence; it is not a means by which
man can transform the universe to suit his own ready-made
pattern of order. Motion, in the Hindu sense, is more of a response to an inner urge which uses the body as a vehicle for
the joy of expression than a motivation toward an ultimate
purpose.

What is the basic reason for thought in the West? Aside from
the fact that the European, like all men at a certain stage of
development, tends to think by nature, he investigates particular facts to find some common denominator in all of them; he
works toward some general law, even if he has no hope of
finding it within a lifetime. He also thinks in terms of time and
space relations, toward some kind of an end; in the course of
his thinking he catalogs events outside himself and reorganizes
them by means of the geometric forms of the mind—again to
create what he calls order out of chaos. We may say, too, that
the product of his thought is a compromise between the finite

---

73. E. Conze (*op. cit.*, p. 22) emphasizes this aspect of the doctrine
of Buddha.

and infinite, what he wants and what he may have from circumstances. Western man has also made use of what he calls revelation, which comes down from a divinity above and is then interpreted for the common man by a priest or another authority. The best thinking of the Hindu is intuitive in character.[74] Once the first intuitive assumption has been laid down he can be most penetrating in working out the ramifications of what ought to be. He has worked out to the finest detail elaborate instructions on how every sanctioned tradition, from performing a sacrifice to love-making, should be carried out, but he has never questioned the objective validity of his fundamental assumptions, e.g., the caste system. So many of his philosophical systems are variations on a basic truth found in the *Upanishads;* the present moment is not to be put into an historical context of past and future, but in the eternal here and now, and so the records of the past have suffered; the names of artists are seldom remembered, and if they are put on record, nothing can be learned about their lives. Likewise, the Hindu has not been so concerned about the improvement of social and political conditions within the range of his finite experience.

To convince another of what he considers the truth or to build up a hypothesis, the westerner fortifies himself with the rules of logic, and we must concede the Hindu can split the finest logical hairs, but, as Keyserling says,[75] his logic is more scholastic than scientific in its results. His strong card in convincing another of the validity of his judgment is the analogy, which is much more alive and pregnant with significance than in the West where it is admired as a thing of beauty but hardly accepted as a logical reinforcement. The European, as he wanders around and through an elaborately decorated temple in south India, finds himself totally confused by a mass of symbols and images scattered about in a riot of disorder, but each one of the decorative objects becomes a living reality within a moment's contemplation for the Hindu, who, like others we have

---

74. N. Tatia: *Studies in Jaina Philosophy*, Banaras, 1951, p. XXIX.

75. *The Travel Diary of a Philosopher* (Trans. by Holroyd Reece), New York, 1925, I, p. 107.

considered, can easily concentrate on and identify himself with one object without being disturbed by the disorderly arrangement of which it is a part. Without metaphors and allegories the finest flower of Hindu literature would fade dismally; Kalidasa is a lofty symbol in the field of poetry, but his life is forgotten. Over the whole geographical surface of India, on the pages of Hindu writing, on the sides and pillars of his temples he has painted pictures inspired by an imaginative conviction but, like the vision of the old man in Kipling's *Kim,* they cannot pass an objective test. But, argues the Hindu, why should they continue to endure as conceivable objects in space and time, as neglected relics, when so many other things pass away? The important aspect is the picture conjured up by the inspired moment or the self-realization experienced in the contemplation of such an image. The important factor is the enduring quality of the spirit within, which looks for no permanent anchor in time and space but simply picks the flowers of experience where it can, knowing that every flower is transitory and can only furnish a momentary mirror for self-identification.

Have the Hindus succeeded in establishing a coordination between the finite subject and object in such a way that one enjoys as much value as the other? The overemphasis on the subjective, the urge to retreat from the object as we know it, the tendency to disparage phenomena, the lack of scientific experimentation, the absence of an historical perspective, and the frequent use of magic argue against a balance between the subject that desires and the object that resists desire and demands a compromise; at the same time there cannot be the problems the West is faced with in dealing with circumstances. The Hindu may say, on occasion, that Brahman is different from the Atman and phenomena, but where everything is fundamentally a part of a single stream and the main current of thought runs with the stream, the water of the river and its delta can create no real problem; the European would call this a neat little game between me and myself. The constant emphasis on a complete identification of the subject with the object and the satisfaction the Hindu derives from such an experience is no encouragement for a subject-object balance on the level of phenomena. This does not mean he ignored all problems of his experience, but he failed to think of objects as worthy of improvement per se. Moreover, since the Hindu subject thinks of himself as belonging to an all-sufficient unity, any fragmentary object pales by comparison; such a preponderant importance assumed by the subject is no asset to scientific thinking.

Another factor speaks strongly against balanced thinking: the Hindu seems to have developed no awareness for tragedy. By a most astute cooperation between pantheism and free will he has succeeded in solving all his difficulties on the subjective plane without coming to grips with the larger aspects on the surface of life. As in his dramas, there may be sad situations of suffering, terror, brutality, but there is no sound reason why a great man should go down to ultimate and hopeless ruin. On the other hand, we must admit the Hindu has a fairly good sense of humor, at times he is a keen observer, and he can apply logic to his thinking—he has created a viewpoint more challenging and self-sufficient than any we have yet considered. Yet all his thinking, brilliant as it is, has functioned within prescribed limits. The problems which arise may seem subjectively great for the moment, but as the man playing solitaire well knows, there is a way of tricking fate at every corner. In the Hindu's favor we must admit he has explored various planes of consciousness where we are more or less helpless to follow him.

The most important type of knowledge for the Hindu is what he learns by intuition which reflects itself into the mind of man for analysis and elaboration. Once a man has achieved self-realization he can then be free to observe facts in objective experience as long as they do not interfere with the accepted assumptions of intuitive insight—the Hindu claims there is no serious contradiction between the two. If the Hindu as a subject were able to isolate himself as another object in experience, he might change his mind about his assumptions on caste and government, but this is next to impossible in such a viewpoint. He is like a statue of Janus: with one face fixed on the identity of his self with divinity he can turn the other face outward without incurring any harm, for phenomena, being basically divine, are not cast from the face of god to be stigmatized as sinful matter; the Hindu may become evil by his own choice and efforts, but mere contact with finite matter need not degrade one who has achieved a self-realization of the spirit. It is also important to realize that the Hindu expends most of his mental energy on the rationalization of the relation between Brahman and the world, but he does not find it necessary to make over the universe between himself and a god apart from the world. The problem of the medieval European was much more serious: for just as Christ, the savior, was a combination of spirit and flesh which was subservient and reflected his perfection, the universe of which the earth was a part had to reflect in its make-up the perfect design of Christian salvation. Since this universe is outside of God and within man's objective world, it must be set up in time and space relationships. Aristotle supplied the perfect forms to which the church added the spiritual content. Who established all this as spiritual and eternal truth? The church and its hierarchy whose revelation was far above that of the common man.

The Hindu, already an integral part of divinity, had no need to squeeze the universe into a geometric design and perfect circles to establish a proper rapport between god and man; nor did he, like the Hebrew, ask his divinity to design a perfect plan for his history. He knew that since Brahman cannot be conceptualized he could not fathom the divine pattern of the universe, for anything of the kind put into words would represent, at best, a half truth.[76] At any rate, his salvation was not dependent on a cosmic design, so why be so concerned about it? Moreover, the *Upanishads* as well as the important sects had emancipated the individual from the dictates of the priesthood, and although the Brahmins recovered some of their power at a later date, every man, as a sharer in divinity, had access to spiritual knowledge. The Hindu, then, was free to

---

76. Cf. E. Conze: *op. cit.*, p. 64.

make his contribution to such subjects as astronomy and mathematics, which were in due time passed on to Europe, without incurring the same embarrassment the Christian suffered when the Renaissance removed the earth from the central point of the universe. After astronomy and other branches of knowledge were removed from the shelter of the church, however, western man found his problems inextricably bound up with the universe at large—the infinite he was striving for was still in the beyond, and so he was left in the midst of the comedy and tragedy of an objective world; this was out of the question for the Hindu, bound as he was to the infinite which prescribed his salvation from within.

The Hindu viewpoint has not been able to by-pass the paradoxes so prominent in the Hebrew and Christian scheme of things, although the thinker is not very conscious of them as stumbling blocks. The reason for this is, no doubt, his ability to escape into the infinite more or less at will, whereas the Christian, unless he is a mystic, must put up with and find his God by passing through the finite, and the thinking necessary to reconcile the finite with his God of perfection brings out these paradoxes into bolder relief. By transferring the infinite to the inner man the Hindu has not been able to explain why Brahma consented to create the finite and why the Atman must be projected into a realm of desire and suffering; nor has he been able to account for the origin of evil, but reasoning enjoys no priority in his program of salvation. Instead of resorting to reasons to bolster his faith in a god with whom he hopes to achieve eventual identity, he is above all aware of his original oneness with god as a *fait accompli*. Why should a reason concerned only with a partial truth be used either to reinforce such a conviction or to upset this supreme certainty so alive within him? There is nowhere in Hindu literature a character like Job complaining to God because of his afflictions, nor do we find an Ecclesiastes groaning about the vanity of things, no Egyptian complaining about the topsy-turvy times, no Mesopotamian trying to learn what sin condemned him to a sad plight, no saint overburdening a scapegoat or chanting his *Mis-*

erere. Why? The Hindu has no way of addressing a god as a person out in the beyond nor has he any right to complain, for every man has a kind of choice of Herakles before him: he may continue in the pursuit of desire or achieve renunciation at any time to realize himself in divinity. Sorrow and suffering may be left behind by ascending a higher level of being, a privilege he is endowed with as a birthright and which waits for his own decision.

For the European the question of free will has always been conditioned by the power of divinity exercised over his creation, but in India it is free of contradiction for a man whose soul is directly connected with or is an integral part of divinity. The paradox of predestination and free will which St. Paul brought to the fore in the eighth chapter of *Romans,* and thereby caused so much embarrassment to the later Calvinists and Milton, dissolves into thin air. If a man is fundamentally divine, why should he wish to act in contradiction to divinty? If he does so, it means he has lost sight of his true nature. This does not explain the reason for evil in the world or why a divinity permits evil to come into existence, but it does account for man's freedom to choose his own destiny which can free him from evil and suffering. The will of a deity need not be so far away or alien to that of man who knows very well what that deity desires or demands of him, for after all, this deity is his better self accessible to his attention at all times.

The immediacy of the infinite, however, has made the Hindu feel much more secure in his subjective viewpoint. Magic, we know, was strong enough among the invading Aryans to furnish the priesthood with a powerful means of controlling their divinities, but much of this disappeared in the *Upanishads.* Later we find gods, demons, and men resorting to ascetic practices to gain their ends, and Buddhists claiming the power of their good deeds are cogent in behalf of those who had passed on; but the Brahman-Atman tenet in Hindu religion took much of the sting out of magic, for how can a man hope to make it effective against the god within himself? He might have used it against his fellow man (and he frequently did so), but he also knew he would be held to account in his future career for any harm he inflicted on a living creature, especially since the god within him was conscious of all his designs. There is no way of practicing underhanded expediency on divinity so closely identified with man. Such a doctrine teaches one to respect the inner man, to avoid gross self-deception, and, since the same divinity is in all creatures, to love these same creatures as a means of fostering a better knowledge of and a higher love for the self.[77]

A number of suggestions have been made to account for the Hindu's conviction about the transmigration of souls, but no single one is satisfactory; certainly the Aryans did not bring it with them. When it appeared on the stage of literature, it was fully developed, which may lead us to believe the germ was already at hand among the native Dravidians. For one thing, it extends the sway of free will over the life of the future, it helps to define good and evil as applied to behavior in this life, it breaks down the barrier the West has built up between man and the animal, and has created a religious sanction for the caste system. Instead of looking at the present life as something uniquely precious and as the greatest possession of man, the Hindu can look at it more *sub specie aeternitatis,* as part of the wheel of existence which he can approve of by his own will. While it has exercised a generally salutary effect on behavior, good deeds take on a compensatory value frowned upon by the moralist who insists that a good act should be self-justified; the disadvantage of such a construction on goodness in action, we must concede, is partially offset by another motive for goodness in action, namely, the universal feeling of sympathy consequent on the renunciation of desire. In the West we have an S.P.C.A., which may ease the conscience of those who support it financially, but, with the possible exception of the pampered pet, it has done little for the beast and certainly has not dulled the taste for a rare steak. In India religion has made a brother of

---

77. *Brihadaranyaka Upanishad,* II, 4 (Trans. by Max Mueller): "Verily, a husband is not dear, that you may love the husband; but that you may love the self, the husband is dear." The writer deals in the same way with the wife, sons, devas, creatures, and all possessions.

the animal; it has encouraged the vegetarian diet. Yet the protected monkey, the holy cow, and the divine cobra can be a
decided nuisance in a finite world where divinity seems bent
on lacerating its own tail. The West looks upon the caste system
as a social nuisance; few seem to realize it is a religious institution, like so much the Hindu reveres as unalterable, inspired
by the transmigration of souls and the doctrine of divinity that
gives a religious sanction to the aristocracy of nature as well
as that of the social structure. These tenets are also supported
by dharma, the rigid, governing law of the universe which
harmonizes with the Hindu's belief in the cyclical sequence in
the movements of the cosmos.[78] Once born in a certain caste the
individual is urged to do his duty within its restrictions, to
realize himself as best he can as a Brahmin or a soldier, a
doctrine which seems to anticipate Aristotle's theory of evolution.
Those reformers who hope to change India must be made to
realize that caste cannot be rooted out easily because the Hindu,
like many others, is averse to such treatment for religious conviction; he will only recognize a change of expression.[79]

Was the Hindu successful in creating a moral compact with
divinity equal to that of the Hebrew and did he live in a universe
that was potentially good or evil? A choice he had, but he could
not choose to leave his god, even if he wished to be independent;
he was so much a part of divinity in the past, present, and
future there was little chance for atheism. He had a moral
connection with divinity more binding than the Hebrew compact, for the agreement and its terms were not made in historical
time but determined long before the birth of any man; this was
a matter beyond his choice. The highest good was a complete
self-identification with Brahman, the lowest evil a complete
apartness from divinity or annihilation, and between these two
extremes the individual was free to develop himself in the
direction of a greater good or evil. Again we find, however, that
his potentiality was concentrated on his spiritual welfare, or

---

78. Cf. M. Hiriyanna: *op. cit.*, p. 109-10.
79. F. H. Ross: *op. cit.*, p. 20.

what the westerner would call the negative side of life, without exerting too much influence on positive experience. In this respect the Hindu was very different from the Greek. Whatever the Hindu did for his world was more consciously designed to benefit his own subjective or spiritual destiny, whose shadow lurked somewhere in the background of all his thought and action.

The Hindu's faith in religious tradition (What is not religious in his tradition?) and his somewhat negative attitude toward finite experience have combined to maintain the same form of government throughout his history. The king has functioned as an absolute monarch, the final arbiter over the destiny of man as a mortal being, and if some rulers like Asoka and Harsha have exalted the office of kingship by playing the role of a benevolent despot, the majority have been a discredit to their position. Divinity, residing within, was allied to the aristocracy of human nature, hence kingship was passed along in the bloodstream from one generation to another. Along with free will, the Hindu has been granted a clear perspective over his present life and its duties in the setting of the eternal and the infinite without developing a sense of self-responsibility so necessary in practical affairs, where his tendency to absorb himself completely in the present moment or in the object enjoying his attentive concentration has made him neglectful of the comparative values of an historical perspective. His trust in the cyclical process of the divine law has made him very skeptical of anything like development or progress. And so no effort was made through the ages to improve on the concept of the oriental potentate. If neither the citizen nor the ruler has developed a sense of self-responsibility for the here and now, the subject will remain a means to an end, and democracy cannot be realized.

The most encouraging feature of the Hindu viewpoint is the toleration accorded to other religions and ways of life. In the West every man is a fragment of the cosmos occupying a separate compartment of time and space where he may endeavor to work out his salvation with the aid of a divinity far removed from his particular area of personal influence. Theoretically, every man's god exercises universal sway over all other men, but actually he is a god, as among the Hebrews, of a chosen few, a race or denomination that knows how to worship him in the proper way; he will also extend his mercies to others if they will conform by listening to his missionaries. Try as he will, western man cannot help shutting his divinity off in a limited sphere whose boundaries widen as his worshippers grow more numerous on earth. Western man is haunted by the fear that the other fellow and his god may crowd him and his divinity to the farther wall of the universe. In India, space and time, reason and order are not reflected into the province of the divine. A pantheistic god extends his being everywhere into Hindus, foreigners, animals, and plants, and sincerity in worship generally calls for respect. Those who worship other gods, we are told in the *Bhagavad-Gita*,[80] are really bowing down before a Hindu divinity, even if they do not worship according to the right prescription, so why suspect or persecute them? It is this aspect of the Hindu viewpoint which will help, more than any other factor, toward a mutual understanding between the East and West.

From time to time we have referred to the prominence of the cyclical process in Hindu thinking. Among the early peoples of the peninsula, and perhaps also among the Aryans after their settlement, there were strong indications of the cyclical movement of the seasons, the same we have noted in Egypt and Mesopotamia. This was succeeded by another movement of much greater importance and dimensions than the stereotyped cycle of the seasons, one which exercised change as reflected in growth and decay, life and death, beginning and end. But none of these terms represent anything final, for death is but the prelude to birth, the end is really another beginning in disguise. The cycle, whose movements expand from within, spreads itself out over the change of seasons, the destiny of mortal man, the workings of the whole cosmic panorama, changes which are not all uniform in their movements, i.e., one

80. IX, 23.

aspect may be in its initial stage while another is ebbing along to a decline. This is symbolized by the Hindu Trimurti, the trinity of divinities who carry along vestiges of former associations in the cosmos: Brahma, the creator, Vishnu, the preserver, and Siva, the destroyer, who is also the god of regeneration. Such cyclical changes are manifested most clearly on the level of finite experience. We must realize, too, there are a number of planes of being and each Hindu, according to his position on the scale, sees reality in a different light; on the highest plane cyclical change disappears completely. In this way Hindu religion adapts itself to the people of all castes, means, and intellectual attainments. All classes of people, whatever their circumstances, abilities, or preferences, may worship the same god or gods on different levels through different modes of expression in whatever way each one may best find spiritual satisfaction, which accounts for the varied and at times confused impression the Hindu makes on the foreigner. Why should there not be difference on the level of sense perception? There are times in the history of their religion when pantheism appears much like a polytheism; and again the worship of Varuna became almost monotheistic for a time—appearances are a kind of afterthought on the part of divinity, which means little as long as each man is true to himself in his own particular position. There are Hindus who can best experience a renewed communion with the divinity in terms of what the westerner calls gross sensuality; again we must recall there is no puritanical separation between good and evil in the objective sense. Good and evil depend on the doing and thinking man, and much, too, depends on the spirit in which he thinks or acts.

After this review we can better understand what the West chooses to call vagaries in the field of Hindu art. We must not look for too much reason,[81] balance, or system in the planning of buildings, and basic lines of construction need not be visible to the naked eye. All phenomena may be regarded as the effervescence of divinity on the surface of reality, and the human

81. H. Keyserling: *op. cit.*, p. 107.

must express himself naturally in the same way. The form it takes is by no means as important as the spiritual *élan* behind the forms. There is little use of looking for a connection between the shape and function of a building where purpose in time and space is irrelevant. Why descry the ruined state of certain structures when change is a part of the universal law governing all appearances? Why ask about the reason for high sikharas when they at least afford surface for the sculptor to fill? Why exclaim against pillars that look like anything but supports or complain about a riot of sculpture without any regard for perspective or spacing, when the Hindu, oblivious to what we call confusion, finds each figure, symbol, or group a potential means for self-identification? He has preserved something of the primitive's ability to make himself one with an object or symbol. Rather than stand off as a separate pair of eyes at a safe distance and distinguish this from that or fit a number of fragmentary parts into a neat checkerboard plan, he pours himself out as a whole man in a straight line of concentration upon one symbol after another, whether he is an artist or an observer. In sculpture one can see how stubbornly the Hindu resists our arbitrary line drawn between good and evil. The movement of many decorative figures is also interesting; where we find the framework confining for a dancer, the Hindu merely wishes to make it clear that the subject is not trying to move from here to there but is merely giving vent to an exhilarating urge which compels him from within—the drive of the spirit takes no thought for direction in motion, the relation of horizontal to vertical lines, the right proportion of decoration to structural line. A normal human form not being enough to contain all the forceful energy pouring out from within, a Vishnu or a Siva must be given four heads, sometimes eight arms. The rhythm we admire so greatly is simply a by-product of a motion that fulfills itself naturally without conscious inhibitions.

And what may we say are the drawbacks of such a viewpoint? First and foremost is the neglect of experience and its manifestations, for while it may be very pleasant and a spiritual comfort to be able to retreat from space and time, it is hard to see how one can expect much of a reward either in a Buddhistic heaven or the next incarnation unless one has made a sound effort to improve this world during his stay. Why should Brahman extend the Atman beyond itself, in the first place, if divinity and the finite are not mutually benefited by such a contact? The spiritual factor in life is generally a salutary influence, but when allowed to get out of hand it can create havoc in time and space contexts. It is also hard to understand how, on the one hand, one can be so tenderly concerned about suffering in man and beast and, on the other, how a character like Krishna can justify the slaughter of war; the warrior's salvation in the next world is a clever but forced way of avoiding the contradiction. Is the total elimination of desire the only way to diminish suffering and evil? How can a saint who remains apart from his fellows to enjoy his own superior self-realization, who makes little effort to teach or help others, and who depends on others for his sustenance justify his birth into this world?

And how can we effect a compromise with this people? Certainly not by force, by preaching or adverse criticism. First, we ought to sweep our own house free of inconsistencies to show others how effective our viewpoint can be; example is still the most persuasive means of influencing others toward the good life. Then we should make a sincere effort to study the eastern viewpoint, not from the condescending height of self-perfection, but on a frankly comparative level. It would also be an advantage to learn something about the history of our own tradition which the westerner has a bland way of taking for granted in his own mind. The rooting out of age-old traditions from a viewpoint is impossible, and why should we strive for a dull uniformity at such a cost? With a sound basis for mutual understanding there is no reason why two different viewpoints should not function in some kind of harmony.

THE GREEK

THE PENINSULA OF GREECE is much smaller than most of the countries we have considered, jutting out into the sea as boldly as the Greeks reached out into a challenging experience. Bathed in the clarity of Aegean skies, the stubborn mountain areas slope down nearly to the coastline and thus leave very little land for the farmer to cultivate; the soil of ancient times was so thin the Greeks gave up the cultivation of grain at an early period in favor of the olive and the vine. For a small country Greece has, in proportion to its size, an extensive coastline that is broken up by numerous inlets and peninsulas, some providing excellent harbors for shipping, a feature which explains why the Greeks became great navigators; their merchant vessels hugged the coast all through the Mediterranean and Black seas and occasionally beyond the Pillars of Herakles. Except for limited areas in the south, most of the grain used by the Greeks came from the Black Sea region and Sicily. The fact that mountains and water presented barriers to communication has been stressed, perhaps too much, to account for the rivalry between Greek cities and for the sturdy individuality of their citizens,[1] for the same factors hardly hampered the unity of the Greek nation of our own times. When we speak of Greece in ancient times we must include the Cyclades of the Aegean that serve as steppingstones to Asia Minor, the islands of Crete and Sicily, and much of the shoreline of Italy and the western Mediterranean. The climate was mild but changeable, the air clear, the landscape varied—everything in their environment encouraged the initiative of this enterprising people.

---

1. N. P. Vlachos: *Hellas and Hellenism,* Boston, 1936, p. 10.

Shortly after 2000 B.C. the Indo-Europeans, a seminomadic people, began to pour into the peninsula from the north and continued to come for some 800 years. The second important group was the Achaeans, the bronze-clad warriors of Homer, who subdued the native peoples and settled in fortified strongholds until more invaders from the same direction fell upon them from the rear. Subsequent bands, one succeeding another, drove out the Achaeans, pushed the Aeolians to the northeast, the Ionians into Attica and the west coast of Asia Minor; the Dorians finally settled in the Peloponnesus. The people they found in the new land were undoubtedly agricultural (at least they worshipped an earth goddess, and echoes of matriarchy predominant in religion and society have survived in later traditions). In Crete they conquered what was left of a flourishing civilization founded on the manufacture and export of bronze implements.

Situated on the crossroads between the sources for tin and copper, the Minoans had built up a powerful fleet of vessels in which they carried their wares to Egypt, Syria, and other parts of the Mediterranean, and they evidently had a navy for the protection of the island. Knossos, the site excavated by Evans, had no defending walls. It was dominated by an intriguing palace structure built somewhat unsystematically around a central court, equipped with running water, bathrooms, light wells and other advantages unknown to the fifth-century B.C. Greek. The building had been burned, rebuilt, and then enlarged, which may account for its apparently haphazard arrangement. The people, as revealed in their frescoes and gems, were lithe and sinewy, lovers of nature in all her manifestations; their preference for rich coloring and chiaroscuro effects and their tendency to reduce man to the level of other creatures stamps them at once as different in viewpoint from the later Greek. With the final overthrow of the Minoans about 1400 B.C. the Achaeans built their strongholds at Mycenae, Tiryns and elsewhere, instilling the old Minoan traditions with a new spirit, while their palaces were constructed on a well-fortified height, the rooms arranged around a dominant megaron which became the ancestor of the later Greek temple. The whole complex was better organized than the Minoan palace but less colorful and less convenient for comfortable living. The children of light from the north suspected the dark shadows, the winding passages, the eerie atmosphere of the Cretan labyrinth.

The political unit of the Greeks was the polis or city state which included a certain area of land to help support the city population, so that all classes and pursuits were represented in the political body. The earliest form of government, described in the Homeric epics, consisted of a king and a council of nobles whose consent was necessary on all important questions; it was not by any means an absolute monarchy.[1a] In the course of three centuries after their settlement the form of their government underwent a number of comparatively rapid changes from monarchy to aristocracy or oligarchy, sometimes to a timocracy, and then often to a tyranny before the restless cities adopted a democracy. During this period there was also a great amount of colonization which we find reflected in the *Odyssey* and the Golden Fleece adventures. Groups of malcontents or unfortunates left home under a leader and skirted the coastline of the Mediterranean and Black seas until they found a favorable site where, if they were successful in beating off the natives, they founded a colony patterned after the mother city. And why so many changes in government and so much emigration? The main reason lay in the steady increase of population, far more than the land could support. The soil of Greece was too thin for intensive grain cultivation,[2] a certain amount of timber had been felled, and in times of stress the poorer farmers lost their land to the rich so that the rich tended to become richer, the poor poorer, and legislation was inadequate to deal with the situation. This brought about dissension and struggle at home, and later, colonization abroad—surely life in the Greek polis was not a dull affair!

Since many of the cities were unable to support themselves by agriculture, industries for the manufacture of pottery, metal-

---

1a. Cf. M. J. Finley: *The World of Odysseus*, New York, 1954, p. 83.
2. Cf. H. Michell: *The Economics of Greece*, Cambridge, 1940, p. 7–8,

ware, and other goods were developed to facilitate trade with grain-growing centers abroad; in the meantime the vine and the olive were substituted for grain. Coinage, first used by the Lydians, was adopted by Greek cities to make exchange easier; the construction of ships was greatly improved; Egypt, a country with great commercial possibilities, was opened to the Greek trader and mercenary soldiers; slaves were brought in from abroad to endanger the position of the freedmen. All these rapid changes within a brief period caused a great number of social and economic upheavals and stimulated thinking, daring enterprise, the growth of the arts, and an overflow of energy and interest that stopped at nothing short of the blank face of infinity. The cities of Asia Minor took the lead in many of these changes, in many fields of cultural expression, even though they were constantly threatened by ambitious Lydians, Cimmerians, and Persians, while Athens and Sparta, the two leading cities on the mainland, began to contend for political and commerical leadership south of Olympus.

One cannot call the Spartan government a form of absolute monarchy, but if one insists on calling it a democracy, it must be considered such with a strongly aristocratic emphasis. Their form of government, their way of life, the Spartans traced to a semilegendary lawgiver, Lycurgus; their original connection with Herakles is even more dubious in the light of recent investigations.[3] The government was headed by two kings, acting as priests, occasionally as judges, and as leaders of the army in the field; the Gerousia, a body of sixty elders functioning largely in a legislative capacity; the Apella, or assembly, composed of all Spartan citizens over thirty years, and the five ephors, the overseers whose power of inspection reached even into the province of the king. The people were divided into three classes: the Spartan citizens who owned the property and served as soldiers; the Perioeci, without vote but serving as merchants, craftsmen, and soldiers; and finally the Helots, the conquered aborigines whose condition of slavery was the lowest in Greece. If, at birth, the child of a citizen was judged to be a physical

3. J. B. Bury: *A History of Greece,* London, 1952, p. 121.

risk to the state, it was exposed. At the age of seven the boy was handed over to a military officer to learn devotion to the state and how to endure physical hardships. At twenty he entered the military barracks, even if he was a married man. And at thirty he was ranked as a citizen but still subject to military service until the age of sixty, when he might be elected to the Gerousia. Like the snail, the Spartan enjoyed a measure of freedom only within reach of his shell of conformity.

Under the complete supervision of his life by the state, the citizen had no manual labor to perform, no business or financial responsibilities, no family duties, for much of his life was spent in public mess halls and barracks. Women, too, had to submit themselves to rigorous discipline both for their own physique and that of their children to come. Very little privacy was granted to the family of a Spartan. The weaknesses of such a system are obvious: the structure of the state, because of the huge number of Helots and Messenians, was unbalanced, hence the Spartans lived in constant fear of revolt. Disparities in property ownership arose, and a Spartan citizen without property was in an embarrassing position, but the greatest defect of their way of life was the narrow grooving of life along a specialized channel, frustrating a full and free cultural expression. And yet Sparta was able to maintain her position and prestige through the best years of Greek history, as long as the bubble of Spartan supremacy floated serene and intact before Spartan eyes.

While Sparta was first and last a land power, the location of Athens near the sea encouraged trade and naval power, which in turn made the Athenian much more familiar with the world outside Attica. When history raises the curtain on this city, the Acropolis has become a sanctuary, the kings, including Theseus and Erechtheus, are glorified in legend, and the city is in the control of wealthy aristocrats oppressing the lower classes. The laws controlling debts and debtors were driving citizens to a state of desperation, and the so-called reforms of Draco were so severe in effect they drove out the worm and left a festering sore. Eventually, in the early sixth century B.C., Solon, the founder of Athenian democracy and a farsighted man, came to the fore with more constructive measures: he canceled all debts and modified the debt and property laws; he gave the Athenians a popular court where magistrates could be called to account, and stripped the Areopagus of its legislative powers; trade was encouraged by introducing coinage; and he forbade the export of grain to higher-paying foreign markets. His greatest contribution was made in the structure of the government, which he divided into magistrates, a senate of four hundred, and the assembly composed of all the citizens, for legislation and the election of magistrates. Although the propertied classes had a certain preference in the election of magistrates, the wealthy bore a heavy financial burden, while the people now possessed in their assembly the sovereignty of the state. The Greek viewpoint had already forged an instrument as lasting as bronze, as powerful as triple steel!

Pisistratus, a capable politician and general, took advantage of a leak in the structure of Solon by forming a coalition of dissatisfied parties to establish himself as the first tyrant in Athens.[4] He was tactful enough not to make any radical changes in the government and at the same time did his utmost to create agreeable distractions to make the people forget he was the single power in the city. He was also careful to concentrate his efforts in behalf of the common people and keep the nobles under control. We are sure that, if he was not responsible for a revision of the Homeric epics, he did show a great interest in these poems; he gave encouragement to the Panathenaic and the Dionysiac festivals, including the theatrical performances; under his supervision a great building program was launched on the Acropolis; he also, by his campaigns in the north and his commercial policy, made Athens a city of repute in the Mediterranean world. His cherished hope of establishing a dynasty was not realized, for after his death two courageous young men succeeded in slaying his son Hipparchus, whereupon the other

4. A tyrant in Greek history is not a tyrant in the modern sense of the term; a tyranny in Greece was a one-man government which frequently turned out to be constructive, although, in general, it was not tolerated for more than one generation.

son, Hippias, withdrew to Persia under the pressure of Spartan aid and the Alcmaeonids, an exiled noble family then living in Delphi. The tyranny in more ways than one was a tactical withdrawal to prepare for a more concerted attack on the barriers opposing a full democratic expression.

Toward the close of the century Cleisthenes, the leader of the Alcmaeonids, instituted new reforms designed both to forestall another tyranny and to make the government function more smoothly. First, he reorganized the tribes and demes to break up the old voting units responsible for the political factions Pisistratus had used to advantage; those belonging to the same demes were now scattered in different parts of Attica. To correspond to his ten new tribes he added one hundred new members to the senate and created a committee of fifty of its members, called a prytany, to take care of the senate's administration, the members elected by each tribe in turn and functioning for one-tenth of the year. The sovereign power still rested with the assembly, which met four times during each prytany's control. The most novel innovation was the vote for ostracism: each year the assembly was empowered, if it so desired, to banish a single leading citizen to safeguard the state from another tyranny, a safety valve that may have removed ambitious citizens from the sphere of politics for a time, but was a disadvantage in that the state lost the services of a capable man who frequently suffered exile growing out of political intrigue. Ostracism was a high price to pay for the gem of political stability.

In the meantime the other city-states, though eclipsed by the reputation of Athens and Sparta, were likewise struggling with problems of trade and politics. Corinth, in a commanding position at the isthmus, planted the colonies of Corcyra, Syracuse, and others to the west and built up a flourishing trade in the same direction, but because she was dominated for many years by tyrants, aristocrats, and the influence of Sparta, she never succeeded in developing the type of democracy we have seen in Athens, which may account for her poverty in cultural expression. She remained on good terms with Athens until the latter deprived her of much of her trade.

The Thebans, after putting aside their kings, remained so long under the control of a landowning aristocracy and later of an oligarchy they made no attempt to embark on a foreign policy until the sixth century B.C.; very little is known about their early history. Her citizens evidently felt secure in their agricultural self-sufficiency until they began to extend their sway over the rest of Boeotia, a policy which brought them into conflict with Athens over Plataea.

The story of the early city of Miletus is clear in its general outlines.[5] Her position on the seacoast made her people seafarers and traders, and when the period of colonization set in, the Milesians sent out a great number of citizens to the coasts of the Black Sea. After the overthrow of their kingship and a long period under a merchant oligarchy, a revolution in 630 B.C. brought the tyrant Thrasybulus to power. Later, in spite of a struggle between classes, the government reverted once more to the aristocracy of wealthy men. When Cyrus, the Persian, knocked at the gates of the Ionian cities, Miletus alone replied kindly to his overtures, so that after the fall of Lydia to his army in 585 B.C. she was able to sit back in smug satisfaction while her neighbors lost their independence.

Aristagoras, the Milesian, in a plan to organize an Ionian revolt against Persia, journeyed to Sparta for aid—in vain—then went to Athens, whose government granted him a number of ships. The Ionians, with the support of the Athenians, marched on Sardis, burned the city, and beat a hasty retreat to the coast, all of which prompted Darius, the Persian king, to subdue Ionia, then plan a punitive expedition against Greece, Athens in particular. In 490 B.C. the Persians crossed the Aegean, first to Euboea, then to Marathon. Here an Athenian force under Miltiades and a few Plataeans, although greatly outnumbered, scored one of the greatest upsets of military history; they took the Persians by surprise and dealt them a disastrous defeat. Ten years later Xerxes, now king in place of his father, mar-

---

5. For the story of their coming to Asia Minor and conflict with the Carians consult K. Freeman: *Greek City-States*, London, 1950, pp. 130–132.

shalled a huge but cumbersome force as well as a large fleet, crossed the Hellespont and then made his way through Thrace and Thessaly to Thermopylae. Here the Spartans, in contact with the Persians for the first time, had an opportunity to show their mettle: at the narrow pass Leonidas and three hundred of his men defended themselves and the road to the south until the last man perished. Thebes then gave up to the Persians without a show of resistance, an act which tarnished its name for years to come. Themistocles, the most resourceful man of his day, advised the people of his native Athens to forsake their homes for the northern coast of the Peloponnesus, and after the city, including the Acropolis, had been sacked, he lured the Persian fleet into the bay of Salamis where, because their movements were cramped, the Greeks inflicted an overwhelming defeat on the enemy. Xerxes beat a hasty and shamefaced retreat back to Persia, leaving his land force under his general Mardonius. During the same year the Sicilians worsted the Carthaginians at the battle of Himera, thus checking the advance of Asia in the western Mediterranean. The next spring saw the Greeks uniting under Pausanias at Plataea to defeat the Persians on land, which put an end to any further threat to the mainland.

After another defeat of the Persians at Mycale, the Ionian cities and islands, now free after years of submission, united in a confederacy under Athens to guarantee their safety against another possible attack from the east. The man responsible for this task was Aristides,[6] called the just, and certainly one of the fairest, most responsible men Athenian history can boast of. While the more wealthy members of the confederacy were contributing ships, and the rest were paying their dues in money to be deposited in a common treasury on the island of Delos, Cimon, the son of Miltiades and the military commander for the confederacy, continued to push the Persians farther back into Asia Minor, until his later partiality toward the Spartans brought on his ostracism. Themistocles, before his banishment,

---

6. The Spartans, under Pausanias, had an opportunity to establish a hegemony over the Aegean but bungled it. Cf. M. L. W. Laistner: *A History of the Greek World from 479 to 323* B.C., London, 1947, pp. 3–4.

had provided Athens with walls both around the city proper and down to the harbor on the sea, a bulwark of defense, coupled with her position in the confederacy, that made Athens the leading city in Greece in more ways than one; on land she was capable of defending herself against Sparta or any other city of the mainland, and on the sea her navy, the mistress of the eastern Mediterranean, protected her lifeline of trade to the north. At this point Pericles ascends the stage to preside over the most glorious period of Greek history.

In the course of time the general attitude of the confederacy changed toward Persia, mainly because the Ionians no longer feared her grasping power, and therefore their attitude toward Athens also changed: since they were now in no need of her protection and the tribute seemed a heavy burden, some tried to withdraw from the confederacy. There were also other factors to be considered: Athens saw fit to remove the treasury from Delos to her own Acropolis, ostensibly to make it more safe, but after 450 B.C. the funds were used to beautify the Athenian acropolis itself; furthermore, many of the disputes arising between the confederates were settled in Athenian courts, where the decision was likely to be handed down in favor of the Athenians. The latter contended that after Athens had borne the brunt of the Persian attack and cleared the Aegean of Persian control it was unfair of the confederates to withdraw, but the terms of the original contract were in favor of the other members, and if Athens forced each one to stay in the league, as she later did, she was thereby converting the organization into an empire, which would place her in an anomalous position. She who had always encouraged a popular form of democracy in Greece would now find herself coercing a large number of dependencies to be subjects in her empire. The policy of Pericles, directed toward making Athens the foremost power in Greece, eventually made the city a political octopus whose democracy was a boon restricted to her own citizens, while her tentacles played the autocrat with her dependencies.

Henceforth a number of confederates attempted to secede, only to find themselves reduced to a very low tributary status.

Pericles also tried to raise the prestige of Athens by land as well as on the sea, but here he found that Sparta and her allies were too much for him. At home he took away the power of the Areopagus over administration and the magistrates, much of which was handed over to the senate, the assembly, and the popular courts whose judges were at times ignorant of the law, and so government was made more and more safe for the demagogue. The effects of such moves were not so apparent while Pericles guided the helm of the state because of the respect Athens cherished for his personal ability, but after his death the *vox populi* carried the state far out of bounds on a number of vital issues. He was able to bring the Ionian Aspasia into his household, although she became a target for his enemies who claimed Pericles undertook the Samian war to please her;[7] he sent out cleruchies, volunteers of Athenian citizens, to act as a restraint against rebellion in the confederacy; the Piraeus was developed and along with it came a growth in trade; under his influence Athens became the intellectual leader of Greece; but his most obvious contribution, to the modern, was the glorification of the Acropolis at the hands of Phidias, Polygnotus, and other artists of the late fifth century B.C.

The immediate cause of the Peloponnesian war (431–404 B.C.) was the intervention of Athens in the dispute between Corinth and her colony Corcyra, which left the former in an embarrassing position; this fact also led to the siege of Potidaea, another Corinthian colony on the other side of the mainland, again by Athens. The Corinthians then succeeded, after the Athenian assault on Megara, in bringing Sparta into the conflict, which consisted for some time in engagements on the outskirts of Greece without breaking out into a major battle between the two main contenders. The Spartans invaded Attica, a strategy they were destined to repeat a number of times, the land was laid waste while the farmers of the province took refuge within the walls of the city, a move that precipitated a major disaster for Athens, in the early years of the war, in the form of a

---

7. Plutarch: *Pericles*, 25.

plague;[8] it cut down more than a quarter of the population and demoralized the people for a time but by no means dampened their enthusiasm for the war. Another setback was the death of Pericles in 429 B.C., a leader they sadly missed for the balance of the conflict. Aegina had been taken over by Athens, but Plataea was lost to Sparta and Thebes, after a dramatic siege. Two new leaders now came to the fore on the Athenian side: Cleon, a tanner and demagogue of the popular party, and Nicias, a slow-moving, cautious and superstitious general. In the daringly successful exploit at Sphacteria under Cleon and Demosthenes, Athenian resourcefulness and strategy won out and at the same time forced a galling surrender on the Spartan forces. Soon after the battle for Amphipolis in the north, which resulted in the death of Cleon and Brasidas, the best of Sparta's generals, Nicias negotiated a peace with Sparta in 421 B.C.

With the rise of Alcibiades, a capable but undependable spoiled brat of Athens, the Melians, an ally of Sparta, were arbitrarily wiped out, and the Sicilian expedition was organized in 416 B.C. to aid the Ionian cities in the west and cut off the grain supply for the mainland enemies of Athens. The whole expedition turned out to be a dismal failure,[9] because, for one thing, Alcibiades deserted to Sparta after he had been summoned back to Athens to stand trial for the mutilation of the herms. While there, he induced the enemy to set up a permanent garrison at Decelea in Attica to prevent the Athenian farmer from tilling his land each year, but his stay in Sparta was short, due to a scandal with the queen of Agis. Persia entered the picture again with financial support for the Spartans. The Athenians won a great naval victory at Arginusae, but in the following year (405 B.C.) Lysander won a decisive victory for the Spartans at Aegospotami, where the last resources of Athens went down with her ships. Athens, now completely exhausted, was invested with a garrison of the enemy, her city placed in the hands of a ruthless oligarchy that ruled over the city with a high hand

---

8. Thucydides II, 49–54.

9. Thucydides (VII, 85-87) gives a full account of the unfortunate fate of the Athenian forces. Consult also Plutarch: *Nicias,* 26–29.

for a number of years, before the democracy was restored. Athens' high-handed treatment of former allies bounced back at her democracy with a damaging resiliency.

An important event, significant for its future consequences, took place in 401 B.C. Xenophon, an Athenian, having joined a mercenary group in an expedition of Cyrus against his brother, the king of Persia, survived the battle of Cunaxa and was able to lead his ten thousand men from the heart of Persia to the coast of the Black Sea. The internal weakness of the empire, reflected in the account of Xenophon, gave encouragement to a Spartan king as well as the Macedonians some years later.

After the humiliation of Athens, Sparta attempted to maintain an empire in the Aegean by suppressing democracies in favor of oligarchies and by curbing any kind of expansion on the part of the cities, but with little success. Her king, Agesilaus, inspired by Xenophon's experience, conceived the ambition of invading Persia and was meeting with fair success when he was summoned home to cope with new enemies. Because of Sparta's high-handed treatment of her allies after the fall of Athens, Corinth and Thebes banded together with their former enemy to make things very uncomfortable for her, even in the Peloponnesus; Athens, after the success of Conon on the sea at Cnidus, was also able to bring together another confederacy and rebuild her walls. On his way home Agesilaus won a very costly victory at Coronea in 394, but was unable to gain any advantage from it, for although the Spartans were eventually able to seize the citadel of Thebes itself, they treated the people in such a degrading manner it is small wonder the Thebans retaliated with a vengeance a few years later. In Epaminondas Thebes found a quiet, resolute man, a first-class strategist, certainly the greatest their city ever boasted, who knew how to guide his city through a number of military tangles, who adopted a solid phalanx formation in battle by which he inflicted an astounding defeat on the Spartans at Leuctra in 371.[10] After

---

10. For a description of the battle and its consequences consult H. Berve: *Griechische Geschichte*, II, Freiburg, 1952, pp. 112–114.

setting free the Messenians, a humiliating blow to Sparta, he defeated their army again by the same tactics at Mantinea but lost his life in the pursuit of fugitives. The power of Thebes, without a replacement for the great general, fell into a permanent eclipse.

Over in western Greece the Sicilians had not recovered from the Athenian invasion when an old menace loomed up on the horizon from the west. The Carthaginians, like the Persians some years before, thinking the time was ripe for the conquest of the Greeks, were well on their way to realizing their ambitions when they were halted by Dionysius, the greatest tyrant of Greek history. Having entrenched himself within an island fortress in the harbor of Syracuse, he successfully beat off all attempts of his city to displace him. Eventually he scored a decisive victory over Carthage and confined the Africans to the western corner of the island. Not yet content, he conducted campaigns on the mainland of Italy to include a number of coastal cities in his empire. Subsequently, in the midst of another Carthaginian war he passed away, like Alexander, after intemperate banqueting, in 367, leaving his kingdom to Dion and Dionysius the Younger, whom we remember not because of any merit of their own but because Plato paid two unsuccessful visits to Sicily at their behest to realize his theory of the ideal state. Finally the noble and at the same time capable Timoleon came from Corinth at the request of the Sicilians, drove many tyrants from their cities, inflicted a severe defeat on Carthage at the Crimisus River and then retired to the status of a private citizen in the neighborhood of Syracuse. At least one Greek leader had learned to shun the sword of Damocles!

Up in Macedonia a new power was growing steadily and surely without arousing too much suspicion among the Greek states. Philip, as a young man, had spent some time in Thebes under the tutelage of Epaminondas, whose lessons in military tactics were not wasted on the impressionable mind of the young Macedonian. Greece also learned, far too late, that he was a cunning diplomat. His early years as king were spent in consolidating his position in his own kingdom, a task no one of

his predecessors had been equal to. Once he had subdued the
tribes to the north and west and had cowed the Thracians, he
began, by adroit diplomacy and shrewd military timing, to hew
away at some of the more valuable Greek outposts in the north.
In spite of the constant warnings of the fiery Demosthenes, who
saw through the moves of Philip, the latter was able to snatch
first Amphipolis, then Olynthos from under the nose of Athens,
whose complacency allowed the Macedonians to steal a march
on her at every turn. For a time Phocis, enjoying a brief period
of supremacy, checked him in his march southward, but in the
end he was able to use this setback as a springboard for a much
more rapid advance. Before making a move he would lay a
well-placed net for his enemies, and once they were unwittingly
entangled, once he was sure of his own position and opportunity,
he pulled the net together quickly and tightly. After the destruction of Olynthos Demosthenes grew more violent without using
much foresight, while Isocrates, the armchair political philosopher, was altogether too altruistic in his attitude toward Philip;
both managed to play into his hands.

Perhaps Demosthenes, from the standpoint of Athenian
democracy, was more in the right, if we remember the behavior
of Philip toward conquered cities, for even if, as Isocrates urged,
the Macedonian had been elected the head of a Greek federation,
how long could Athens have retained any independence under
a successor of Philip? [11] The temptation to weld Greece into an
empire would have been too great. At any rate, the whole matter
was settled in Philip's favor at Chaeronea in 338 B.C. where
the Greek allies were outmaneuvered, Demosthenes and many
other Athenians running from the scene of battle.

All the Greek states were brought into a union whose major
purpose, it developed from a meeting at Corinth, was to invade
Persia to avenge all the insults that power had hurled against
Greece. On the eve of the great undertaking Philip, who had
taken a new wife, found himself involved in family trouble
because of the birth of another son and met death at the hands

---

11. Cf. J. B. Bury: *op. cit.*, pp. 723-724.

of an assassin; the agent behind the crime was never brought
to light.

First, Alexander had to put down a number of revolts in the
north and south where the young man, a master of his father's
military tactics, showed himself equal to the task. Thebes, more
than any city in Greece, felt the full brunt of his wrath. In 334
he crossed the Hellespont and defeated the Persian host at
the Granicus River, a victory which left him, after a few minor
engagements, master of all Asia Minor. After taking Miletus
and Halicarnassus he moved on to Issus, at the gateway to
Syria, where Darius met him with a huge force in the following
year, and again the cavalry, headed by Alexander, and the
solid phalanx carried the day, the whole army of the Persians
being put to flight as soon as their king turned his back to the
battle. To gain control of the Persian fleet and the coast of
Syria Alexander moved down to Tyre, the nemesis of more than
one conqueror in the East, a move which taxed all the resources
of his siege engines, all the courage of his men before he could
take it. After adding Gaza to his conquests he entered Egypt
without any difficulty. He laid plans for the later cosmopolitan
center of Alexandria and then made an astute political journey
to the oracle of Zeus Amon in the desert; here he was recognized
as the legitimate heir of the pharaohs, a procedure necessary to
hold the respect of his oriental subjects; we may be sure that
Alexander never thought of himself as a divine being.[12]

One more battle on the plain of Gaugemela in 331 broke
the back of Persia and its king, who met a sad end soon after
his wild flight to the east, leaving Babylon and its heavy fortifications an easy prey, before the Macedonians descended on
Susa and Persepolis, the capital of the empire. Here the palaces
of Xerxes were burned, the statues of the tyrannicides despatched
back to Athens; here too Alexander adopted the policy of
amalgamating the East and the West by taking on eastern cus-

12. C. A. Robinson (*Alexander the Great*, New York, 1947, pp. 115-
116) takes a different view of the matter; Cf. also E. Suhr: *Sculptured
Portraits of Greek Statesmen*, Baltimore, 1931, pp. 48–50; W. W. Tarn:
Alexander the Great, Cambridge, 1948, p. 43.

toms and dress and encouraging his army to do the same. Many of his soldiers, however, were reluctant to follow suit. The way then led to the Far East, through Sogdiana and Bactria to the fabled land of India. One of his most difficult campaigns was that against Porus, a leader of indomitable courage, whose elephants were a disadvantage to his own ranks in the battles on the Hydaspes, whose courage, however, earned the highest praise and respect of Alexander after the battle. At this point the Macedonian veterans, weary of the long expedition, refused to march farther east, and their reluctant leader was forced to conduct his troops back to Babylon by land and sea. In 323 B.C. he died after a carousing celebration prior to a planned expedition to Arabia.

Athens and other Greek states, overjoyed at the passing of Alexander, shook off the yoke of Macedonia, but their freedom was short-lived; Antipater soon quelled the revolt and Demosthenes was driven to suicide. Ptolemy took over Egypt and Seleucus received Syria and the territory to the east for his share. Henceforth the history of the eastern Mediterranean is a series of dynastic wars between Egypt, Syria, Thrace, and Rhodes, while the mainland remained quiescent, resting on the glories of the past until 146 B.C., when Rome made Greece another province in her empire.

When the first Greeks invaded the peninsula, they found, as we have seen, a way of life different from their own; this was especially apparent in the field of religion. It has long been surmised that many of the states of Asia Minor, e.g., Phrygia, Lycia, Lydia, and Caria were matriarchal at this time and perhaps remained so for some time after the Greek invasion. The religion of the island of Crete was dominated by a female goddess, a very stern-looking lady holding serpents on her outstretched arms, and from Minoan frescoes we learn that women played a very active role in outdoor life, especially if that activity was dictated by a religious motive. Another divinity, a youthful male, assumed a subordinate position, sometimes that of a sky god who came to visit the great mother in spring and then vanished with dying nature in the fall. The worship of a similar pair, Attis and Cybele in Asia Minor, survived to the days of the Romans, who brought the cult to their city during the Second Punic War. The Aryans, whose religion and society were dominated by the male, must have waged some bitter conflicts with the mother-worshipping natives who forced the Greeks to submit to a compromise in a number of localities. Where can we find traces of such a compromise? We need only examine the story of the Amazons, the marriage of Zeus and Hera, the stay of Herakles at the court of Omphale to realize that the Greek god had to stoop low to conquer, and in many cases the old relationship between male and female survived in a new significance. Pre-Greek religion also seems to have been closer to earth, associated with the fertility of the soil, plants, and animals, and many of the divinities, who took on a new dress and function among the Greeks, were female; Artemis and Aphrodite are outstanding examples. Many of the struggles of Greek mythology are reflections of the war of religions before the Olympian pantheon was generally accepted.[13]

The Greek gods of the Homeric epics still preserved definite connections with the aspects and phenomena of nature, even after the compromise effected with the native population and their emergence as anthropomorphic beings. There is nothing lofty about these divinities; there is nothing of the sublimity of Yahweh, nor did they make such cruel exactions on their worshippers as Cybele or Ishtar. Above all, they were human, living in a heaven of their own and subject to limitations in the form of responsibilities to each other and fate, but also enjoying privileges beyond the power of man. Toward their worshippers they were benevolent as long as they received their due and man remained within his duly appointed sphere. Like events and circumstances in a changing world, they could reward the patient effort of man with a certain degree of happiness and chastise excess in the form of the "slings and arrows of outrageous fortune." Their humanity and their interest in the lot

13. G. Thomson: *Studies in Ancient Greek Society*, London, 1949, p. 178.

of mortals constituted their greatest charm: they laughed and wept, they practiced deception on each other, grew angry and felt regret, they fell in love with god and man, an experience fraught with both joy and sadness for the latter. There was also a family organization on Olympus, a patriarchal institution in which Zeus was called upon to settle disputes, sometimes to mete out heavy punishments.

Zeus, the father of the gods, ruled over his family, over the known universe by virtue of the thunderbolt he hurled with such devastation. Like the father of a family, he could be gentle to the weak, he could be influenced by the wiles of women, he could shake the earth with his wrath—an old sky god, no doubt brought down by the Aryans from a region where the manifestations of the heavens meant more than the moods of the earth. Hera, his wife, was probably an old earth goddess, redressed to make a respectable spouse for Zeus; and like a model matron, she had no extra-marital relations, she presided over the rites of marriage, and could be a jealous thorn in the side of her wayward husband. Poseidon, the earth-shaker who presided over the sea, was especially fond of the horse, was worshipped both in towns along the coast and inland; his origin is unknown to us.[14] Hades, another brother of Zeus, was the dark god of death, the lord of the underworld and the husband of Persephone. Neither of the brothers was too patient with the overlordship of Zeus, which they regarded as a form of tyranny, but in view of his power they could not be too insistent in their demands.

Aphrodite, as old as any divinity in the Aegean, became the daughter of Zeus, the mistress of love and beauty; Eros a venerable and ancient god of the poets, became her adopted child. Because Apollo as healer, prophet, and musician had definite associations with shepherd life, it is likely he was brought down from the north by the Greeks to Delphi where, we have good reason to believe from mythology and art representations, he had to fight for the lordship of the most sacred

---

14. J. E. Harrison (*Mythology*, Boston, 1924, pp. 39–41) traces his origin to Libya. The Near East seems to be a much more likely place.

center of Greek worship. Artemis, formerly a fertility goddess whose worship as such was continued at Ephesus, became a chaste patron for young girls, a goddess of the moon and the hunt; as a sister of Apollo she was often associated with him in mythology and religion. Hermes can be traced to the shepherds of Arcadia, but for the Olympians he served as the messenger of the gods, a conductor of shades to the realm of Hades, a protector of merchants, travelers, and thieves. Hephaestus, as a former fire god in Asia Minor, carried on as a master craftsman for the Olympians. Athena too was once a fertility goddess associated with the serpent and the owl before the Athenians made her a reserved virgin presiding over war, cultural pursuits, and workers in the crafts. Dionysus, the youngest in the divine family, came from Thrace to Delphi, then to Athens, bringing the vine and wine in his wake; the Athenians made him a more sober devotee of the theater. Other less important divinities were Demeter, goddess of the harvest; Ares, a swashbuckling god of war; Hestia, an old guardian of the hearth; Asclepius, master of healing; and Pan, the capricious spirit of nature, respected especially by shepherds. There were also the nine muses, the graces, the hours, the fates, of whose origin little is known, and countless satyrs, nymphs, dryads, harpies, furies, and gorgons which owe much to the rich imagination of the Greeks.

Heroes belong in a class by themselves. We are now quite sure that Greek heroes—all heroes, in fact—were not, by origin, glorified men raised to an exalted level after death but personifications of forces in nature, e.g., the sun, which benefit man in the course of the year.[15] The Greek thought of a hero as the son of a mortal and a god, one with divine aspirations but mortal limitations, inclined to overreach the boundary of his privileges and so rouse divine jealousy; eventually the hero had to descend to Hades with mortals. Herakles, the most prominent of all, is a confusing combination of hero and god, for as a hero he accomplishes superhuman feats against monsters and giants, but as an old survival of the sacred marriage he is subservient

---

15. Lord Raglan: *The Hero*, London, 1936, pp. 131-132.

to a female goddess.[16] Others include Perseus, Jason, Theseus, and the warriors of the Trojan saga. The hero, generally speaking, was a man of exceptional ability, one who displayed outstanding courage in the face of all obstacles, even of the prospect of a gloomy sojourn in Hades. What could be more precious to the Greek or his hero than a full, rich life in the present, crowned with well-deserved fame?

The Greek, as a rule, worshipped out in the open before an altar, a marked contrast to the eastern dark holy of holies; he also worshipped in caves, in groves, at festivals, on mountain tops, at oracles. Sacrifices included animals of various kinds, bread, cakes, fruit, and flowers, as well as the pouring of a libation of mixed wine and water. The temple was not the place of worship we have found in so many of the eastern civilizations but a shrine where a god could reside on occasion, where his statue was housed. The priest was not a sacrosanct person with a monopoly on a privileged channel of revelation running from divinity to man, nor had he any right to coerce others with the weapon of religious authority; he was simply an average citizen appointed for a given length of time to supervise the sacrifice and worship in a way most approved by tradition. The frequent festivals in honor of divinities took the place of our Sunday. There were national festivals at Olympia, Delphi, Nemea and the Isthmus as well as annual celebrations, e.g., the Panathenaea and the Dionysiac festivals in Athens. And what pleasure did the gods derive from such honor and worship? Being very human they were flattered with attention, they enjoyed sharing in the communal meal at the sacrifice, above all, the odor of burning fat.[16a] Beyond the prayer, the service at the altar had nothing so solemn as the worship of eastern divinities. The Greek respected the majesty in divinity and at the same time the dignity in man.

---

16. *Odyssey* XI, p. 601. Homer is uncertain whether to call him a god or a hero.

16a. R. B. Onians (*The Origins of European Thought,* Cambridge, 1951, p. 279) equates this fat with the "stuff of life," also (p. 293) with ambrosia.

Before every important undertaking a sacrifice was offered and omens were interpreted to learn about the will of the gods, although the latter were not too binding and many of the intellectual and political leaders must have been sceptical of all forms of divination. Omens were taken from the flight of birds, the movement of animals, any sudden or exceptional phenomenon. There were also oracles. At the ancient shrine of Zeus at Dodona the priests found the will of the god expressed in the rustling of leaves on an ancient oak, but the oracle at Delphi, the most influential of all in the best days of Greece, took advantage of a cleft in the rocks whose vapors, when inhaled by animals or humans, produced a strange and unaccountable behavior. The Pythian priestess, so-called, sat above this cleft until, in a state of ecstasy, she uttered strange sounds which the priests interpreted in verse form. The verses or oracles, purposely cryptic and capable of different interpretations, were composed by a staff of priests open to bribery, hence the leaders of Greece, who put little faith in the oracle, frequently used it to dupe the common people at home and thus gain their own ends.

The lower world was the dwelling place of the dead, a further development of the Mesopotamian kingdom of Nergal. The future life, whether people practiced inhumation or cremation, was hardly a cheerful place for man or hero, as we learn from the eleventh book of the *Odyssey*, a place where the souls or shades wandered about listlessly, without strength or consciousness, unless they were given the blood of a sacrificial animal to drink.[17] Here reigned the dark, gloomy brother of Zeus and his bride Persephone; here was the boatman Charon who ferried the shades across the Acheron; here the three-headed dog Cerberus stood guard; here dwelt the god of sleep, the judge Minos, the furies, and other dreaded creatures. It housed Sisyphus, Tantalus and Ixion, arch offenders against the gods in the early days, as well as Giants and Titans worsted in struggles with Zeus and his family. Where was the approach

17. M. P. Nilsson: *A History of Greek Religion*, Oxford, 1949, p. 138.

to Hades located? There is no agreement on this point, but wherever the landscape presented a barren, primitive area, like that around Lake Avernus, the ancients put it down as an entrance to the lower regions. The Greeks had no great fear of the dead, because there was no way by which the shades might return to the light.

There were also two popular cults centering in the regeneration of the earth and man, cults that were no doubt survivals of the days before the invasion. The Eleusinian Mysteries, celebrated at Eleusis in Attica, included a ritual based on the story of Demeter and Persephone, the rape of the latter by Hades, the long search of the mother, the return of the daughter, and the gift of grain. It was a cult definitely based on a vegetation myth, for Persephone was on earth with her mother for all but four barren months of the year when she stayed with her husband in the world below.[18] The nature of the ceremony at Eleusis, which took place by torchlight at night, was not divulged by any of the initiates—we know nothing certain about the rites, which probably included in their presentation a parallel association between the ascent of Persephone to the light and the regeneration of man, an experience demanding a standard of moral behavior as a condition; the initiated would also have a happier lot in the world of shades. The Orphic cult, more obviously connected with the regeneration of man, was built around the figure of Dionysus as Zagreus, the reborn god, and the sinful nature of man acquired through the blood of the evil Titans. Man's highest aim in life, they believed, was to rid himself of his sinful nature and achieve complete self-identification with divinity; it also included a series of transmigrations.[19] It demanded faithfulness in observing the rites about which we are ignorant in this case also, and right conduct, even in the face of injustice from others in the family or society. Orphism, whose connection with Orpheus is undetermined, was a religion of the common people, a solace in times of need or oppression.

18. M. P. Nilsson (*Greek Popular Religion,* New York, 1940, pp. 52–54) gives an excellent interpretation of the myth.

19. H. J. Rose: *Ancient Greek Religion,* London, 1946, p. 94.

Greek religion, because of its lack of priestly authority and its attitude of noninterference in secular life, offered no serious obstacles to the development of independent thinking about man and his relation to the universe at large. Much of this thinking came to light in the Ionic cities in the early sixth century. These early efforts are interesting because they represent the first projections of man's thought into the cosmos, organized as an orderly arrangement of objects propelled by regularly recurring movements acting upon these objects. There is much that has been carried over from thinking dominated by more primitive notions: the cycle of creation and destruction, the relation between the microcosm and macrocosm, the belief that all concrete matter is imbued with life, hence hylozoistic, and the so-called vortex. One thing the modern is likely to forget in his amusement over so much simplification, is that all this pre-Socratic philosophy was brought forth not only without scientific instruments but before the thinker knew anything about the distinctive difference between the subject and the object, before man knew anything about the processes of thought so familiar to us from the study of psychology.

Thales of Miletus, one of the seven wise men, said water is the fundamental element of the material universe, that all things come from water and return to it again; the force required to make these changes he thought of as one of the constituents of water itself. As he stood on the shore of the sea he saw how much water there was on the surface of the earth, he realized how much water there is in the living organism, that an embryo is kept moist, that wells and springs bring up water from the depths of the earth. Anaximander was bold enough to think of the material universe as infinity whose boundless, potential qualities are its most distinctive features; from such a universe one world after another could be formed. Another outburst of his imaginative thinking conceived of the first theory of evolution, through changes brought about by the environment of a creature and the latter's initiative in responding to nature's challenge—man was first a fish, then an amphibian on the seashore before he developed into a biped. Anaximenes,

the third Milesian, settled upon air as the primary principle
of a changing cosmos; what's more, he was certain he knew
how air produced what we find in the world and then dissolved it all: like Watts, he saw water apparently giving way
to air under the action of heat and, transferring it from a particular to a general aspect of the cosmos, called condensation
a creative force, rarefaction a destructive one. The Milesian
theories about geography and astronomy, though interesting,
are not as creative or significant for the development of thought.
Whatever we may say about their generalizing, which is the
most natural type of thinking, they laid a firm basis from which
later thought could ascend to the abstract or expand further
on a horizontal line.

We now pass to several men who sought for a general principle by eliminating difference on the horizontal plane of experience, and to do this meant the subtraction of quality to arrive
at a common feature of all objects. Pythagoras rejected every
disturbing quality in favor of quantity and then endowed
number with the power of magic to control all other aspects of
things. Like the Chinese in the moral field, he measured the
length of sounds necessary to produce harmony on a musical
instrument and then supposed the same principle of harmony
could be applied to the human body for the preservation of
health. He was evidently of the conviction that a harmony of
quantities was latent in the whole universe, waiting for man's
discerning eye, a kind of magic of numbers that did little for
the development of thought, although the by-products of his
efforts contributed much to mathematics and music.

Parmenides raised his common principle so high above the
finite it was beyond all description, beyond the reach of conception; "being" was nothing positive, no attribute can be
assigned to it—its nature came very close to a nirvanalike
reality[20] which could be contemplated rather than visualized.
All the difference and quality of our experience were deceptive
and what could be learned from it was unreliable opinion,

20. This has been very adequately expressed by B. A. G. Fuller:
History of Greek Philosophy—Thales to Democritus, New York, 1923, p. 150.

whereas true knowledge, once all variation was subtracted, explained what was in "being," but all this was beyond expression. Since motion was the cause of change, it had to be denied as an attribute of "being," a thesis Zeno did his best to support with his antinomies. Again the by-products of the latter's work reveal for the first time in conscious thought the eternal paradox between the finite and infinite, a contradiction we have found haunting man's thought and action from his very beginnings. In the efforts of these three men we sense a tendency to rationalize the eastern viewpoint, and had they been able to support their tenets with priestly authority, they would have set up a hierarchy in Greece or southern Italy.

Heraclitus of Ephesus brings us back again to the ebb and flow of finite experience, to the constant change he called more real than any kind of permanence conjured up by the subjective mind. The whole universe was forever threshing back and forth between two possible extremes; into this conflict every creature had to hurl himself if he wished to keep abreast of circumstances, if he wished to make his character his destiny. Instead of a static "this" or "that," all things, including man, were in a state of eternal becoming, and therefore positive effort and a defiant attitude were necessary to cope with such a world. Fire, which, he claimed, made up the mind and life within us, was put down as the most important element of the cosmos, perhaps because of its heat and constant flickering motion. Like Pythagoras, he lived in a world of opposites, but, unlike him, his means and extremes can hardly be sensed or measured in the midst of so much change.

Empedocles found his universe made up of the standard four elements, but his important contribution came by way of two forces, transferred from human emotions to the world at large, as agents of creation and destruction. These forces are love and hate. All matter was lifeless (so we find it also in later philosophy), depending on some outside force to move it, to use it. He also entertained the religious motive of reincarnation[21] and the good behavior associated with it, but this

---

21. K. Freeman: *God, Man and State*, Boston, 1952, p. 84.

side of his doctrine is not too clear from the fragments. Both Heraclitus and Empedocles were aristocrats of the active intellect, opposed to those whose apathy made them surrender to a static universe.

Democritus of Abdera had a much more developed theory of materialism. His world was made up of countless indivisible units he called atoms, moving in a downward course at the hands of impersonal gravity. The most natural movement, for one unacquainted with the true relation of this motion to the earth, was a descending pull which brought the atoms together by chance. His doctrine is one of determinism. The atoms are qualitatively the same but they vary in size and shape, those of a similar make-up uniting with their own kind to form the world as we know it. In living he proposed a program of moderation that anticipated Aristotle's golden mean.

Anaxagoras was also concerned with the composition and motion of the cosmos, tracing the matter of visible and invisible things to small seeds which, however, differed from one another qualitatively. The motion that brings together seeds of the same quality does not operate by chance; it is directed by the *nous,* or cosmic mind, which also sets a purpose or a goal toward which all seeds must move, and keeps them in order as they move. His philosophy is, then, teleological, not deterministic. The *nous* is separate from the rest of the physical world; it is different, but how different is not too clear from his words.[22]

Up to this point man has been treated as simply another unit of the cosmos, subject to similar movements of creation and destruction and composed of similar materials, another creature washed up on land by the sea of creation to compete with the animal in a potential world. It is important to realize that this cosmos, whether composed of four elements, seeds, atoms, or created from water or air, is an entity made

---

22. This question has led to considerable speculation on the part of the authorities. Cf. W. T. Stace: *A Critical History of Greek Philosophy,* London, 1920, pp. 98-99; also W. Jaeger: *Die Theologie der fruehen griechischen Denker,* Stuttgart, 1953, pp. 182–183.

up of parts which are more or less separate and on their own, not the mere manifestations of an underlying reality we found in the experience of the Hindus. The fifth century B.C. brings with it a new anthropocentric emphasis which may be explained as a result of the Persian wars, the spirit of the new Athenian democracy, or it may be regarded as an important reaction to the many and varied cosmic theories of the pre-Socratics. The Greek, like all thinkers, was interested in arriving at a dependable and workable truth behind the changing aspects of experience without, however, giving it a strong subjective push. Because the pre-Socratics proposed so many theories, the possibility of coming face to face with such a truth appeared to be fading on the horizon, some no doubt concluding there was no truth in the objective world. Religion with its gods functioning as definite objects in nature imposing common standards of belief and behavior was now losing credit with the intellectuals. Consequently the thinker turned to man himself to learn about truth.

The Sophists, as we hear from the ancients, were famous educators traveling around from city to city to teach the younger men—but this side of their efforts has been eclipsed by their sophistry, their expediency we hear so much about from Plato. Protagoras formulated the statement that man is the measure of all things, which means the subject, in thought, is a law unto itself requiring no objective standard at all. Gorgias, who followed in the same line of thought, went so far as to say that nothing exists, although he never forgot himself while defending such an argument. This doctrine appealed to the immediate desires of human nature, especially to the young people more than happy to consign the restraints of their elders to oblivion, eager to find a means of persuading others to their own viewpoint; this need the Sophists were at hand to supply by way of rhetoric and eloquence. And if eloquence was not powerful enough to gain one's ends, what then? The Sophists were ready with a corollary to the effect that might makes right. The man with means to coerce should satisfy his desire without any feelings for the other party, in defiance of any moral code; and if he had no means, he was privileged to acquire those means by any form of deceit in his repertoire of devices. We can easily understand that, if such a philosophy had been universally adopted, it would have spelled confusion in state and society, but as long as such responsible characters as Aristides stood at the helm of politics we can be sure the Greeks were not all Sophists in the early fifth century. However, while men taught that knowledge was mere opinion and morality was self-interested expediency, there could be no promise of all the contributions of the Periclean age. There are two big reasons why Greece was not swallowed up in the confusion of subjective relativism. The first was the faith in themselves aroused by the victories over the Persians; certainly there was something good in the teachings of the past to justify so great an upset at the expense of a great empire. The second was Socrates!

The Athenian gadfly, the son of a sculptor, spent his life in search of the truth, and if he did not find it to our satisfaction, he certainly pointed out the road to its discovery. Married to a woman with the reputation of a scold, he spent his whole day abroad teaching young men and conversing with anyone who might come his way. He took no pay from his students; perhaps Xanthippe was justified in complaining about his negligence of the family. From the *Symposium* of Plato we learn he served his country as a brave soldier, and from his own defense we hear of his activities in the state; he repeatedly refers to his "daimon," an inner voice he obeyed on all occasions, a voice some think of as inspired revelation and others claim was no more than keen insight or sound judgment after careful reflection. Because he was so curious, so insistent in his quest, so frank in disclosing false knowledge, he became an object of hatred to those who failed to understand his motives. In 399 B.C. he was forced to drink the hemlock in prison.[23]

Socrates' aim was the discovery of some dependable truth more permanent than the shifting quicksands the Sophists found in objects, and he was sure he could find it in the human being. Instead of probing into the sky, the earth, and the matter of

---

23. Plato (*Phaedo* 65-66) gives the account of his death.

the pre-Socratics, he used a question and answer method to pry into the mind, letting the other talk at will, to find out first how much the other knew and then to help both the other and himself along the road to sound knowledge. He used induction to arrive at a correct general statement, he emphasized definition and comparison to lay bare a truth common to more than one mind and couched beneath all the superficial opinions of sophistry. To us all this is a matter of course because we engage in the process as though it were a part of our natural endowment, but to Socrates and his students it was a startling discovery that became more and more engrossing; he was as sure as the alchemist he would be able to use his newly discovered knowledge to save mankind from many of its ills. It was, then, easy for him to leap to what we call a hasty conclusion: knowledge is virtue, as he put it; the men who knew what was right ought to do the right thing. He did not realize, of course, how easily knowledge can become a means in the hands of evil as well as of good men, how weak an arbiter the knowing man can be over the moral man. He also concluded that if knowledge can be taught, virtue can likewise be taught. In Athens, where thought was still young, it was easy to think of goodness as a next-door neighbor to knowledge, both ready to cooperate against the common foe. These errors simply testify to Socrates' great faith in universal knowledge as a common good, in reason as a means of finding it, a faith he succeeded in handing down as an heritage to others.

Plato, revolted by the execution of his teacher, turned away from much that Athens had stood for, although he set up his Academy on the outskirts of the city and remained there most of his days. The student inherited the truth of Socrates, which he proceded to sublimate to such a degree that his idea or universal was far removed from the particular in experience, while the latter became nothing but a remote reflection of its genuine counterpart, a separation that carries us back to Parmenides' "being" and "nonbeing"; but Plato was much concerned about man's role in this scheme. His opposition to the Sophists led him to confine all their knowledge to the shadows of experience where the flux and flow of Heraclitus reigned supreme. There were, then, two types of knowledge for Plato: that of shadowy experience to serve as a steppingstone to something higher, otherwise man lost his way in a confusion of error. The higher level of knowledge demanded a more rigid discipline in dialectic, an ability to discern ideas and classify them—ideas which were innate in every man but required rediscovery on the part of the patient searcher, ideas which were true and clear to the soul in a previous state[24] but had lost their clarity when the soul descended into a mortal body. The acquisition of true knowledge became a process of reasoning recollection.[25] The teacher, as illustrated in the *Meno,* must help to extract this knowledge from the hidden depths of the mind; the rest the student must do for himself. Plato had, of course, the same difficulty all thinkers encounter when they try to reconcile a perfection in the infinite with the changing aspects of the finite, a gap which cannot be bridged by reason; here he resorted to the myth or the allegory.

Plato's ideal state was also a kind of revelation dictated from above, so perfectly fitted together it had little chance to survive in experience. The division of classes is a reminder of the old caste system of India; its authoritarian character and structure have much we are familiar with in both fascism and communism. The rigid control over the citizen's life, his choice of occupation, his rank in the state show traces of Spartan influence, and the arbitrary dictates coming down from above snuff out all independent thinking, any self-responsibility among the citizens below. The separation of good from evil in art, literature, and music would bring about a state of aesthetic starvation hardly fit for a community of eunuchs. Plato's two journeys to Sicily made him aware of the inadequacies of his state, which prompted him to compose the *Laws* to fill in the gaps.

The supreme idea in Plato's hierarchy is that of the "good." Therefrom he derives the greatest beauty, the principle of right

24. P. Shorey: *What Plato Said,* Chicago, 1933, pp. 201-202; cf. also the *Katha Upanishad,* 3, 3-9.

25. *Republic,* pp. 514A–518C.

conduct; it also becomes the point of departure for his teleology. After the soul had passed through a series of incarnations and had stood the test required to merit salvation, it was in a position to identify itself with this supreme idea of goodness, dwelling henceforth in a perpetual state of blessedness. It is no exaggeration to say that Plato has rationalized, as far as it can be done, the general eastern attitude toward reality and experience and may also be considered a prophet of the Middle Ages. His direct successor in Greek thought is Plotinus.

Aristotle set up his school of Peripatetics in the Lyceum, also in Athens. He had spent many years in the Academy of Plato, and then, after a short absence from the city, presided over his own school until the death of Alexander, when he fled from Athens because he was counted as a pro-Macedonian. He was familiar with every branch of knowledge of his time, he investigated new fields of study, invented new terminologies, and may be considered one of the greatest minds of western civilization.

In the *Metaphysics* Aristotle struck directly at the heart of his subject and the underlying difference between his thought and that of Plato by defining substance in terms of the universal and the particular. He made it clear (and this is important) that the universal and particular must be in conjunction if one expects to learn anything about substance, that reality cannot be dealt with as a universal which is not grounded in a particular;[26] this is what made Aristotle a scientist in our sense of the term, while Plato, because his idea was so far removed from experience, remained a more subjective rationalist. Once Aristotle had explained the relations between the universal and particular he proceeded to analyze their history in reference to what he calls "causes" by which he explained both the logical necessity and the time and space development in the career of a substance. He then drew these causes together into a new division, that of form and matter. Form is the actual, matter

---

26. W. T. Stace: *op. cit.*, pp. 265–66. There are still teachers in America who believe that Aristotle devoted all his time and intelligence in the Lyceum to paraphrasing the works of his teacher.

is the potential aspect of substance upon which form imposes its stamp, form being more predominant in some substances than in others. In his *Physics* Aristotle first defined time, space, and the different types of motion before he laid down the general law that every substance, in its motion, is striving for a higher condition of form. He then invented and defined the terms "organic" and "inorganic" before he described his scale of being. The latter includes inorganic matter, the plant, the animal, man, and the heavenly bodies, and regions where we can hardly follow his imagination, however logical it may be.

Like the ethics of most great thinkers, that of Aristotle is directed toward the happiness of the individual. Following the line of thought which links the ideal and the material closely together, he recommended a modest modicum of earthly goods and pleasures as an asset in the pursuit of higher, more intellectual values. After a careful consideration of each virtue and vice, he developed his theory of the golden mean as a guide for all ethical action. He opposed Plato's communal living in favor of the family as the unit of the state, and the government of this state was given a more potential and democratic foundation consisting of citizens who were capable of holding office. Far from constructing an ideal state, he explained the make-up of the principal types of states on Greek soil and then pointed out the merits and defects of each one. Along with an analysis of the different arts, he arranged them, in his *Poetics*, on a scale of merit according to the element of universality contained in each one. Philosophy, of course, ranks higher than poetry or history because its subject matter is less bound to the particular.

In the fourth century B.C. the Greek cities, partly because of exhaustion after the Peloponnesian War, partly due to a prevailing scepticism, paid more attention to the family, the neighborhood, than to the gods, the city, or the cosmos. The thinkers of the day were ethical philosophers concerned more about the good and evil of practice than man's relation to the world at large. The Stoics, under Zeno, reduced the universe to a material monism which included everything from the loftiest concept to the lowest bit of inert matter, but at the same time they superimposed on this monism two forces, reason and passion, constantly pulling against one another. "Live according to nature" meant to follow the path of reason. This inconsistent doctrine was as awkward as the theology of Persia: Ahura-Mazda must conquer in the end, but in the meantime he and mankind must struggle against the evil Ahriman. Since the Stoic admitted no free will, man's lower desires must eventually conform to the laws of reason. *"Ducunt fata volentem, nolentem trahunt."* He also tended to divide the universe into good and evil, those things which appeal to reason and those things which cater to sensuous desire. He asked his followers to cling to one and to shun the other, and thus he prepared the citizen first for empire, then for hierarchy, neither of which encouraged the responsibility of free judgment or decision necessary for a potential man living in a potential world.

Epicurus borrowed his metaphysics from the atomists. His aim was to remove the fear of the gods and of death from human life, dispelling both with the aid of his materialism. While the gods are made of finer atoms, they are too busy with their own affairs to pay much attention to man. Once a man is dead, he is once more broken up into atoms, so why not be free "from too much love of living"? Cultivate the higher virtues, especially friendship, extract the greatest possible pleasure from every event or moment, not only in the fleeting present but also in anticipation and memory; at the same time reduce your needs to a minimum and avoid the excesses of hedonism.

The last strained effort to construct a system of thought was that of Plotinus, the Neo-Platonist. First he described his god or the "one" as an infinite, eternal, perfect being, and to explain its relation to the rest of creation he resorted to a device already somewhat familiar in Plato's writings: the god overflowed into successive circles or emanations called the *Nous*, the world soul, the individual soul, reason, vitality, and inert matter, those most distant from the creator being more evil. His bridge between the finite and infinite and his explanation for the origin of evil are rationally inadequate, but for the religious-minded of his day it was sufficient. And how could man, born in the most

distant emanation of matter, return to a self-identification with
the divinity whence he originally came? By practicing the virtues, by following reason and intuition, and finally by ecstasy. In
this way a mystical religion was grafted on Greek philosophy
to fill a gap the fifth century was never conscious of. The ladder
by which the Neo-Platonist returned to his god was, in Christian
times, replaced by the figure of Christ, a personality the common man could understand more easily than an ascent on the
ladder of Hellenistic and Roman mysticism.

The epics of Homer, with their models of courage and resourcefulness, with their fund of information on all phases of
Greek life, became textbooks in education, not only in moral
example but in the heroic outlook on life which later blossomed
forth dramatically into tragedy. Although ascribed to the name
of Homer, whom the Greeks thought of as an Ionic writer, the
two epics are part of a large body of heroic poetry much of
which has been lost. It is indeed surprising that these works
preserve such a persuasive unity[27] for the modern reader, despite
the efforts of scholars to break them up, handed down as they
were from mouth to mouth, recited by bards at the courts of
kings, and probably not written down before the sixth century
when most of the events in their background had been completely forgotten. Like the *Vedas,* they came into being in the
childhood of culture when war, conquest, and valor were uppermost in man's estimation, but this is not the only picture of life
we find painted in heroic measures. We find the family of the
gods well established on Olympus, ready to take part in the
struggles of men, not only as interested observers but as more
distant and older relatives of the human family. They take sides
in the fray—even find themselves wounded. They protect their
favorites, although they know Troy must eventually fall and
Odysseus must somehow reach his Ithaca. The genial humanity
that saturates both human and divine levels and which is described with a reserved sympathy removes the characters from

27. J. A. Scott (*The Unity of Homer,* Berkeley, 1921, pp. 268–9) argues
for a single Homer.

an impersonal aloofness to a point where they stand in a united bond with all mankind, man and god facing similar problems on different levels. And yet each figure is a type whose contours are brought to mind again and again by epithets, by speeches, by their towering stature against a comparatively insignificant background. The great characters are tragic and most of them, with the exception of Thersites and Paris, are virtuous in the Greek sense, compounded with one failing sufficiently unrestrained to bring them to ultimate ruin.

The *Iliad* goes back, mythologically, to the strife between the three goddesses for a prize of beauty; historically, to some upset in the Greek world which drove the Achaeans from their mainland strongholds to Asia Minor. As in a symphony, the author proclaims boldly and simply the theme of the wrath which he repeats and develops in varied situations, bringing out the good and evil in other characters, weaving a pattern of glory and sorrow, of mighty exploits, grieving women, until it reaches a climax in the duel of Achilles and Hector. It is not a mere recital of a series of consecutive events that transpire in a given framework of time and space but a highly dramatic presentation of conflicting emotions, each figure and episode offering potential material for later tragedies. The phenomena of nature with which the poet was familiar—its bees, flowers, streams, herds of cattle, its wind and storm and flood, its mass of nondescript men—are presented as a colorful tapestry setting for such Titanic figures as the swift-footed Achilles, the wide-ruling Agamemnon, the far-darting Apollo, and the earth-shaking Poseidon. Each character is allowed to display his best or worst on a momentous occasion: Agamemnon leading his army, Odysseus speaking in council, Ajax defending the ships, Paris in the duel with Menelaus, Achilles fighting with Hector—before each one suffers the consequences of his failing (the fate of most of the heroes is described in companion epics not known to us). In spite of the sadness of a tragic performance lurking behind the whole narrative, the glory of the present engrosses actor and reader, except for an occasional moment of regret that "the paths of glory lead but to the grave." The tale contains highlights of the tender devotion of women, the longing for the homeland, greed for spoils, the cruelty of slaughter, underhanded trickery, the vanity of pride, the transience of human achievement and glory—all presented in attractive outlines against the cloudless serenity of a Greek landscape. It looks back to barbarian customs of a primitive period and it reflects the ages of bronze and iron. When Poseidon[28] insists that Zeus has overstepped his bounds, it points to the democracy of the future.

The *Odyssey* gives us a pleasing contrast to the action and turmoil of its predecessor by carrying the reader through a panorama of romantic adventure, strange peoples and customs, the quiet moods of nature, the aftermath of a devastating war. Historically, it reflects the age of colonization when the Greek became acquainted with new peoples and traditions, but in each case the magic of the barbarian must yield to the resourcefulness of the Greek's experience and ability. The whole stage, while acted over a wider geographical area, comprises fewer characters and divinities. The main figure, Odysseus, carries in his wake the blessing and bane of the ten years' war, continually haunted by a yearning nostalgia for wife and home. In a sense, the memory of the war combined with the sufferings of the hero increase the element of pervading sadness. The theme is announced again at the very beginning, but Odysseus is not brought into the foreground before the reader is made familiar with the distress of his family in Ithaca, and a contrast is drawn with the peace reigning at the courts of Sparta and Pylos. In the sylvan setting of Calypso's isle the hero's longing to return home at any cost is pitted against the desire of the immortal, doomed to loneliness in her island paradise. Not until he relates his adventures to the court of Alcinous do we learn of his taunting the Cyclops, the main reason for his persecution by Poseidon. Back home he is still the man of many devices, the master of strategy against the suitors of Penelope. Throughout his wanderings Poseidon is his *bête noire,* Athena his ever-present help in trouble, while Zeus remains the final court of appeal on remote

---

28. *Iliad,* XV, 184–199.

Olympus. The *Iliad* taught the Greeks how to behave toward other men, the *Odyssey* enjoined the rules for family loyalty;[29] Achilles was the paragon of warriors, Odysseus a model of shrewdness, Penelope the patient, faithful wife.

Hesiod was not at one with his world, as Homer was; he became a teacher because he saw many features of his life he disapproved of. Instead of seeking an escape in the Orphic view, however, he accepted the Olympic pantheon and added a new interpretation. A man of the Boeotian soil, deprived of his inheritance by a scheming brother, he made Zeus a defender of justice, patient and long-suffering but prepared to mete out a full measure of punishment in the end.[30] He is no poet of the aristocrat at court but the voice of the common peasant eking out his livelihood from the stubborn land, the capricious climate of Boeotia. The *Works and Days* was inspired by the harsh treatment he received at the hands of his brother whom he warns to repent in time, although he is ready to forgive him a crime committed in ignorance. To explain the evil state of man he recounts the Prometheus myth and the descent of Pandora; he tells of the five ages of man in the course of which man has caused much misery for himself. The gods were not entirely guiltless but man must take a large share of the responsibility. Then he exhorts the peasant to work hard in spite of all obstacles; he dispenses advice on how to conduct his household, when to sow and harvest, how to spend the winter months. As a didactic poet he was not interested in colorful imagery or lyric flights; he writes in a matter-of-fact style such as a peasant might use in giving advice to his son. The *Theogony*, written in the same style, is the earliest treatment of mythology in Greek literature.

The unsettled conditions in Greece of the seventh century reduced many a man from wealth to poverty and drove many citizens into exile because of economic upsets reflected in the

---

29. L. A. Post: *From Homer to Menander*, Berkeley and Los Angeles, 1951, p. 21.

30. He wants to find some ethical connection between the Olympian gods and nature as well as the life of man (cf. Jaeger: *Paideia*, Oxford, 1939, I, p. 63).

rapid changes in government. This discontent in Ionia and the islands found expression in lyrics and elegiacs. Some were very bitter, while other poets, riding along like Anacreon on the tide of good fortune, gave themselves up to the joys of the present. Alcaeus and Sappho, both of Lesbos, stand in the first rank of Greek lyric poets whose work has come down to us in fragmentary condition but whose reputation among later Greeks and Romans we cannot ignore. They have given us the famous Sapphic and Alcaeic meters so popular with their followers, especially Horace and Catullus. Disregarding all the legend which has clustered about their names we can call Alcaeus, the political exile, a capable singer of a wide variety of subjects, while Sappho confined herself to impassioned lyrics on love and wedding songs. Anacreon, as free and wanton as the air he breathed, sang of love and joy, the wine and vine for the entertainment of himself and anyone who offered him food and luxury; he was a lighthearted singer of fair-weather songs; he wrote for no cause except the sensuous enjoyment of immediate pleasure. Arion, the originator of the dithyramb, and Alcman, the Spartan composer of choral odes, are known to us only by legend and a few fragments.

The elegy, which developed along with the lyric ode, dealt with any subject of contemporary concern, subjects we should expect to find, for the most part, in prose; the song of sorrow, which passes for elegy in modern verse, was only one form of it in Greece. Solon used it to justify his political reforms, and Xenophanes made it a medium for debunking the mythology and religion of his fathers. Tyrtaeus saved the day for Sparta by writing war songs to inspire the citizens in a revolt of the Messenians and henceforth his poetry was most popular in that land of military prowess. Theognis wrote with a bitter pill in the corner of his mouth, because a change in the government of Megara had sent him into exile—an aristocrat looking down upon the new democracy as a political degradation of everything worthwhile in the past. Archilochus of Paros used iambics as well as elegiacs for his personal and vicious attacks, wandering from place to place, kicking furiously against the pricks of fortune and, like so many literary men, he threw away his shield before fleeing from the field of battle.

Stesichorus and Simonides were two of the greater lyric poets of Greece, but again we are handicapped by the meager survivals of their efforts. The singer who looms up high on the horizon both then and now is the Theban Pindar. Poetically educated in Athens, he became the master of the epinician ode composed in honor of a victor in one of the great national festivals, at the time enjoying their greatest popularity. He was an aristocrat writing for the wealthy princes of Greece, doing his best to glorify the family and traditions of the victor, and certainly it was an achievement demanding exceptional ability to repeat this theme of praise for one prince after another and at the same time to make each one a work of art. The structure of his odes is often as architectural as a Beethoven *allegro*, the transition frequently as abrupt as the angles between the wall and roof of a temple, his metaphors as copious as they are brilliant, his language compact and austere. More than any lyric poet he had the rare ability to convert the commonplace into the sublime, his Olympian flights soaring beyond the sentiments, the passions of personal concern. But who was the real Pindar? Did he have any sympathy with the man of the street? Was he truly an admirer of the tyrants of Sicily? Was he a devotee of the Olympian pantheon or an Orphic?[31] His poetry is our only evidence, and we have no right to demand too much consistency from a lyric poet. There are times when he seems to be carried away by the pomp and glory of princes, the prestige of mythical genealogy, and then with an abrupt turn he laments the transient character of all that life has to offer. In the light of what he has written, the true Pindar, passing from one mood to another, is difficult to discern. Bacchylides, the rival of Pindar, might have become a major lyric poet of his day had he been able to move out of the shadow of the Theban.

Herodotus has been called the father of history, for his pred-

---

31. I am inclined to agree with H. J. Rose (*A Handbook of Greek Literature*, London, 1934, p. 121) who believes Pindar's allegiance belonged to orthodox religion.

ecessors, the logographers, were not primarily interested in either the actions of men or the critical evaluation of events. His field includes the world as he knew it west of India, and we may be sure he traveled through much of Asia and Greece for his material. The strange account of Scythia makes his visit there somewhat doubtful. His subject is the Persian wars, the great conflict between the colossus of the East and the small city-states of Greece, which he carries back to the Trojan War (he does not think of this war as a cause). Like Homer he maintains a connection between divinity and man, the latter fulfilling his destiny under the watchful eye of the former; like Homer he is especially interested in men, and like the great epics his history is permeated with a tragic atmosphere.[32] Before he can begin with the Persian conflict he finds it necessary to inform the reader about Lydia, Egypt, Babylon, and Scythia, accounts including what he saw, what he heard from others about geography, origins, government, art, and customs, a concept of history more comprehensive and nearer to that of the modern than the viewpoint of Thucydides. Certain of his tales have raised question marks in our minds, but Herodotus cannot be accused of deliberate lying, because language difficulties, lack of records, his enthusiasm for the moral interpretation made errors and exaggerations unavoidable. He was as accurate as we can expect of a pioneer and consistent with his times in the extraction of a moral lesson from history; moreover, he has given us a colorful narrative punctuated with dramatic episodes, persuasive speeches, battles, and marvels, each described in the rhetorical style most appropriate—one can easily understand the fascination he aroused in the Athenian audience at a public reading in the theater!

Thucydides, the historian's historian, makes us sit up straight and pay close attention to his carefully balanced sentences, the polish of his rhetoric, his strained efforts in the direction of exactness. He is the most objective of all historians. He had, of course, the advantage of having lived through the events he was describing, of having suffered from the plague, of being person-

---

32. M. Hadas: *A History of Greek Literature,* New York, 1950, p. 113.

ally acquainted with the leaders whose speeches he reports, of being a general familiar with the military tactics of the day, so that his account rings with the realism of history in the making. But what impresses us most is his knowledge of human nature and the devastating frankness he employs to bare its secrets, its motives, its inconsistent waywardness, its lack of foresight; the tragedy of history lies not, in his opinion, in violating divine ordinance but in crass ignorance or stupidity. His subject was the Peloponnesian War which he regarded as the most significant conflict,[33] even though a disastrous one for his native city, in all history. His training with the Sophists had made him skeptical of divine intervention in human affairs, it gave him a polished style which he never misused, and it made him a penetrating observer of the human animal. He set up a standard for all historians to emulate!

Xenophon's writings are our only dependable historical source for the fourth century, before Alexander's conquest. He was a practical, straight-forward country squire whose military experience and life on an estate qualified him to write a prescription for success in either of these fields. His enthusiasm, however, for Sparta and Agesilaus left the role of Thebes completely in the shade. The *Anabasis* is both interesting and informative, it enticed Greek leaders to invade the Persian empire, but it is neither penetrating nor elevating, and what he recorded about Socrates is somewhat like what Sir Roger de Coverley might have said about Locke or Leibniz. As a personality he was, like so many Athenians, a many-sided character, capable of committing himself creditably in many fields of endeavor.

The theater, for Athens, first became a recognized institution in the celebration of the Dionysiac festivals under Pisistratus. The performance centered around the dithyramb, about which we know little except that it had a variety of meters and treated some familiar themes in the career of Dionysus. Eventually a structure was erected, containing a proscenium and stage buildings, before which was an orchestra for the action of the chorus

33. J. T. Shotwell (*The History of History*, New York, 1939, I, p. 199 ff.) forgets that Thucydides is writing only about the Peloponnesian War.

and seats for the audience. A man of sufficient wealth and leisure took over the duties of training the chorus of fifty members as a service the state required of men of such endowments. Thespis was the first playwright to compose plays under his own name. He also detached a member from the chorus to support a different view from the rest and so gave an impetus to dramatic tension and conflict. The chorus served to create a suitable atmosphere for the predominant mood, it warned actors of the future and repeated what had taken place. It introduced newcomers and personalized many of the functions of our stage machinery. The main character of a tragedy was a great man, also good enough to enlist the sympathy of the audience when he fell, but with one weakness that strained at human limitations until it brought him to ruin; the Greek was not Puritan enough to conceive of either a wholly good or evil individual. One might also say that a tragic hero strove to transcend the finite character of his life, that the infinity of his desire clashed with the limitations of human nature and brought him inevitably to a fall.

Aeschylus added a second actor and emphasized the stage effects to fit the godlike characters he presented to his audience. As a veteran of the chief battles against the Persians, the moral construction he put on the victory over presumptuous barbarians lived on not only in his *Persians* but was transferred as well to the conflict of other plays. Like the battle of Salamis, the struggle between Zeus and Prometheus is Titanic, almost cosmic in scale. His figures are monumental, superhuman because of the divinity working in them; but here we must recall that a god is not a perfect being, although sufficiently great that heroes hesitate to question the power and decision of Zeus: they recognize both the primitive wrath and the tender mercy of the Olympian, and since divinity is so immanent in the life of man, both the characters and their conflicts are placed on an awesome level. Sophocles brought in the third actor and so increased the possibilities for dialogue in the presentation, possibilities he himself exploited. For him the conflict of any play centers in man as a human being, which places greater stress on the potentiality of man's character than on the divine element within him;[34] therefore it is especially appropriate that the famous choral eulogy of man should be recorded in the *Antigone,* a play dealing with the conflict between the ruler's position in the state and the citizen's individual duties. Divinity is still there but its constraining power yields to the human aspect of man's power of decision, or we may say divinity now becomes more human in the influence it exerts.

Euripides is sometimes regarded as the most modern of the three playwrights, due to his straining at the conventional forms of tragedy, but above all because he looked within the human psyche, at all the conflicting desires and emotions that play havoc with the best laid plans. In the development of his conflicts he, like Thucydides, reveals a penetrating and at times morbid curiosity, he turns his characters inside out, as it were, and before he reaches the end of the play the threads of the irrational are so inextricably knotted he resorts to the *deus ex machina* for a resolution. For his purposes, then, the female of the species was most fascinating as a character study, which no doubt explains why women were among his most compelling figures. The education of Euripides among the Sophists trained him in the use of specious argumentation and the study of feelings responsible for human rashness, for inconsistencies in action. The *Medea* is the finest example in literature of the conflict between the East and West in ancient times—between Jason, who consciously or unconsciously rationalizes his motives, and Medea, who frankly lives out the driving needs of her nature without mental reservations, without seriously considering the consequences for the future.

Although Athens did not have as much to do with the first developments of comedy as with the forming of tragedy, the *komos* or village farce was popular in early Attica where the Athenians were quick to realize its possibilities at the festivals. We know it best in the form Aristophanes gave it, containing an agon, a duel between the two opposing sides, and a parabasis in which the author airs his own opinions. Almost any subject

---

34. W. N. Bates: *Sophocles,* Philadelphia, 1940, p. 17.

that might be reckoned as a public issue was brought on the stage by Aristophanes, including political figures, the war party, Socrates, the courts, playwrights, even the gods; moderns are often shocked at what they believe is a blasphemous sacrilege, but in Greece the human gods, possessing a healthy sense of humor, gladly took part in the fun and frolic of the festival. Aristophanes was a genius in wit, also most capable in molding his wit into exquisite lyrics; he believed that if anything is worth while it can stand the test of ridicule; otherwise let it cover its face and run. Beneath his comic veneer and what we choose to call bawdiness he was a very serious aristocrat with the best interest of Athens in his heart. In the fourth century, social man—the man of the family, the neighborhood—took the center of the stage in what is known as New Comedy, of which Menander was the chief exponent, bequeathing to the modern theater many of its devices and stock characters: the identical twins, the triangle, the lost child, the clown or slave, the miser, and the spendthrift. Menander[35] was a dramatist rich in invention and imagination, a very popular writer in his own day, and one who has been copied or redressed all the way from Terence to Thornton Wilder. Social intrigue, consoling sentiment, neighborhood gossip, unexpectedly pleasant surprises took the place of the biting wit and political satire of the fifth century B.C.

The teaching of the Sophists, especially of Gorgias, was largely responsible for the prominence of rhetoric and oratory in Greek education. Where success in politics depended on the persuasive ability of a speaker to sway the assembly there was bound to be an emphasis on form, in many cases to the detriment of content, an emphasis that continued long after the heyday of the Sophists. It appealed strongly to the immediate desire of human nature and was also fostered by the ear of the Greek, more sensitive to the lack of balance and polish in language than we are. A great number of speeches that have come down to us were delivered in court, where they were given orally, or, in case the party was not a capable speaker, could have been

---

35. Gilbert Murray (*Two Plays of Menander*, New York, 1945) has reconstructed and translated two of his plays.

written by a professional speech writer and then read before the jury. Such a writer of speeches was Lysias. We hear of him as the son of Cephalus, the wealthy metic who played host to Socrates in the opening pages of the *Republic* of Plato; in the *Phaedrus* the same author has invented a speech which he assigns to Lysias.[36] Like Walter Scott, he set to work at an advanced age, after the Thirty had stripped him of his wealth, to mend his fortune by writing speeches. His style was influenced by Gorgias without resorting to redundant, flowery embellishments. His language was usually clear and much to the point and he was not inclined to minimize the facts in favor of emotional effects. His best effort is the speech against Eratosthenes, his arch enemy and one of the Thirty, bold enough to remain in Athens after 403 B.C.

Demosthenes, at the other extreme, was the fiery patriot of the fourth century, perhaps the most emotional of all Greek speakers. His portrait shows us a man of slight build, his right arm free of the garment for gestures, the features of his face concentrated with emotional intensity. After early years of hardship, which included a fight for his inheritance and a rigid training in speaking,[37] he developed into an aggressive crusader, and to his credit it must be admitted he had more foresight than many an Athenian for the good of the city beyond her borders. The major speeches of his youth failed to achieve their goal: Megalopolis was left to the mercy of the Spartans and Rhodes was lost to the cause of democracy. When Philip rose as a major threat in Macedon, Demosthenes used all the resources of his eloquence to make Athens conscious of her plight, but he failed to rouse her from a satisfied complacency. He berated his fellow citizens for preferring their own amusements to the city's welfare, for spending more on private homes than on public buildings, for standing by until Amphipolis, Olynthos, and all of northern Greece fell into the hands of the astute Philip. In 338 the allies were defeated at Chaeronea, Demosthenes running

---

36. Cf. P. Shorey: *What Plato Said*, Chicago, 1933, p. 199.

37. Plutarch (*Demosthenes*, 7) tells of the rigorous discipline he underwent to overcome certain weaknesses.

from the field with many of his fellow soldiers. His greatest personal triumph was *On the Crown,* an apology for his whole career in politics, which sent his opponent Aeschines into exile. As a stylist Demosthenes was alone, as he was in politics; he availed himself of every device in the rhetorical bag—rhythm, metaphor, exclamation, oath—regardless of rules, as long as they produced the desired effect. His language, bursting forth like a tornado, was reinforced with startling gestures and facial contortions that must have left his audience in a rhetorical daze. The modern regards him as a somewhat showy and tactless individualist and so he was, but he was, in the main, honest, true to himself, and always a fourth century Athenian. It is tempting to speculate on the effect such an orator might have made on the Athenian assembly a hundred years earlier.

Isocrates, another student of the Sophists, had a difficult time finding attentive ears for his teachings, partly because he remained outside the sphere of practical politics, partly because he seemed, to all Athenians, out of tune with the times. Having lost an early inherited fortune and shunning the *bema* for a number of reasons, he founded a school of rhetoric that netted another fortune, perhaps from the wealthy students attending it. He remained active to the year of his death in 338 B.C., after the victory of Philip. He wrote rather lengthy speeches, polished for publication, which he addressed to monarchs and states whose interests were more or less remote from those of Athens, but in spite of the political nature of his subject matter, Socrates, in the *Phaedrus*[38] of Plato, expresses the hope that the rhetorician will some time turn to philosophy—at a time when the latter and Plato were already along in years. We cannot learn what the orator thought of this questionable compliment, but we do know he included his own interpretation of philosophy in the discipline of his dialectic. In the *Panegyricus* he urges all Greece to unite under Athens against the Persians; the *Areopagiticus* urges a return to the democracy of Cleisthenes and the council of the Areopagus; the *Antidosis* is an apology for his

---

38. 279 A.

school and past life; the *Panathenaicus* lavishes praise on Athenian accomplishments at the expense of Sparta. His writing follows many of the prevalent rules for rhetorical polish, but excelling in long periods surprisingly clear in spite of their length; he cared nothing for the emotional outbursts of Demosthenes. While Athenians read his work with interest, his warnings fell on deaf ears; his policy was a farsighted one, but who in Athens cared to trust his city's fate to the hands of Philip or Archidamus of Sparta? Subsequent events taught the followers of Isocrates that he had been too altruistic, and undoubtedly Demosthenes had the last bitter laugh when Antipater, in 322, humiliated Athens and drove him to suicide.

The pre-Socratics have left us only fragments quoted by later writers, and much of that is in verse. Hardly anything has survived from the writings of the Sophists and, of course, Socrates wrote nothing. Plato started out as a poet whose fondness for rhythm and meter cropped up later in the metrical prose of the *Phaedrus*, whose greatest contribution to philosophical prose is the dialogue, no doubt adopted from his teacher; this form he developed into an effective and smoothly flowing exchange that, transferred to dramatic conflict, would have been a credit to Sophocles. Plato was also most capable in imitating the style of others, especially Lysias and Gorgias. Aristotle cannot be called a stylist in any sense of the term, but we cannot forget that what we have may not have been intended for the eyes of posterity. Plotinus has given us the *Enneads*, which are frustrating to the analyst with a critical eye; he writes like a man lost in a mystic vision, which he describes from all angles in accord with a strictly subjective point of view.

After the death of Alexander, the Hellenistic period produced a wealth of writers recording, for the most part, the afterthoughts and variations on earlier themes. The cream of their poetry is contained in the rich collection of the *Greek Anthology*, while a noble effort in the epic, though somewhat strained, was made by Apollonius Rhodius in the *Argonautica*. Beyond Arrian, the imitator of Attic historians in his record of the exploits of Alexander, and Polybius, the authority on Rome and the Romans of the third century B.C., most writers in this field were mere court historians. A new medium, the romance, was probably borrowed from the East; the motivating interest was a sensuous type of love drawing a number of characters through an accordion plot of fantastic adventures to a happy ending.[39]

The most original poet of the time was Theocritus. After reading a few of his idyls, it can readily be seen that he imbibed the atmosphere of the pastoral in childhood, something which cannot be learned from a Boucher tapestry or a piece of Dresden china. He was also a versatile artist in the sense that he was able to apply his medium to a variety of subjects and moods: the mourning for Daphnis, the magic of the rejected lover, the festival of Adonis, the amorous clumsiness of a Polyphemus, the singing contests of shepherds. Although he spent much of his time at the court of Philadelphus, he was more than an artificial Alexandrian, for the freshness of his images, the charm of his settings, which he drew from his memory of Dorian Sicily, have made Theocritus the paragon for all pastoral poets; he achieved as much for his muse as Menander for the comic stage.

Satire was born from too much looking backward, after the enthusiasm for the old ideals had faded. The imitators parading the dried husks of the past called forth the criticism and ridicule of the debunker, a role most capably filled by Lucian, born in Syria but an Athenian by adoption. After learning rhetoric and giving it up as a life pursuit he settled down in Athens where he devoted himself to satire in the second half of the second century A.D. In despair of finding the truth among the host of hypocrites, each wearing his doctrine expediently on his sleeve, and not being philosopher enough to set out on his own quest, he undertook to strip the whole show in the form of the dialogue, the medium for which he is best known. He also lampooned both religion itself and those who pretended to believe in the old gods. In *The True Story* he has taken the historian to task by outdoing the exaggerations of such writers, those who made no

---

39. An excellent example is Chariton's *Chaereas and Callirhoe.*

distinction between miracle and fact, in a rollicking tale that carries his characters through the heavens, the isles of the blest, around to the other side of the world. There is nothing lofty about the eclecticism of his style, but he had a genius for clothing old modes in a new dress, for pouring old wine into new bottles. He could not have counted for much except in an artificial age when Greece was losing its anthropocentric anchor of responsibility and looking for the shadow of substance in love, mystic religions, miracles, and philosophical fads. We must give him credit for one original stroke which seems to have escaped the eye of the critic: in *The Praise of the Fly* he contributed the first familiar essay of European literature, that intimate, whimsical conversion of the commonplace into something delightfully important.

The first century A.D. produced Plutarch, the biographer whose moralizing and dramatic episodes have made him the most popular of Greek writers in translation. The parallel arrangement of Greek and Roman notables is misleading to the modern, a defect his comparisons cannot atone for, but this shortcoming was of no consequence to the ancient reader. Since he was unable to find much of anything personal in the records of his heroes he had to content himself with anecdotes, with the reflections these men made on the society and events of their times. Plutarch was a pious man, one of the last of the pagans, which undoubtedly accounts for so much moralizing, the hallmark of propriety in his day and in the late Renaissance; but beyond his simple sincerity, an asset in teaching moral precept, there is nothing remarkable about his style. He is practically our only source for the Egyptian myth of Isis and Osiris. His apology for demons[40] is an effort, consonant with his times, to account for the evils of experience. It tends to purify the gods and so removes them from that delightful association with men the earlier Greeks could not dispense with.

One word about the work of criticism that passes under the

40. Cf. K. M. Westaway: *The Educational Theory of Plutarch*, London, 1922, p. 35.

name of Longinus. Who he was and the immediate reason for writing the treatise we cannot fathom, but it is comforting to find a man in this age who could see clearly the monarchs of the forest in the midst of so many dying trees; who avoids dividing writers into nice good boys and naughty reprobates; who is able to distinguish true greatness from its sentimental or sensational counterpart. Despite the silence of the ancients on this work it has a ring of genuine resonance which has carried with it a strong influence on the moderns.

The Greek artist borrowed the alphabet of his art from his predecessors and immediate neighbors, but within a short time he stamped it so indelibly with his own expression that the original groundwork could no longer be recognized. The natives of the mainland provided him with little he could use. After coming down from the north he was exposed to a great variety of art production on the island of Crete, in the Aegean, in Asia Minor, and Egypt. The ruins of Knossos with their colored frescoes, light and shadow effects, strange arrangements must have filled him with awe and misgiving, although he certainly learned much there in the way of design and architectural structure. We can see the influence of the Minoan in the megaron the Achaeans built at Tiryns, especially in the columns and decoration, in the beehive tombs, in the lion gate at Mycenae, and the countless small objects covered with the afterthoughts of earlier design. And how did the Greek change what he found? He simplified or abbreviated the decorative element of his building so that the functional lines of support stood out boldly, he systematized the arrangement inside and broke up the interior space, he transferred the emphasis from the interior to the exterior, thereby minimizing the effect of chiaroscuro. In painting and relief he gradually eliminated most of the decorative patterns the Minoan had used for filling empty spaces or he subordinated them to the human figure to conform with his anthropocentric viewpoint. Nature became either a remote setting or disappeared altogether in favor of human nature. For the carving of man in wood or stone he went to

Egypt, where he found a rigid symmetry, a formal law of frontality he copied for a while before he learned how to instill movement into the muscles and joints. From Asia he learned about the genesis of the Ionic order and certain lessons in modeling which had seeped into Ionia through Persia from Mesopotamia.

The Doric system of architecture which developed from such a façade as that of the Tiryns palace was known as the masculine order because of its more ponderous members and the simplicity of its lines. It was especially popular among the Dorians of Sparta and Magna Graecia. Its shaft rose directly from the stylobate, the top step of the foundation or stereobate, and its ascending drums tapered gently as they rose toward the entablature, having a slight entasis or swelling as well as vertical channelings running the whole length of the shaft. At the top of the column we find the capital, composed of an echinus which eased the transition to the horizontal line, and a rectangular abacus. Thereupon rests an entablature of three members: the architrave, a heavy horizontal member left plain[41] because it carries the weight of the ceiling; the frieze made up of triglyphs and metopes, the former a survival of the ceiling beams of wood which originally jutted out at this point; and the cornice projected out over the rest of the entablature to protect it against rain. Below each triglyph was a regula with six guttae projecting downward; above each triglyph and metope and projecting from the cornice were mutules, again with guttae attached. The metope's rectangular field was reserved for a sculptured relief, and above the entablature was a gable whose triangular space was filled, in the best period, with sculpture almost free from the background; this was bounded above by a raking cornice for the protection of the sculptures. From the east to the west gable ran a tiled roof decorated with acroteria and antefixes.

Nearly the whole temple was painted, but bright colors were

---

41. An exception may be seen in W. B. Dinsmoor: *The Architecture of Ancient Greece,* London and New York, 1950, p. 87, fig. 33.

applied only to such parts as the metopes, triglyphs, antefixes, and sculptured figures. There was no binding material to hold the blocks of stone together; clamps and dowels kept the individual slabs and courses from falling into a dusty heap. Before marble was generally used for building, the architect availed himself of wood. In fact, columns of wood existed as late as the time of Pausanias[42] in the second century A.D. The earliest type of temple consisted of a cella, the main body of the structure, with projections of the walls, first at one end, then at both ends; these projections were known as antae. There were also prostyle and amphiprostyle temples (with columns running across one end and both ends, respectively). If columns surrounded the entire building, it was known as a peristyle temple. The general rule stated that a temple should face eastward, its principal doorway placed at that end which housed the statue of the divinity; therefore the altar, located outside, was at the eastern end. There were more elaborate arrangements of columns, there were round buildings furnished with a peristyle, but most structures in this category belong to later periods.

The oldest temple of the Doric order is the Heraeum of Olympia, built perhaps before the beginning of the seventh century, whose wooden members survived for a long time after marble became the common material of construction. The interior was novel in that every other column was joined to the cella by a partition wall, giving the effect of a series of chapels on each side of the central space. Next in date comes the temple of Apollo at Corinth of which only a few columns remain. The Dorian temples of Sicily and Magna Graecia afford a variety of examples, including the colossal Olympieum at Girgenti with its engaged columns and Atlantides to support the massive superstructure, the temple of Apollo at Selinus with its deep porch and three doorways suggestive of Etruscan influence, the temple of Poseidon at Paestum, one of the best preserved and one which adheres closely to the Doric canon. The example at Segesta is interesting because, in its unfinished condition, it tells us some-

---

42. V, 16.

thing of the architect's procedure. All of these temples were built of limestone, all had low and heavy columns supporting a massive entablature. The great shrine of Apollo at Delphi cannot, because of so many destructions and rebuildings, be adequately reconstructed, but the treasury, of which Olympia and Delphi had quite a number, has survived in a good example of the Doric order, namely, the little temple built to house the Athenian dedications to Apollo, a well-preserved and pure example of a temple in antis. The Doric in its fullest flower is represented in the fifth century by the temple of Hephaestus in Athens, which owes its preservation to its use as a Christian church; nearly all its features of construction, except for changes made by the Christians within, are as the fifth century Greek saw them.

The Ionic or feminine order received most of its inspiration from the East[43] where we have already seen an early version in an Assyrian relief. The slender shaft with the its slight entasis rises up from a base whose Attic formula dictated one trochilus between two tori, but in eastern Greece it was much more involved and varied. The channelings of the shaft were brought out, not to a sharp edge, but to a flat surface called an arris, and the volute, the most distinctive feature of the order, was placed between a small echinus and an equally small abacus to form the capital. The entablature included a pleated architrave, a continuous frieze extending around the temple (a mainland feature), and a cornice from which extended the dentals or former wooden beams of the ceiling. Above were the pediment and raking cornice. This order, which also had wooden prototypes, was characterized by more orament and refinement, particularly in the capital and moldings, found at their best in Asia Minor, e.g., the temple of the Ephesian Artemis where the lower section of the shaft was sculptured in relief. On the mainland the purest example was the amphiprostyle temple of Athena Victory on the Athenian Acropolis. The Corinthian order, which

---

43. Egypt also made an important contribution (W. B. Dinsmoor: *op. cit.,* pp. 59-60).

was used sparingly in Greece, was much the same as the Ionic except for a more florid capital consisting of an arrangement of acanthus leaves, appearing in Athens for the first time on the monument of Lysicrates on the street of the tripods, where the columns are engaged. Here we should also mention the Treasury of the Siphnians in Delphi, an early temple of the Ionic style whose entablature is supported by patient, good-natured ladies dressed in the eastern style of drapery so popular in the sixth century.

The Acropolis, the sanctuary of Athens, had been devastated by the Persians before Cimon and Pericles made their plans for new buildings. The Parthenon, the greatest achievement of Greek architecture, was begun by Ictinus and Callicrates in 447 and completed some fifteen years later by tapping the funds of the Delian Confederacy that Pericles had already removed to Athens. Two large Doric temples had already been built in Greece and so could serve as models: the temple of Aphaea on Aegina and the great shrine of Zeus at Olympia. The Parthenon, except for an Ionic frieze on the cella wall inside the peristyle, was a Doric temple with a prostyle of six columns at each end, the peristyle made up of eight columns running across the ends and seventeen on the sides, counting the corner columns twice. The whole structure above the foundations was of Pentelic marble. A study of its lines reveals that nearly all the surfaces were slightly curved to correct certain optical illusions, although other reasons have also been suggested[44] for such refinements. The Erechtheum, an Ionic structure north of the Parthenon, was never completed according to the original plans but was nevertheless one of the most attractive of all buildings in the Ionic order and one of the most popular in our own time because of its porches, both the one on the north, destined to become an inspiration for Greek revivalists, and the south porch, minus the frieze and supported by six caryatids. The interior, on different levels, had shrines dedicated to Poseidon, Athena, and Erechtheus. Dwarfed by the Parthenon in size, its original plan

---

44. D. S. Robertson: *A Handbook of Greek and Roman Architecture*, Cambridge, 1945, pp. 115–118.

altered by political maneuvers, it was still the most original in imagination and the most refined in ornament of all Athenian creations of its kind. The Propylaea by Mnesicles, also incomplete, has a picture gallery on the north side which originally contained paintings, a south wing sadly abbreviated to make room for another shrine, Doric columns facing the approaching visitor both on the east and west, while those flanking the inner passageway leading to the Parthenon were Ionic.

Whatever we may say about the formality of the exterior, the cramped space of the temple's interior, it was a reliable index to the meaning of Greek life; it mirrored something of the geometry of his mind, it stood obviously aloof from nature; and was as clearly defined as his personality against the backdrop of kaleidoscopic color of the East.

Theaters abounded everywhere in the Greek cities, the best preserved being that at Epidaurus. The theater proper containing the seats for the audience was laid out on the slope of a hill and divided concentrically with the orchestra by a diazoma, the whole area of seats spreading out fanwise from the circular orchestra which contained the altar of Dionysus and was connected with the diazoma as well as the upper seats by long passageways. On the other side of the orchestra was the scene building with its façade of engaged Ionic columns and wing buildings, one on each side, leaving only a narrow space on the upper level of the proscenium, which makes it unlikely that the action of the play took place anywhere but in the orchestra.[45]

The gymnasia at Olympia and Epidaurus were expansive structures built around a central court separated from the building proper by a peristyle. The Telesterion or Hall of Initiation built at Eleusis by Ictinus, one of the architects of the Parthenon, was a large, rectangular structure faced with a porch running the full length of one side and enclosed by fourteen columns. Within, the walls were lined with rows of seats facing the center, the roof supported by a large number of

---

45. Cf. M. Bieber: *The History of the Greek and Roman Theatre,* Princeton, 1939, p. 139.

columns, an arrangement as awkward, for the viewer, as a spectacle observed through a picket fence.

The following century saw the erection of the Mausoleum, the tomb of Mausolus of Caria. A massive podium, surrounded by a continuous frieze, supported an Ionic peristyle over which was a large pyramid crowned with portrait statues of the king and queen in a quadriga—in ancient times this monument counted as one of the seven wonders of the world. The fourth century saw the greater development of a two-storied porch furnished with the Doric order below and the Ionic above, and the private house in such cities as Olynthus and Priene. Presenting a barren wall to the street except for a door and an occasional high window, the rooms of the house were generally grouped around a central court. In later examples lower rooms sometimes faced the street, in which case they were rented out as shops.

Much of early Greek sculpture was fashioned of wood, numbering many old cult statues of divinities held in high regard in later times, but none of these has survived. The early sculptor looked to Egypt for his models. The types of the archaic period include the seated figure, the standing nude male, the standing draped female and the flying figure, most of which show the influence of Egyptian frontality.

The portrait statue of the seated Chares follows a rigid rule of symmetry and balance, while the body, part and parcel of the throne, is roughly modeled above, but below is tightly encased in drapery with folds indicated by parallel incised lines. An excellent example of the second type is the young athlete (or Apollo) in New York.[46] One glance reveals that the sculptor carved and conceived of his figure from four different sides, which accounts for the flatness of the back, the chest, and sides of the face, while the advanced leg, the frontality of the figure, the lack of expression in the face, and the firmly clenched hands also have Egyptian affinities. Despite the crude facial features, the use of incised lines to indicate shoulder blade and elbows, this young man has a vigorous quality the later sculptor might

---

46. G. M. A. Richter: *Kouroi*, New York, 1942, fig. 19–21.

well have envied, much of which is already lost a century later
in the Apollo of Tenea, a figure that makes a desperate effort to
break the bonds of convention. The hair has soft, wooly waves
like that of the barristers of England's courts, the eyes pop forward and leave some distance between the lid and brow, the
attempted expression of the archaic smile draws the corner of
the mouth up toward the high cheek-bone; there is an awkward
flatness about the frontal anatomy, the knee cap is dug into,
not modeled out from the marble of the leg. Many of these
figures were made on the islands, those of a more compact,
muscular structure belonging to the southern tradition.

The standing draped female is well represented by an early
figure, generally called Hera, from Samos. Again the modeling is
pretty well covered by tight-drawn garments incised with conventional folds, the lower figure encased in a heavy rubberized
cast from which the toes are allowed to peep below. The left
hand was originally held between two very high breasts.
Another with a flat instead of a round effect is the Nikandra
statue from Delos, a primitive figure with a triangular face and,
except for the breasts, a boardlike body. A further development
of this type is the series of obviously staring but smiling maiden
figures found in the ruins of the pre-Persian Acropolis, again
representing a number of different schools of the islands and
the mainland, the majority clad in the rich Ionic fashions popular
in the sixth century B.C. There is a great divergence between
examples of what is called the Chian school and the one clad
in Doric fashion,[47] but all show a remarkable freshness and love
of life. Here we must mention the color appplied especially to
the garment borders, eyes, and hair, a feature characteristic of
all Greek sculpture and unusually well preserved in the Acropolis dedications. As ludicrous as the faces may seem,[48] their
apparently genial disposition, the eager curiosity popping out
of their faces, the gay colors of their finery reflect an age of
prosperous well-being before the Persian invasion. The Victory

---

47. F. Gerke: *Griechische Plastik,* Zurich and Berlin, 1938, pl. 32–3.
48. The improvements in technique are listed by G. M. A. Richter:
The Sculpture and Sculptors of the Greeks, New Haven, 1930, p. 72.

of Delos makes a courageous attempt to solve the problem of motion. She has the same flat forehead, high cheekbones, and archaic smile; the upper part of the body is a triangle whose apex is the breast line, the waist a kind of pivot upon which the upper part of the body turns, and to create the feeling of motion the artist found it necessary to lengthen the right leg. Although the motion is produced by exaggerated effects, there is originality and imagination in the type.

The early fifth century, notably after the Persian invasion, found the Greek artist able to cope with the anatomy of the body and the features of the face, except for the eye and the corners of the mouth, the last to yield to his persistence. The Tyrannicides, as unsatisfactory as is the group in Naples, have corrected most of the crudities of the past and at the same time preserved a severity in the treatment which is an heirloom of the archaic period; there is also something forceful and uncompromising about their directness that one misses after the middle of the fifth century. The cire-perdue process in the bronze technique also developed apace through these decades.[49] The Charioteer of Delphi has the same severity of the Tyrannicides and a concentration that permeates the whole body and the stately folds of the garment; the artist has succeeded in preserving the human dignity of his creation by the conservative treatment of posture and dress, for the concentration of the face, the straight, forward body, tell the story persuasively in spite of the casual rhythm in the folds of the upper garment playing around the shoulders and upper arms. The potentiality of Greek character is now emerging to the surface as it gradually sheds the severity of the archaic style. Greek art achieved one of its greatest moments in the bronze Zeus of Artemisium, a work that preserves all the archaic period had been striving for as it looks ahead to the best work of the fifth century. The magnificence of the torso, the poised balance, the controlled rhythm of the movement would have made any Greek artist of the century proud to claim it.

49. D. K. Hill (*Catalogue of Classical Bronze Sculpture in the Walters Art Gallery*, Baltimore, 1949, XIII) says Phidias may have discovered it.

Myron, in his Discobolus, has pushed the old law of frontality completely off the horizon, but he keeps the motion of his figure in control by using a closed design whose every line turns within to the center or hub of the wheel of action. He is also well aware of the important historical moment in an action sequence, when the subject has completed one stage and is ready to begin another, so that the observer can easily see the past and future in clear perspective at this moment of transition from the backward to the forward thrust. In the Athena and Marsyas the moment of transition between the throwing down of the flutes and the rushing gesture of Marsyas is intensified by the dramatic crisis in the episode, supported by a contrast between the reserved calm of the youthful Athena and the abandon of Marsyas; this feature is to be repeated less convincingly in the later Apollo and Marsyas relief from Mantinea. We can hardly measure the genius of Phidias today because the chryselephantine works, for which he was so well known, have not survived, and the Olympian Zeus, which created a name for him in Greece, as well as the Athena Parthenos[50] are not to be estimated by mediocre copies in our modern museums. The Athena Promachos, the towering bronze defender on the Acropolis, could be seen by sailors as they plied their ships around the promontory of Sunium. The Lemnian Athena, her features well defined, her face beautifully modeled, is everything in general but nothing in particular, an example of the potentiality and adaptability Pericles was fond of praising in the Athenians. She absorbs all our likes and dislikes and still retains an individuality of her own.

We can judge Phidias to some extent by the marbles of the Parthenon, but first we must review the development of temple sculpture. For us the first important pedimental sculptures are those of Aegina, executed in the early fifth century. The sculptor had learned how to work out a composition of figures within the bounds of a depressed triangle, so that only the central figure could stand up erectly, the rest, whether crouching or reclining

---

50. C. Morgan (*Hesperia*, XXI, 1952, pp. 333–339) dates the Olympian Zeus definitely before the Athena Parthenos.

in the corners, constrained as if by magnetic force, to pay homage to the goddess in their midst. The guardian Athena, or Aphaea, as the case may be, stands as a silent but welcome arbiter, on each side of the temple, over fighting contestants. All of them except for the presiding goddess are admirably modeled, displaying, in spite of their less than life size, a remarkable power of physique, but the symmetry is monotonous, the warriors are somewhat cramped in their positions. At Olympia, some years later, we find artists with a more adventuresome spirit, a more fertile imagination. A general view of the east pediment, representing the principal figures of a local myth, portends something of ominous significance reflected in the prominence of Zeus, the drawn-up chariots, the skeptical or foreboding figures bringing up the rear. At the west end a commanding, majestic Apollo, with lingering archaisms, dominates a life and death struggle between centaurs and men. The contrast in mood between the pediments is a welcome change, the variety in symmetry is still more pleasing, and the daring modeling brings the observer into the presence of action that is primitive and overpowering. The metopes here are the most impressive in Greek sculpture because of the treatment of the figures and the variety of design within such restricted limitations.

The Parthenon pediments, which Phidias supervised, apparently exhausted all the possibilities of such a triangular space. Again we find a comparatively peaceful scene at the east end and a conflict at the other, but if the Birth of Athena appears tranquil, it is because we cannot properly reconstruct the central scene whose momentous character is reflected in the figures on each side. It is no mere episode taking effect in a certain framework of time and space but an awe-inspiring occurrence on a panoramic scale in a universe that reaches out to the farthest limitations the Greek could conceive of. Every aspect is interpreted in human terms, every movement is ennobled by the drapery as it ripples over the limbs to increase the rate of motion, every line has a mission in uniting the figures, in their varied but easy positions, into a composition of cosmic and dramatic significance. Without overt display, devoid of emotional bubbling, each figure contributes its own share to the whole with consummate ease.[51] The west pediment, because of its fragmentary condition, cannot be reconstructed except from vase paintings which are by no means adequate. The frieze, placed in a difficult position, is a careful study in perspective, lighting, grouping, and motion, each effect subordinated to the general impression, a pageantry of Athenian citizens of all ages and rank doing homage to their divinity in a respectful ceremony that asks no man to kowtow in the dust.

Polyclitus, of the Argive school, was first of all interested in the human body as he saw it in the gymnasium, representing it in an easy walking posture, the weight mostly on the right foot, to demonstrate his execution to advantage. The Doryphorus, which served to illustrate his canon of proportions, the Diadoumenus and the Amazon are standing in the same position, but none of them, copies as they are, does justice to the man chosen to fashion the chryselephantine statue of Hera in the Argive Heraeum. Cresilas made a portrait of Pericles for the Acropolis, which we have in a number of copies that preserve the same generalized, potential features of so many late fifth century creations, all worked into the face of the *strategos* Athens had looked to for guidance in the golden age. Paionius has given us the Victory the Germans found in Olympia. Effective as it is, the drapery calls so much attention to itself in the same obvious manner as the Victory balustrade of the Acropolis, the composition as a whole suffers.

The fourth century is ushered in by the Peace and Wealth of Cephisodotus. The Doric peplos, the hair and posture of the figure take us back to the previous century, but the softening of the face looks ahead to the future. From the hand of Scopas we have nothing original except the four heads from the temple of Tegea, which certainly show the influence of his emphasis on the pathetic, on the exploitation of the inner man, already foreshadowed by Euripides; it answered the needs of the century

---

51. Hans Schrader (*Pheidias*, Frankfurt am Main, 1924, pp. 240 ff.) assigns the east pediment to Alcamenes, the west one to Paeonius.

and made him a popular artist. His heads, in conformity with the southern tradition, are broad, the eyes are thrown back deeply into the sockets, the lips slightly parted, and at times the head is tipped back on the neck. The shadows thus created over the eyes combined with the unrestrained movements of the body made Scopas the ideal sculptor for satyrs, bacchantes, and other followers of Dionysus. The Demeter of Cnidus, with its *sehnsuchtsvollen Augen,* also comes nearer to Scopas than to any other artist.

Praxiteles, the Athenian who hired a model and a painter in his atelier, was the dominant figure of the century. Perhaps the most popular work of antiquity was the Aphrodite of Cnidus, of which we have a fairly good copy, adequate enough to bring out the gentle flow of rhythm of his relaxed bodies, the utter lack of self-consciousness in his faces, the melting glance of the eye—qualities distinctively Praxitelean which no other artist has been able to reproduce satisfactorily. The Hermes of Olympia, if not from the hand of this sculptor, is surely close to his work in style.[52] Even in copies of his work we can easily see the common traits—the faraway, absent-minded expression of the face, the curve of the body leaning against an upright support, the lighter proportions of the body itself, the accent on more youthful figures of the gods, e.g., the Apollo Sauroktonus, where the drapery serves more as an accessory than a covering for the body. The figure at rest, however, is not a denial of life; the Satyr in the Capitoline museum has paused for just a moment to concoct a malicious bit of deviltry before continuing on a mad, capricious rush through the forest. The relief of this century gains somewhat in action but loses much more in execution and composition. The Doric temple at Bassae, which contained an early example of the Corinthian column, also had an Ionic frieze showing the battle of the Greeks and Amazons, a late fifth century relief which can be profitably compared with

---

52. This work has been the subject of much controversy in recent years. The latest contribution is that of R. Carpenter (A.J.A., LVIII, 1954, pp. 1-12).

one picturing the same subject on the Mausoleum of Halicarnassus. In the latter the sculptor has repeated the same motive
again and again.

Lysippus was a prolific worker, one who preferred bronze to
marble as a medium. The two copies of his originals, the Agias
and the Apoxyomenos, hardly do justice to a man known for
vividness of expression and finish of execution, but some conception of his style may be gleaned from the Naples Hermes,
even if it is dangerous to call Lysippus the artist of the original.[53]
He was also the official sculptor of Alexander the Great, for
whom he executed a number of portraits, the most faithful copy
being the Azara herm in the Louvre. Though a weary cam-
paigner, he still preserves something of the sensational showi-
ness, the bravado of his youth—the shadows of his face never
lengthened to disillusionment. It is hardly likely that Lysippus
accompanied the Macedonian on his tour of conquest, nor was
it deemed necessary for a sculptor to have his model at hand
for a portrait, a statement supported by the statue of Demosthenes by Polyeuctus, made a number of years after the orator's
death, yet one of the most natural portraits in the history of
Greek art. Alexander, however, established a new tradition in
portraiture by borrowing traits from the gods and Herakles, a
practice on his part which makes an identification difficult unless we can distinguish the part in the hair and other physical
marks mentioned by Plutarch.[54] The most celebrated of his
portraits by Lysippus was the famous Alexander with the
Lance, which must have expressed a high measure of pompous
dignity and thus set a fashion for many of his imitators in the
Hellenistic and Roman periods.

Alexander carried the various modes of Greek cultural expression from the mainland to different parts of Asia, and art
followed suit. His successors set up new focal centers in Alexandria, Antioch, Pergamon, and Rhodes, whose people took

53. F. P. Johnson: *Lysippus,* Durham, 1927, p. 182.

54. E. Suhr: *Sculptured Portraits of Greek Statesmen,* Baltimore, 1931,
pp. 67ff.

over what Greece had developed but without understanding the viewpoint behind its creations. This viewpoint was already rapidly disappearing in the old city state. It is imperative, then, that we judge their work not by what we observe on the surface but in accord with the motivation behind it. They admired the anthropocentric view but were unable to maintain it; they often wanted to be responsible beings living in a potential world, but they also wanted something beyond it with more enthusiasm; they thought they were living an integrated life within the limits of moderation, but intense desire had a way of distorting this balance in its own favor. One line of endeavor, one way of doing things, left other possibilities in the shadow; in art this meant specialization. Each school looked back at the past of the mainland, and each one had its own way of recreating the old ideal, each one also became more self-conscious of what it was striving for, of its difference from other schools. In spite of all the diversification, eclecticism, emotionalism, and self-conscious display, some isolated works can still stand up on their merit and rise above the aesthetic provincialisms on the exterior.

The Victory of Samothrace captures the attention of every visitor to the Louvre. It is so eclectic it can be associated with no school of the past. The drapery swirls in heavy masses around the legs to give a powerful sweep to her movement. It is definitely a sensational product of an unknown artist, but it has a majestic stateliness that appeals to the modern as it no doubt did to the Hellenistic Greek. A hand, recently discovered on the original site, was empty. Another example of eclecticism is the Melian Aphrodite with its serenely smiling face, its moving torso, and legs firmly supporting the action above—all adding up to the creation goddess spinning her golden thread of prosperity for the benefit of mankind. The Borghese Warrior is definitely a showpiece for skill in anatomy. The outstanding portrait of the period is the Hellenistic Prince. Whoever may have been the model, it is the nearest approach we have to the Alexander with the Lance of Lysippus. The natural curve of the well-developed physique is sufficiently offset by the straight line of the lance and the hard determination of the face, all that a

Roman general would care to incorporate in his portrait for the benefit of posterity, but who can be sure it is a Roman?[55]

The Pergamene altar was erected to commemorate the victory of the Greeks over the Gauls, who threatened to engulf Asia Minor in the late third century B.C. The monument was built in Pergamon by Eumenes II and furnished with a large frieze depicting the struggle between the gods and giants, much of which has survived in a large number of original fragments dealing with the important phases of the struggle. The obvious strivings, the emotional and physical sufferings of the combatants struggling with a blatant sensationalism, the deep shadows and Scopaic features added to the confusing drama, every available space taken up with half-figures, with accessories—we find almost everything in the expression of this baroque frieze that was forbidden to the sculptor of the Parthenon relief. The Dying Gaul is a single piece taken out of its setting, but as it is, we find it one of the finest expressions of restrained suffering in Greek sculpture. The Rhodian school, famous for its Colossus, preferred the large, more complicated and technically difficult, graphic description of mythological episodes (like the Laocoon and the Farnese Bull) executed by highly skilled craftsman, picturesque in their details when viewed from a distance, but a close examination finds them disappointing. The Alexandrians exploited the gentle, dreamy qualities of Praxiteles, reflected both in the Chian girl's head in Boston, which in Christian times might easily have passed for the portrait of a visionary lost in ecstasy,[56] and in the quiet mood pervading their landscape reliefs; even in the soft lassitude, the relaxed contentment in the faces of the Ptolemies.

Too little painting has survived from ancient times to warrant much discussion here. Our secondhand knowledge comes from literary sources, vase paintings, and later work at Pompeii, Herculaneum, and the Fayoum. We are told the Greek painter

55. R. Carpenter (A.J.A., XXXI, 1927, pp. 160–168, and *Memoirs Am. Ac. Rome*, XVIII, 1941, p. 93) suggests Lucullus.

56. G. Dickens (*Hellenistic Sculpture*, Oxford, 1920, p. 23) calls it *morbidezza*.

worked in fresco (certainly not that of the Minoan), tempera, encaustic, and mosaic. Polygnotus, the master of the fifth century, is known to us from a lengthy description of two large paintings in the Lesche of Delphi, from which the archaeologist has traced his influence to a vase in Orvieto.[57] His was evidently a severe style wherein the human figure stood out sharply from the background, the details of the landscape abbreviated as much as possible, where distance and depth in terms of perspective meant little in a composition devoted to the portrayal of character or *ethos* of great men. In the fourth century Zeuxis and Parrhasius vied in reproducing nature as accurately as possible, if we may believe the accounts, with the aid of light and shadow effects; their wider range of color probably made their work something more than colored drawings. Apelles, the painter of Alexander, was the most skillfull and ambitious of them all, one whose work called forth the most lavish praises. The best reflection of the ancients' skill in mosaic is the Battle of Alexander and Darius from Pompeii, now in the Museum of Naples.

Vase painting was not reckoned among the arts by the ancient critic, but for us, in the absence of painting, it reflects much that has been otherwise destroyed and tells many an interesting story about religion and daily life. Many of the large cities like Athens and Corinth had their potters' quarter where these vessels were fired, painted, and then exported to all parts of the Mediterranean. The archaic period substituted crude geometric human figures for the stylized flowers, plants, and animal friezes inherited by the Ionians from the Mycenaean era, and as the human became the center of attraction, mythology soon monopolized the subject matter of the Athenian master until we come to the François vase of 575 B.C. The black-figured style, in which the objects were painted black, leaving the background in the natural color of the clay, reigned supreme until 525 as a superb art of delineation, the details of garments and facial features added in incised lines and light touches of color. The Execias cylix, showing Dionysus sailing over the sea, is the

57. M. Swindler: *Ancient Painting*, New Haven, 1929, pp. 199–201.

highlight of black-figured composition, the scene admirably
fitted into its framework. The red-figured artist enclosed his
spaces with a black line, sometimes reinforced with a relief line,
to define his figures and objects. Brygus creates a forcefully
dramatic Iliupersis, his drapery plays a more prominent role,
and scenes from everyday life become more common, but, as
we have seen in sculpture, a decline sets in as soon as accessories usurp too much space and attention. Another technique,
employing a white background for more sensitive drawing and
delicate coloring, was mostly confined to funeral vases.

That the ancient Hellene was a remarkably distinctive individual was as evident to the Persian in the army of Xerxes as
to the student of today; that he was much more different from
each one of the eastern peoples than the Egyptian from the Mesopotamian will readily be admitted by one who has brought
their viewpoints within the range of a comparative perspective.
What has produced this difference which is found not only on
the surface but also beneath any apparent similarities with other
peoples? To say one is European and more active while the other
is Asiatic and more passive is merely giving names to things
we find on the surface. To speak of individualism in the Greek
is the amateur liberal's way of putting his finger on an obvious
manifestation whose roots go down much deeper into the unknown. To attribute it alone to climate or the irregular coastline makes the Greek a pawn in the hands of irrepressible
circumstances. Can we find an explanation by examining more
closely our own way of thinking and living? To a certain extent;
but while the modern owes his intellectual heritage to the
Greek, his spiritual tradition goes back to the Hebrew, a unique
combination that would yield little fruit for making an appraisal
of the Greek's distinctive role in ancient times.

What has brought about that balance between subject and
object which started the European on his long career in abstract
thought, on the one hand, and in physical science, on the other?
Why did he first look at the earth, air, fire, and water, the
serpent in the grass, the eagle in the air, the stars above, the

fish, the fly as respectable objects worthy of his attention, objects of value apart from what they could contribute to his practical benefit? Why did the Greek first become consciously aware of the mental processes necessary for systematic thought? What is back of the individualism as well as the democracy that created a revolution in government? How did he develop a historical perpective? What is the meaning of the tragic view of life? What made him lay so much stress on man, not as a subjective giant but as a compromise between his desires and limiting circumstances?

It is true that, once he had learned something of the pleasure of exercising his reason, of exploring into the processes of the mind, many a Greek neglected to apply his new discoveries to the plane of practice. Does this mean the Greek made no progress in the field of thought? Does it mean he left the burden and bulk of the scientific basis for thinking up to his modern successor? It is sad that some of our modern critics take the discovery of the mind itself for granted and wonder why the Greek failed to give us our modern discoveries in science. The pre-Socratics made a valiant attempt to explore the material world, but because of a lack of mental equipment, more indispensable than advanced scientific instruments, the ancient had to wait for a further awareness of his own faculties. Likewise, we take the great achievement of democracy as self-evident in Greek history and then curse the Greek for the evils consequent upon excessive individualism. It is true that in many respects the Athenian neglected to apply the principles of his democratic ideal, that he converted the Delian confederacy into an empire, but the mere discovery of democracy as a form of government and its application, even on a small scale, looms up much higher than the shortcomings attached to it in an age when absolutism was seldom questioned in any field of human endeavor.

We have seen that magic played a paramount role in the life of all early peoples, eastern and far eastern but especially among Egyptians and Mesopotamians, whose viewpoint placed the infinite within reach of man's desire, eternally seeking for means to control the constant change of experience. Such a device served as an asset in keeping certainty and security within the control of the subjective agent impatient with the problems presented by finite time and space. The Greek too had an abundance of magic in his background,[58] but when his viewpoint developed a potential man dealing with a potential world, magic remained within definitely circumscribed limitations. In the East, however, magic was not merely an occasional matter of divination to learn the future, to throw a sop to the superstitious, or to work indirect harm on an enemy. It carried its methods into other avenues of human endeavor where its surviving effects were still more harmful (we have already explained why many of its pitfalls were avoided by the Hebrews and Hindus). At this point we are in a good position to summarize the noxious method and effect of magic which supplied an immediate answer to a demand for uncompromising certainty and also kept the mind a slave to the tyranny of subjectivism. Above all, magic dictated expediency in thought and action. It made the subject the self-deluded prey of its own demands and robbed the object of its due rights; if the latter was a human being, he lost his dignity; above all, it restricted theory to a single approved direction between a definite cause and effect and prevented its further development independent of a specified practical result. Every subject was, then, constantly on the *qui vive* to exploit his environment for his personal benefit, to use other men as a means to an end, and consequently the means which might have contributed so much to the eventual advance of the subject was subordinated to a stereotyped method functioning between impatient desire and its satisfaction.

Transferred to the field of religion it means that no matter how powerful a particular god of phenomena may claim to be, his power is contingent on how he reflects or fulfills the desire of the subject pulling the strings behind the curtain. Every devotee can, by means of this magic, make or unmake a divinity, which can loom up very high on the horizon of the worshipper's viewpoint if that divinity can become identified with his desire.

---

58. Plato: *Republic*, II, 364B.

Such a man, if he is powerful enough by the grace of emotional appeal, can become a priest whose efficacious self-identification with his divinity can in turn develop into an even more powerful subjective device for using others as a means to self-aggrandizement. Instead of allowing the worshipper to appeal directly to his own conception of god, the priest builds up a form of worship, a theology which makes him the indispensable representative through whom divinity can be solicited. This simply means that one supreme subject takes command of a host of smaller subjects whose desires are now channeled through the priest to their desired end in the divinity. It means too that the priest now controls god in one single direction, and by means of revelation, which can inspire fear or love, enslaves the worshipper spiritually, and may even exploit him politically and economically. Of course, one may say it makes no great difference as long as the desires of exploiter and exploited are satisfied, and we must concede the priest will be bound to satisfy the needs of the worshipper, but in the meantime a well-balanced spiritual relationship between the worshipper and his god is out of the question, and the former surrenders his right of direct appeal to his god in favor of an opiated fulfillment of a burning and immediate desire for certainty and security.

It cannot be emphasized strongly enough that the subject was loath to recognize that the certainty and security he cherished at such a high price were but the creations of an intense desire projected into the infinite and eternal. Prone to self-deception, he was the last to realize that his world of static dependability would eventually involve him in its own decay. He was like a man in a tree reaching for fruit with one hand while he saws off his limb of support with the other.

In government we find much the same procedure. Each member of the state would like to be the big subject or ruler of the people and will become so if he can gain sufficient power to force others to carry out his bidding. Once in the saddle of power there is little compromise with the ruled; in return for a questionable protection the common citizen of a "brave new world" must be absorbed into a reflection of the ruler's will.

Absolutism is the outcome of such an application to the theory of ruling whereby the ruler controls the form of government and forces the citizens, deprived of the right of decision, to identify their wishes with his own. In Greece too there were subjective aristocracies, tyrannies, and oligarchies constantly threatening the city-state, but there was one overwhelming difference between the political absolutism of Greece and that of the East: the latter was strongly reinforced by religious sanctions, so that often the ruler, sometimes an ex-priest or under the control of the priesthood, maintained his position not only by centralizing the secular power into his own hands but by the magical support of religion; this made it invulnerable to any kind of attack. In Greece the ruler could not enlist the support of religious authority, which accounts for the rapid changes in government, for the people's initiative in suppressing any objectionable authority. There a man had to command the respect of his people by his ability instead of resorting to primitive methods of magic, a fact which explains why the Greek tyranny rarely lasted more than one generation.

The field of knowledge supplies a similar example. The craving for certainty induced the subjective mind to forget about an object that required too much experimentation and supplied no ultimate, final information, in favor of what came down from authority above without qualification; revelation was so much more consoling than trial and error methods. Small wonder that science could neither come into being nor thrive under the spell of such charming expediency! Science, as we shall see, must depend on a much healthier adjustment than subjective expediency can effect to create the theories and machines of modern times. Where magic was able to extend its method into the theory and practice of the East, the view of man's world in which the subject absorbed the object so completely and only one object at a time, was monistic, for although there was actually an object in this unbalanced equation, it counted for little. The one world discouraged much attention to particulars and therefore any comparison between either the particulars themselves or between the whole and its parts. The object might change but the degree of concentration and absorption was still strong, so that polytheism meant, for the most part, a transfer of focus from one god to another.

The Greek, too, found himself in a finite world of change but took an entirely different view of his situation. How did he succeed in converting the ever-changeable into something at least relatively permanent? How did he manage to anchor himself to some kind of security? The answer to this question reveals the distinctive adjustment he made with his world, which set him apart from all eastern peoples. As a subject he refrained from identifying himself with an infinite either outside or within himself and so avoided many of the perils of absolutism in every field of human endeavor. Had he, then, no awareness of the infinite as a factor in his living? Did he try to deny its existence? No, but he was not inclined to let it become a ruling factor, a subjective dictator in his life. When Anaximander spoke of the *boundless*, he thought of it as the source from which everything in the universe was created. Parmenides first drew a sharp distinction between being and nonbeing, the finite and infinite, but after removing all qualities or attributes from being, he paradoxically asserted it had the shape of a sphere;[59] nor is there a creation *ex nihilo* by an omnipotent divinity in the teachings of these two men. Zeno, in his paradoxes, has also made a contrast between the finite and infinite. I think one may safely state that the Greek first brought the difference between the finite and infinite into the light of consciousness, that even Homer[60] and his followers were aware of their implications, but seldom did they sacrifice the here and now for something without limitation in time and space. Much is made of the fact that the Greek avoided the irrational in mathematics,[61] and if

---

59. W. T. Stace: *A Critical History of Greek Philosophy*, London, 1920, p. 47.

60. R. Mondolfo: *El infinito en el pensamiento de la antigüedad clásica*, Buenos Aires, 1952, pp. 40 ff.

61. O. Spengler: *The Decline of the West* (Trans. by C. F. Atkinson), I, New York, 1926, p. 65; T. Dantzig: *Number, the Language of Science*, New York, 1939, p. 101.

this may be called a dread, it also means he was cognizant of its existence.

We have already seen that a finite world cannot exist for the mind of man without implications of the infinite and eternal behind it—as soon as we push the universe to an outer limit we must concede the possibility of something on the other side. The Greek, however, was not so much concerned about the long range questions for their own sake as learning about them *through* his immediate, finite experience. He was a particular fragment amid a large number of other fragments, one who neither asked any favors of a perfection beyond his experience nor placed himself in bondage to any kind of subjective authority claiming to reveal the secrets of the infinite. Although he was an imperfection in need of other men and things for improvement, he saw no reason why he should barter his own choice and opportunity to achieve improvement for a short-cut method via the religious or political authority of an absolute nature. To succeed in complementing his own needs he had to think and act, to learn more about himself, about other men and the world he lived in, and then to discover why they thought and acted as they did. For the orientals of the seventh century B.C. the Greek was altogether too restless, too active, too curious, forever threatening the *status quo* of the older civilizations. The Greek was young, his world was young and full of promise, it had so many possibilities of bringing about a state of universal happiness—but not by a denial of life on the horizontal plane.

It was man's world, and when the Greek saw, as Sophocles did when he wrote his *Antigone,* how far man had left nature behind, he called him the most wondrous of all beings. But this was man who had come into contact with all kinds of experiences to make himself many-sided and adaptable, the ideal Athenian of Pericles' time. And since he was a limited creature without any absolute authority within reach to control other limited persons and objects, each one of which had certain privileges and responsibilities, he had to respect the limitations imposed by time and space; once he transgressed them, he had to take the consequences. After the Persian wars he realized how superior he, the Greek man, was to other men, but in spite of his pride, other men outside Greece were included in his horizontal point of view. It was man bounded by birth and death with very little concern for afterlife, man subject to change in circumstances, to the changing moods of other men—a potential man creating his own sense of security within the finite and constantly coping with new problems to maintain it. If we could place ourselves in the shoes of the Athenian of 460 B.C. who saw how far the man of his city had come during the previous two centuries, we could understand why Socrates thought he could learn nothing from nature outside of man, why the Greek painted the image of man on every sign post of his life. It must have seemed to many at the time that man was on his way, intellectually or practically, to uncovering the secrets of the universe through the study of the finite.

The most important encouragement to the development of the potential man as the final arbiter over his destiny was the nature of Greek religion, and here we come up against a common misunderstanding among moderns. Of course, religion was important to the average man of the street,[62] but it was a very different religion from that of the East. First, let us review these differences that contributed so much to Greek endeavor in other fields. The priest, far from being a sacrosanct individual chosen by the voice of god to act as his special deputy on earth, was merely another citizen delegated by his fellow men to fill another office; this office demanded a knowledge of ceremony, sacrificial and otherwise, of festivals connected with the worship of a particular god, but it in no way allowed him to mount the pedestal of authority over other citizens or to become the mouthpiece for any revelation. We hear of no tyranny exercised over the mind by a priest in either the religious, the political, or the intellectual spheres, for without the infinite to support his claim to superiority there could be neither revealed knowledge nor absolute authority. There was no creed to tell the individual exactly how to think of his god and to define his obligations to

---

62. G. L. Dickenson: *The Greek View of Life,* London, 1907, p. 10.

that god; the temple displayed its greatest beauty to the world outside, reserving no fearful, awesome, mysterious chamber within as a holy of holies for the exclusive communion of god and priest; the altar was outside the shrine where it served as the center of worship. The Praying Boy faces his divinity with outstretched arms, not as a contrite petitioner overburdened with sin, ready to bow his head and bend his knee in the dust before the representative of the absolute.

There were, as we all know, quite different elements in popular religion, but neither Orphism nor the Eleusinian Mysteries were permitted to trespass on man's freedom of thought and self-development. There were men like Pythagoras, Parmenides, and Plato who emulated the East by setting up an absolute authority over all phases of life, but the fate of the Pythagoreans in Italy became an object lesson to all who wished to mind god's business for mankind in general. There were oracles that became mouthpieces for political graft as well as centers for popular superstition. Athens was known as the most religious city in Greece,[63] and at the same time the most productive in the arts and independent thinking. What greater commendation can we make in favor of any religion? Alcibiades, spoiled brat that he was, offended the Athenians (so the report goes) by mutilating the herms of the city before setting out on the Sicilian expedition. Is such a crime to be condoned by the modern who agrees that the British justly arrested Bismarck for whistling on a Sunday? Any man was free to absorb himself in the sublime, to worship Zeus, or play the skeptic as he liked, as long as he did not interfere with the right of another to make his own choice. This was the tolerant message of a religion emancipated from both a priestly tyranny and the subjective authority of the infinite, where every man was, in a sense, his own priest.

There are those who may reject the moral side of Greek religion for the obvious reason that it lacked consistent integrity—the justice of one divinity was not always the justice of another and man became a pawn between the two standards,

---

63. Pausanias, I, 17, 1 and I, 24, 3.

whereas the Hebrew Yahweh drew all these vagrant strings together into his own person. In a sense the criticism is valid. When Hippolytus offended Aphrodite, Artemis, his true love and ideal, stood silently on the side while the other brought the young man to his destruction. The moral precepts of the Hebrew God recognized no such a split. But experience was on the side of the Greek: one can be very loyal and true to one friend, so loyal and true that a serious misdemeanor, even the murder of another, can lie somewhere along the fringe of single-hearted or single-minded loyalty; the tragic consequences could be appreciated to the fullest extent by the father of Hippolytus. The Hebrew, facing a similar situation, could either hope and trust that somehow, somewhere, Yahweh had a secret, long-range purpose behind the adverse turn of events, which would eventually redound to the good of his subject or he, like Job, could hurl his defiant questions against the ramparts of heaven only to be overwhelmed by the roar of the whirlwind.

With such an advantage in his favor the Greek was able to put a new construction on knowledge. He found himself face to face with all kinds of problems which, as we have seen, represent conflicts between the subject and object, between what we want and what we may have. He found, if he wanted to be honest with himself and fair to the object, that he would have to compromise, to work hard to get along with men or to learn something about an object of any kind. When the Greek set out on his search, he had none of the advantages we have and perhaps a few more prejudices to discard. He had no scientific instruments, no libraries, he had no mind ready to deal with knowledge. There is no doubt that the processes of thinking were already latent in many eastern civilizations but had been slumbering under the influence of magic. Now that the methods of magic were pushed aside, it was still impossible to gain any ground in investigation, unless the thinker was acquainted with what each mental process could reveal and then could use them in reference to a definite end. Since the Greek of the seventh century was ignorant of these processes, he had to learn about them as he dealt with the objects of learning, by setting up a balanced equation between subject and object, whatever the nature of the object might be. The mind, as the Greek handed it down to us, was an outgrowth or a digest of countless impacts of experience on the thinker. As a part of the subject, it sought to impose a certain order on the world beyond, but the mind itself, whether the subject was willing to admit it or not, was also influenced by the objects out in experience. The order such a subject imposes cannot be anything like the static arrangement of the East, because in a balanced subject-object relationship of finite members the mind is fully aware of the constant change going on in both subject and object and therefore must be forever on guard to preserve even a relative order. The Greek started out, then, with a subject capable of dealing more fairly with an object; he also had an avid curiosity and, like all creatures, a longing for certainty which he expected to find somewhere in phenomena.

The pre-Socratics learned about all kinds of concrete objects they could see, feel, hear, smell, and taste, but they had difficulty in distinguishing between what they seemed to be and what they really were because they had not learned much about the nature of quality. They discovered that the basic material of the universe could be earth, water, air, fire (four different elements), or atoms, or seeds, and that the motion necessary to bring about change in creation and destruction might be inherent in matter or propelled by love and hate, by chance, or a cosmic mind. The changing processes in the universe might be interpreted in the light of determinism or teleology. In the course of these investigations and speculations they found some strange objects in the earth, the sea, and sky, all of which they tried to fit into a pattern of unity and significance. And where was man in this great panorama? While he was really the prime mover in this great learning process, he had not yet reached a state of self-consciousness as a subject nor was he aware of his importance as the owner of a mind; from our view he was just another object of change, being created and destroyed in an endless cycle.

But one thing in himself he could now appreciate, namely, the meaning of sensation and observation by which he could learn about tangible objects.

The early philosopher, like the magician, was prone to make use of the analogy and invest it with power—with far less dangerous consequences: the process of condensation, the concepts of love and hate, even that of the mind were projected into the cosmos where they were expected to function as effectively as in the small orbit of man's immediate experience. The philosopher, however, did not create or seize upon a cause and effect sequence in his own circle to *imitate* with subjective power, he was not inclined to groove his analogy into a narrow channel of practical expediency, nor did he control any religious authority for standardizing his thought and imposing it on the minds of others. The sparks flew from his anvil of thought, minus any searing effect, to illumine the efforts of those who wished to make their own contribution.

And how did this knowledge by observation differ from that of the primitive? The latter, in the investigation of his experience, was limited to what might be of practical benefit to his way of life, and as soon as he had reached this frontier of observation with the aid of magic, he asked no further questions; any notion about religion or the cosmos he may have achieved was somehow linked to a practical result which is one reason why curiosity never roamed too far afield and theory was never allowed even a shadowy independence. The Greek, as we know, observed natural phenomena because he was curious about their ways and how he could fit them into a pattern of unity regardless of their bearing on practice; but he too found himself thwarted in his search for truth because he had not yet found a common denominator in the mind he could use for further thinking on the level of theory. A series of observations cannot be of much value for further thinking unless the subject knows how to extract some common value to be used later for comparison and as a standard for checking further observations.

There is no reason to doubt that the primitive was able to reason in his own simple way to make his tools, to till his soil, to lay his plans,[64] but he was not able to look into his own mind to see what was going on there. A consciousness of mental processes, which the Greek was looking forward to but had not yet achieved, enables the thinker to distinguish between a casual observation, a hasty opinion and a general truth, each one of which must be given its own particular value. Moreover, it builds up a confidence in the eventual efficacy of thinking, something of which is necessary to free it from the tyranny of the practical particular. The Greek eventually taught us how to check on our reasoning in terms of universals and particulars and so paved the way for a greater independence of theory in modern science, whose by-products may or may not benefit us in practical problems. After the days of the Greek, theory eventually led the way, shedding a number of by-products for practical use as it advanced.

What the Greek had found in his objective investigations was contrary to his expectations. Like so many people in search for certainty, he hoped to find, within a reasonably short time, a unified secret behind all the change, the cause and effect, the action and reaction in phenomena, one he could use to satisfy his desire for security in experience. Instead of discovering some kind of common bond for further thinking, the mass of facts brought forth so many different explanations and ways of looking at things he began to despair of finding his secret among concrete objects; he was unable to go on in his program of thought with the sole support of observation. Observed facts, however interesting and fascinating, could not, taken by themselves, cast the reflection of the general or common denominator of truth on the mirror of man's mind which, as yet, had no way of learning about objective truth in this sense. Then the opportunities of a democratic government and the teachings of the Sophists came into the Athenian picture. Why bother about the world at large as long as one can find some kind of permanence in success among men, and many of the citizens

---

64. B. Malinowski's comments (*Magic, Science and Religion*, Boston, 1948, pp. 10-18) on this subject are especially interesting.

were fools who could be used as means to an end. Attention drifted away from objective knowledge in favor of rhetoric, language, and deception, and as a consequence the Greek had to give up temporarily the balanced subject-object relationship he had learned to use, in exchange for a new kind of expediency. Another factor in his loss of faith in the objective was the inability of his mind to distinguish between the hypothesis and an established truth, hence all the suggestions of the pre-Socratics were temporarily thrust aside until the mind was able to formulate a common denominator as a standard for testing all the information and conclusions the thinkers of the past had accumulated. The discoveries of the physical world lay on the surface of sensation which was powerless to subject them to a thorough-going analysis or build them up into a synthesis. The Greek chose to discard objective facts for a time and concentrate on himself.

The field of research was now transferred from the cosmos, which included man as another infinitesmal unit, to man himself, who had initiated the search for truth. It resulted in a subjective approach to reality which at that time meant mostly politics and religion where man, as the measure of all things,[65] turned his guns of skepticism on truths the Greeks had considered unassailable long before the search for objective truth began. Viewed from the standpoint of the history of thought, sophistry was apparently a retreat, but actually it was a strategic withdrawal at the opportune moment. It was, of course, a reversion to the procedure of magic which urges every man to see truth in the mirror of his own desire, to justify it by persuasion or, on the level of practice, by force. Here, however, the process was on the conscious plane where a man could see it going on much like an introspective panorama extending from the original intention to its moral consequences in practice, and this made it so much more culpable to the man of sound moral background. It encouraged men to think as animals act, to stake

---

65. Cf. B. A. G. Fuller: *History of Greek Philosophy*, New York, 1931, II, p. 23.

everything on superficial opinion, the deadly enemy of Parmenides and Plato; and in many cases the Sophists and their students were successful in their ventures because the outsider had no standard for evaluating the truth of opinion which, as the tool of the subject, manipulated the object more or less at will. We said the retreat to a point where man functioned as the subjective lord of thought and action was a strategic asset, because the road to a common denominator for testing knowledge led through opinion to another hitherto unexplored region of the mind. Opinion was based on the individual perception which the thinker now learned about as the second step after sensation in the learning process, together with its merits and disadvantages. Another merit of sophistry was the increased emphasis on man as the owner of the mind, its sensations and perceptions.

What was the chief difference between the subjective expediency of the Sophists and that of earlier magic? The latter was so grounded in religious sanction that it developed a static uniformity for the sake of security and therefore it was out of the question to drive a wedge into its foundation; that of the Sophists developed on the surface of finite experience where its shortcomings, its futility, soon became apparent to a growing mind. Like the flux and flow of Heraclitus, its birth and death were within view of each other. It was devised by man and could be changed by man without violating an *ipse dixit* of the supernatural.

Naturally, the expediency of the Sophists would have brought the intellectual life of Greece into a state of relativistic chaos and government into anarchy had it continued to hold sway any length of time. We have cited the Persian wars and Socrates as the agents responsible for a turning of the tide to the great achievements of the fifth century. After Salamis and Plataea the Greek began to be conscious of something great which had been built into his character in the past, a discipline much older than the recent teachings of the Sophists, traditions which could play the role of a respectable object in his future thinking. What it was he could not say because it had never penetrated the level of consciousness; surely it was something which had been growing since the days of Homer and made him feel it was right as right could be, if it had made him superior to the Persian of the East, something that persuaded the Greek that truth was not a monopoly of the subject living and desiring in the immediate present.

The man who brought a new type of truth from its hidden depths, not only for the Greek to see but for all subsequent ages to benefit by, was Socrates, for it was he who restored the balance of subject and object on a much more permanent basis. He went around his native Athens and probed into the minds of all who were willing to talk to him. Most people were severely jolted by his persistent questioning until he became an object of hatred. A large majority, looking only on the surface and hugging their disillusionment, condemned him as another Sophist, but Socrates was not to be put off the track by such accusations. Although he had no name for it, he was looking for a type of truth he knew had been in the mind for a long time and which could be used as a dependable criterion to test the validity of all kinds of knowledge, whether that knowledge was born in memory, perception, or observation. Here let us register a healthy reminder: Socrates was a very religious man who, so far as we know, fulfilled the requirements of traditional religion without feeling himself the least bit restricted in his intellectual adventure; in fact he was able to saturate his mission with a religious purpose.[66] He was the arbiter over his own religious life which imposed no restriction on the liberty of others to do the same.

Socrates went on examining the opinions of others or what they perceived to be the truth, he looked at them from all angles, he compared them with each other, he judged them in accordance with their effectiveness in action, and in the course of all this probing he found there was a common element behind all perceptions of the same category of things, whether concrete objects, moral virtues, or intellectual truths, and this common element he called truth in the highest sense of the

---

66. I recommend the reading of Korolenko's *The Shades—A Fantasy.*

term. This truth, which we call the concept, he was not always able to see in clear outlines, but he saw enough of it to recognize its importance. What did this discovery mean in the acquisition of knowledge? It meant the subject could now use another and more profitable common denominator *in the mind* to form a new balance for constructive thinking, one which would eventually counteract the destructive influence of the Sophists. But to arrive at this truth one had to wade through a great number of perceptions and observations before formulating a concept common enough for men to respect as a truth they all shared in. Henceforth when a man spoke of courage, wisdom, justice, piety, cow, man, or centaur, he knew that behind all the opinions that spring into thought at a moment's notice there was something common in the minds of all men that, once it had been clearly defined, could serve both as an object for thinking and a criterion for further investigation. Socrates, of course, knew he had not found absolute truth; it was as true as anything in finite experience can be; it was comparatively more true than the flash of perception. From now on one could think not only in terms of abstract truths but include also concepts of concrete objects from the world at large. Now it was possible to continue with phenomena where the pre-Socratics had to leave off, because of the lack of a unifying element which had always been there but could have no value for man until it was consciously crystalized in the mind as a workable truth.

But this was by no means all the concept contributed to human thought. Given the possibility of formulating concepts of right behavior, a man could no longer be a law to himself.[67] This process could be made the basis for drawing up a law code, rules for social propriety, principles of government—any general rule which would tend to hold men together in some kind of harmony without impairing a healthy roominess within these limitations for the enjoyment of personal values. Since the conceptual formulation enjoyed both a comparative security and order and at the same time could be altered to suit a change

---

67. The first book of Plato's *Republic* discusses this point with reference to the concept of justice.

in conditions, it could be maintained in harmony with experience and also help to ward off any threat of absolutism. It was also a *sine qua non* for the advancement of reason. Given the universality of the concept and a number of particular aspects or attributes (whether in the form of opinions or observations), the thinker could then form syllogisms, think deductively or inductively to learn more about the truth behind other particulars gleaned through observation; then a theory or hypothesis could be built up in the mind and checked by further observation in nature at large, a procedure the pre-Socratic could not follow because there was no way of agreeing on a common denominator until the formulation of the concept.

If objects and objective facts could have compared notes with one another and revealed to man's mind what was more universal or common, what was peculiarly particular in their nature, the Greek would not have deserted observation of the physical world for sophistic relativism which led later to the concept of Socrates. With the aid of the general and particular, however, men could compare knowledge gained by observation with that of perception, they could place perception over against conception and so learn the difference between more stable truth and more relative facts in the objective universe or opinions dictated by human desire. Reason was not invented by Socrates; he brought it to the threshold of consciousness where the thinker could see it in operation, apply it to practice, and control its behavior in further thinking; he made it a convenient and constructive tool for all later theorizing. Here we may repeat with greater emphasis what we have already pointed out: magic was so bent on a practical end it channeled theory through a stereotyped groove of cause and effect sequences which prevented the development of reason, it had likewise no interest in the object per se. Clear, objective, scientific thinking could not develop from the expediency of magical methods, but only from a well-balanced subject-object relationship in which the object, whether concrete or conceptual, was held in the same high respect as the subject.

Thales and his followers had chosen a manifestation of objective experience to serve as a respected object in their thinking about the cosmos, but little advance in thinking about such objects could be made without a common denominator formulated in the mind of the thinker himself. Once a common denominator, conceptual or otherwise, was recognized, it was important to keep it within range of finite experience where it could mirror and be subject to constant change on a horizontal plane. If it should be abstracted from the finite, like the number of Pythagoras or the being of Parmenides, there was always a danger of elevating it to the level of the infinite where its truth, in addition to being sacrosanct, would become a tool in the hands of some powerful subject who, in turn, would set himself up as the high priest of its revelation. Fifth century Greece was given a new, balanced subject-object relationship in which the object remained in the mind of the thinker and adapted itself to the demands of a potential universe. This was the great contribution of Socrates!

One would naturally think the Athenian, now that the value of the mind and the usefulness of reason were clarified, would return to the observation of natural phenomena and continue where the pre-Socratics had left off—to explore the fields of science as the modern has done since the days of Francis Bacon. There are two reasons why he failed to do so: the great discovery of the mind made him feel it was all-sufficient in itself, and so the mind fed on its own material without being brought to bear upon the immediate problems of society and the practical needs of living. The second reason was Plato, who, in his bitterness over the death of his teacher, revolted against much of what Athens had stood for in the past; he worshipped his teacher and sublimated his concept to an exalted level. The idea left experience so far behind that the latter preserved only a shadowy resemblance to what Plato called the highest reality. Knowledge was no longer equated directly with the facts and concepts drawn from experience but became a kind of recollection which could easily pass over into subjective revelation. The philosopher king was an arbitrary authority over all affairs secular and divine, the citizen having no right of appeal. As soon as reality winged its way too far from finite experience, the interpretation of its meaning became the subjective property of a chosen few, while balanced thinking broke down.

Aristotle realized that no matter how logically necessary a process of thought may be, it cannot have value for man in the world of experience unless the universal and particular, the concept or idea and its concrete counterpart are closely linked together. In this way the object can remain a common denominator the thinker may use in scientific investigation and at the same time he can preserve a sound balance for all thinking. The metaphysics of Aristotle is the accumulation of a long development, extracting the most significant concepts of all his predecessors to build up his comprehensive system. But why do we not find more thinkers following the example of Aristotle in fields of scientific investigation? Beyond a few well-known pioneers in Hellenistic times, little effort was made to take advantage of Aristotle's dictum about the nature of substance, because the schoolmen were still bent on finding the ultimate secrets of the universe in the mind itself, because the late fourth century brought with it a strong moral emphasis which weakened the potentiality of man in a changing world, because the initiative the Greek showed after the Persian wars and through the fifth century was now on the wane.

Greek thought, in the fourth century B.C., had reached its highest state of development. With a clear picture of Aristotle's substance in mind the thinker could subject his whole experience to definition, comparison, and classification. He could organize general concepts drawn from observation, opinion, or a combination of the two, then test them in the light of particulars, both abstract and concrete. Aristotle and some of his followers were able to examine, as no Greek before them, every branch of knowledge, every aspect of their world in the light of a scientific approach. But had not every man done this, more or less, before Aristotle? Indeed, but now he had a clear picture of himself as a thinker, he knew why, in terms of a broader perspective, he was thinking and he knew how to test the validity of his thought—his thought was now organized to meet the demands of a changing world; his thinking had continuity, a significance beyond the attainment of an immediate desire in a narrow frame of time and space. As the Greek was struggling with the problems posed by his objective experience, he beheld, as in a mirror, a revelation of his own mental faculties in operation; his efforts in thinking, in addition to teaching him how to learn in the objective sense, became an ascent to a fuller self-realization.

In his supervision of the affairs of the Delian confederacy the Athenian was apparently of the conviction that democracy was a possession peculiar to the citizens of Attica, one which only the Athenian could properly appreciate; for the islanders, he assumed, it was a gem they were incapable of estimating fairly, and since the Athenians had brought it to light and availed themselves of its advantages, why not convert it into a monopoly? Athens failed to realize that others might learn, by way of education, to develop a democratic viewpoint, that a broad education is necessary to keep the spirit of democracy alive. Above all, she forgot that her democracy had grown by dint of sheer effort in thought and action; once they relaxed, the greedy ogre of subjective desire dangled the tempting bait of stereotyped security and certainty before the longing eye.

We are now in a position to appreciate why the Hindu and the Chinese were unable to take advantage of the contributions of their best thinkers and apply them to their own pressing social and practical problems. The latter, in spite of almost modern advances in thought, was unable to break through certain moral sanctions tradition had been building up for centuries in government and social decorum; magic with its philosophy of expediency had helped to mold these sanctions and so laid a restraining hand on balanced thinking. The Hindu, despite the brilliant thinking of his philosophers and organizers of knowledge, was unable to break through the postulates of subjective, intuitive dictates; consequently, instead of scientific thinking directed to the solution of practical and social problems we find a highly enlightened form of scholasticism, dedicated to a withdrawal from the problems of positive experience. In the case of the Hindu, the arbitrary subject controlled the intuition both in its direction and the object it absorbed, and because its dictates were more permanently pleasing to the subject they were put down as true, much more true than any information derived from a compromise with a changeable object. The Chinese followed much the same procedure with the traditions he built up and extended into the moral and practical spheres of his life. In each case certainty in the field of knowledge, and security for the future took precedence over the spirit of adventure and the challenge of a finite world.

The modern little realizes what a debt he owes to this rapid surge of development in the balanced thinking of the Greek, because he takes his heritage too much for granted. It cannot be stressed too emphatically that such a subject-object relationship, so indispensable to later scientific theory, could not have come into its own where religion and its priesthood fail to mind their own business; it requires the full and free growth of potential man in a changing universe. After the fourth century some Greeks sought for salvation in transcendental experience, a tendency encouraged by oriental influence now growing apace after the invasion of the East by Alexander. The finite world was soon to become a mire of sin, and the object of Socrates' thought degraded beyond recognition.

In the eastern civilizations we have discovered how religion, in one way or another, exercised some control over the choice of the ruler and the type of government in power. In China and Egypt the ruler was a son of divinity and so bolstered the connection between subjective man and authority imposed by the infinite above. The people at large were taught to listen and accept, not to raise their voices to make a decision; it was decreed by heaven that their position in life was fixed and would always remain so. In Greece there was neither a man who had descended from the infinite to rule over the people nor a religious authority to preordain the form of government and rank of the people. In a finite world each man is endowed with, first of all, what nature has given him, and this must be taken for granted; but over and above this grant each one can improve his natural endowment by thought and effort, he is given the same potential privileges and responsibilities as another and is expected to take advantage of his privileges and assume a full share of responsibilities. The field of government also calls for a man of potentialities who must develop himself as far as possible, a citizen capable of holding office, so that even when he is not holding office, he will know how the magistrates should fulfill their duties. The rulers are merely citizens raised to a higher position in the state for a time to protect the citizen in carrying out his duties, not to deprive him of personal rights.[68]

In Greece the government in the form of an aristocracy or a tyranny had to be very capable and diplomatic in dealing with the people to maintain its position, for the sword of Damocles was suspended over its head. In a democracy the citizen was on the same level with the holders of office; this fact gave him a broad perspective over the state—its area, its citizens, its policies, in conformity with his pluralistic or comparative view on life in general. Whether a citizen in or out of office, the Athenian was expected to deal with either another citizen or the state as a whole as responsible objects possessing as much dignity as himself. If the majority of citizens, both then and now, loses its potential character and decides to use the government as a means to an end, if it is more in love with immediate security than with its right of decision, someone is always ready at hand to push out democracy and relieve the citizen of both privilege and responsibility in every respect. Democracy is in the people, not in a form of government.

In Greek life the whole was the sum total of all its parts without absorbing the parts to their own detriment. The Parthenon is above all a monument of architecture calling on the arts of sculpture and painting to play their role in decoration, but far from losing their individuality, these subordinate arts maintain a certain distinctiveness as they contribute definitely to the harmony of the whole, and if a piece of sculpture is detached from a metope or pediment, it can still stand up on its

68. This is the problem presented by Sophocles in his *Antigone*.

own merit without crying out for architectural support. How different in this respect is the temple of Karnak, on the one hand, and the Gothic cathedral, in another period! In the Greek theater, too, we can be sure that one art was not permitted to tyrannize over the others, that declamation, music, and dancing moved along in some kind of harmony instead of blurring their distinctive outlines in the fusion of a Wagnerian music drama. Much the same relationship held good for the democratic state placed over against the citizen. Instead of occupying a higher position sanctioned by caste, wealth, or religion, the ruler was no more than another unit in the state, holding an office that required him to help all citizens enjoy their privileges within their rights and to carry out their obligations effectively, but not to infringe on either their rights or duties—all the citizens, plus the ruler, made up the whole state. This is the lesson taught by the *Antigone* of Sophocles!

The Greek has given us a concept of moral responsibility, one which requires a potential man in a potential world as a *terminus ante quem*. If each individual is potentially good or evil and everything in his world is good or evil in the same sense, it is squarely up to that individual to do all he can to make himself and his world better; if he does otherwise, he must be ready to assume responsibility for his commissions and omissions; he has the right of decision vested in himself. This brand of responsibility cannot flourish under an absolute form of government, under a priesthood that sends down its decisions, like revelation, from above for the benefit of those who have never learned how to make their decisions. An absolute form of government cannot afford to encourage its citizens to rise from one social status to another. The Athenian also had to bear in mind the limitations imposed on him by society and mortality in the here and now; he was bound to respect his neighbor's right to enjoy a full life, the laws imposed by the state, the general restrictions of experience. There is no reason for believing that even the majority of Athenians could boast of such a high standard of character, but as long as Athens could produce such men as Aristides, Themistocles, Cimon, Thucydides, Cleisthenes and Pericles, there was plenty of justification for self-responsibility. And such a standard was upheld by a man like Aristides in spite of no prospect of reward in the afterlife and in the face of political ostracism.[69]

It is easy to see how this ideal relaxed in the fourth century and then broke down more completely in Hellenistic times. The concentration on moral philosophy with its tendency to separate good and evil, to look back at the fifth century with a nostalgic longing for something the Greek no longer knew how to foster, to focus attention more exclusively on distant goals, heralds the approach of absolutism. The Stoics divided man's experience into those things that conform to the dictates of reason which they called good, and those things which appealed to the emotions which were put down as evil; the Epicureans claimed certain things inspired fear in man, and once these things were removed, the good would become apparent. As soon as the objects and pursuits of experience are neatly divided into good and evil, the burden of decision is removed from man's weary shoulders; the universe is no longer potentially good or evil, it *is* either good or evil and remains so. Eventually the evil is tarnished with the taint of sin and the good removes itself so far from the morass of sin on the other side that a guide or interpreter undertakes to lead man from the mire to a subjective identification with what is infinitely and eternally good. This role is taken over by the priest in a plan of salvation laid down by the mystic Plotinus.

Tragedy, another concept developed by the Greek, we have not been able to find except in Mesopotamia (and occasionally in China) where we took for granted that Gilgamesh filled its requirements at the end of the epic. It has no way of thriving where man's connection with the infinite is firmly entrenched or where salvation is assured in the next world. A tragic atmosphere permeates not only the stage in Greece but also the Homeric epics, its view of history and life in general, because these people concentrated all their efforts on the finite; since

---

69. Plutarch: *Aristides*, 7.

they could reconstruct the infinite and eternal only in terms of the evidence of finite experience, the next world was anything but a cheerful place. A tragic character must be able to face uncertainty with a challenge. He must be a great man with such a share of goodness in his make-up that the reader or audience would sympathize with him, regardless of the error he has committed to bring about his fall. All human life is veined with a tragic flaw, but the effort it requires to accomplish something great before it all ends makes it noble as well. In a potential world the villain, because he is a close approximation to absolute evil, cannot find a place, and hence he never mounted the Greek stage. The problem of tragedy is essentially human, human striving for what is forbidden in a life bounded by limitations.

We are told that tragedy, especially that of Aeschylus and Herodotus, was based on the concept of sin, often inherited by later generations, which called forth the jealousy of the gods and the ultimate ruin of the offender. If that is so, and there is plenty of evidence to support it, the Greek effected a successful bit of grafting of an Apollonian lesson from experience on the older tradition. Can we find both of these attitudes reflected in Greek tragedy? From the old inscription on the temple in Delphi warning against excess, down to the golden mean of Aristotle, men were cautioned against violating the natural limitations of experience lest she bring them to ruin in war, by disease, in a conflict with society or nature at large. The tragic hero is one whose desires have a way of straining against these limitations until they kick back at him or, to use language already familiar to us, the hero, the son of a divinity and a mortal, has desires and ambitions that exceed his human limitations and therefore bring him to a tragic fall. He stands on the scale between the extremes of behavior, where he is the arbiter of his own potential existence; if he moves too far either way he must, in spite of an otherwise noble character, pay the penalty.

The potential man of the fifth century was not one who spent his days running away from absolute evil and chasing absolute goodness but a man who, by his own judgment and initiative, was able to improve himself and others morally and intellectually, all of which had to be done within the limitations of experience to avoid the consequences of *hybris,* which drove one to exceed these limitations. Much has been made of the inherited curse which stalks the future of the tragic hero, but we also note that many of the heroes confess their own shortcomings leading to their eventual fall. The triumph of this potential man over any inherited curse is boldly proclaimed by Sophocles in the *Oedipus at Colonus,*[70] when his exiled hero rejects all responsibility for the murder of his father and a marriage with his mother, because these crimes were committed in ignorance; he can be called to account only for what he has consciously and wilfully contributed to his own detriment and that of others. A man's worth was estimated in terms of what he could do for himself and his world instead of resigning himself either to a mental and moral status somewhere between Galahads and villains, saints and devils, high and low caste, aristocrat and slave, or to a blood curse inherited from an ancestor. The concept of the villain which may have taken its cue from a practical application of Gorgias' *nihil est* belongs to a *Weltanschaung* that includes black devils and pure white angels, where men tend to accept what life has decreed for them; instead of willing to make himself and his world potentially better, the villain may only better it in spite of his evil nature or as an unconscious by-product of evil intentions. The man who cherishes no respect for any kind of an object may develop into an Iago or a Mephisto, *der Geist der stets verneint,* and therefore hates anyone that either has or thinks he has something of value which he, the villain, does not wish to strive for or may not have.

Much the same applies to the very good man, the reformer bent on rearranging all men and things to fit into an artificial construction relative to what he calls goodness. In his fanatical efforts to draw a sharp line between good and evil, he and his

---

70. 960–99.

goodness become so good they are positively good for nothing, and much evil arises as an unconscious by-product of his efforts. Both the reformer and the villain may avail themselves of sophistic expediency to gain their ends, because they are more than sure other men are not wise enough to see the light, an attitude which brings back the magician in a new guise, in a new setting. The Greeks, being more closely identified with the finite than any other people, knew well how to deal with its relative potentialities. Goodness must be something consonant with the good of an object as well as the subject, and the goodness cherished by other people who have the ability to think and decide for themselves constitutes an object every subject must respect. He must construct a moral and at the same time a mentally balanced subject-object relationship between himself and every man he deals with; on the scale of the golden mean he must avoid pushing his subjective desires to either extreme to permit every thinking individual to make a contribution to what is best for the common good at a given time. Both the world and standards of good and evil change in the finite, as the Greek knew; the man of sound judgment and clear decision can best deal with men and things that are not reckoned as absolutely good or evil but can be made relatively better or worse as time goes on. A static utopia, even in our times, must remain above the clouds, and black hells will always be consigned to the dark, mysterious bowels of mother earth.

The monistic, vertical line of vision of many eastern peoples helped them in their conviction that they were the chosen race in the eyes of divinity, while foreigners were regarded as a footstool for their own feet; we learn nothing about these neighboring people unless they appear as slaves or captives in sculptured reliefs. In Greece the horizontal view, directed over all the particulars of experience and prodded by an avid curiosity, included all the peoples of the eastern Mediterranean and beyond; such is the historical perspective of Herodotus. The mere fact that Persia had been an arch enemy did not exempt her from cultural interest; many customs of these Persians were greatly admired, especially by Xenophon. The two fifth-century historians realized the importance of keeping an even balance between the historian as subject and the objects of his investigations, but the court historian of Hellenistic times often sacrificed the truth of his object for subjective glorification; history in this vein lost its tragic significance and atmosphere. The emergence of a historical perspective and the writing of such a clear, objective, impersonal account by Thucydides shortly thereafter, are phenomena which can be accounted for only by the Greek view over a finite horizon.

There is plenty of evidence of humor in the cultural expression of Greece, much more than in the East; there is little or no trace of it in the writings of the Hebrews and Mesopotamians. We find two types very popular before the coming of Christ: irony, best represented by Socrates, and satire, exploited by Aristophanes and Lucian. Our own ignorance about the psychology of humor makes it difficult to make any significant comparisons, but it is hardly possible that the Greek ever appreciated laughing consciously at himself; this seems to be one of the great contributions of the modern to the western viewpoint.

Art is the best mirror we can find for cultural expression. In the first place, the Greek artist was interested in the general aspects of his life, i.e., the battle of the Alexander mosaic could be any encounter between Alexander and Darius. This tendency is also expressed in generally accepted types which seemed to sum up the history and character of the figure for artist and public in a kind of *Allgemeinheit,* as Winckelmann put it. The figures are encased within a firm outline to emphasize their formal character, to call attention to limitations, but the form need not remain the same for the figure that seeks improvement through effort; like the Greek individual, it has no way of throwing off limitations completely but grows onward and outward, in accord with the demands of the finite. Unlike nature which, attractive as it may be, still remains as it is, or better, follows the same movements year after year, the figure of Greek art stands out in strong contrast to the panorama of colorful growth in the background; the temple with its straight

lines, its boast of order and symmetry, must have appeared like
a hybrid to a lover of nature, and the human figure, as we have
seen, is usually left without the details of a setting. It was an anthropomorphic art from the archaic to the Hellenistic period: for
two centuries it struggled to emancipate itself from nature at
large and establish definite types; after a short period of experimentation with the face and anatomy, it blossomed forth into
the potential figure of the fifth century, the many-sided embodi-
ment of the Socratic concept, whose general roominess absorbs
so many of our specialized enthusiasms without losing its impersonal balance. The head of the Lemnian Athena includes so
much that is basically common to our observations and opinions,
to our angelic aspirations, our narrow assumptions of what man
ought to be. When we turn away from its presence, it leaves us
with a common denominator for further thought and a kind
of tolerance born of a pleasant reasonableness the Greek had
found in a rich, finite experience. After 400 B.C. the same figure
seems to reach out emotionally for something it no longer owns.
In contrast to the passive, introspective figure of India, whose
motion is generally devoid of purpose and direction, the Greek
individual is active, fully aware of his relationships in time and
space and moves onward to a definite goal.

The artist was proud, even in the case of vases, to add his
name to the work of his hand, and this in spite of the low
estimation attached to workers in the plastic arts. The Greek
personality, in the best days, was to be viewed from the
outside where one could see how it met the challenge of circumstances and molded itself in terms of its contacts with men,
events, and things; the inner life was not considered so worthy of
exploration. There is, in our sense of the term, no such a thing
as an autobiography in Greek literature; in fact, when Plutarch
set out, at a late date, to write biographies, he found nothing
in the way of personal data. His work is a strange collection of
legendary anecdotes and moral didacticisms which made his
work so popular in the Renaissance. The Greek, however, knew
what each one of these great men meant in his own framework

of time and space, of contacts with events and other men of his time.

It is a mistake to think the Greek was hardly able to make a beginning in scientific achievement which the modern rapidly brought to a riper fruition in theory and practice. It is true that Plato turned the direction of thinking into rational speculations where science, as we construe it, was abandoned as a negligible pursuit, and it is also true that technical workers were placed on a low social scale, but we who look on the surface can easily forget how the Greek struggled to explore the capacities and faculties of the human mind, to free it from the trammels of magic's subjective expediency, and to set up an even balance between subject and object without which the modern could not have advanced so rapidly. This is the important contribution of the Greek genius to the development of thinking, which it left as a precious legacy to posterity.

Leben heisst streben!

THE CHINESE VIEWPOINT

CHINA, LIKE INDIA, succeeded in maintaining the continuity of its cultural expression and viewpoint from a very early period into modern times. The early development of this viewpoint, before the Shang rulers, is as much of a mystery as that of any early people we have considered; when we manage to catch sight of it through the efforts of the archaeologist, the people already have a language, a social organization, a way of life that is unique and distinctive, and if many of its features changed from one invasion to another, from one dynasty to another, there was always a solid core which could only be described as Chinese. It was comparatively late before the modern European learned much about China, because the people were not anxious to open their gates to the foreigner, and moderns were loath to take the writings of Marco Polo seriously. Today, after China has been overrun and exploited by foreigners, we wonder how a nation of people that had maintained its position through so many centuries collapsed like a mountain of toothpicks at the approaching breath of the European. Why did a people who had been so practical in many respects show themselves so impractical in other ways? Why should a people with so much wisdom in their heritage be positively nonsensical in its application? Why should a people brilliant enough to invent printing and gunpowder long before the European, never take advantage of these assets? They have been called democratic by some observers and yet they have behaved most undemocratically. For a long time men in government positions were scholars required to pass examinations on the cultural achievements of their past, but all this neither made a change in government structure nor encouraged a sense of moral responsibility in the people.

The Chinese of the empire believed they had arrived at the most perfect state of cultural expression, a prejudice true of many early peoples but especially true of the Chinese; European foreigners were barbarians without sense or taste. In a sense they were right, but such a perfection can become vain and hollow as a floating bubble. A number of principles had been applied in their creations over such a long period they took on an aspect of dull repetition, if not to the native, at least to the outside observer. There was one approved way of supporting the superstructure of a building that went unchallenged through centuries, although another type might have served their purpose better and added a welcome variety. The practice of divination, the funeral rites, the structure of government, the education of young men had reached such a state of proper perfection they were more burdensome than useful—museum pieces in the center of a busy, modern thoroughfare. One cannot say, however, that the Chinese people, as a whole, were allowed to remain contented with their lot throughout their history. As in India, foreign tribes came in periodically from the border regions, but in each case custom and convention were strong enough to subdue the invaders; tradition was never seriously threatened. This may have been due to the primitive character of the invader of China compared to the more advanced Muslims who came into India in large numbers, and it may also be credited to the more tenacious social structure of China.[1] To live in the midst of this people and remain outside of the family organization must have been virtually impossible and, furthermore, it was their social system that preserved them internally when many another survival from the past was ready to fall like an overripe plum. It will be interesting to learn how successfully the Communists can cope with the family of modern China.

There is no feature of the Chinese way of life stronger than

---

1. The inhabitants of northern China, from neolithic times to the present, belong to a single racial type. There is no skeletal evidence for an invasion (H. G. Creel: *The Birth of China*, New York, 1937, p. 51; cf. also F. C. Jones: *China*, Bristol, 1937, I, p. 13).

convention; in fact, it was a part of their religious outlook.
There was a proper way and a wrong way of carrying out every
procedure in action, a right and a wrong way of thinking,
writing, painting, dealing with other people according to rank,
worshipping the gods, treating one's wife, children, superiors,
and friends. The correct formality of procedure in action took
precedence over anything like a display of intimacy or affection,
to such an extent that family life appeared to the foreigner like
an austere institution devoid of familiarity. This may be putting
it a little strongly, but a representation of family life as it is
known in Renaissance or Romantic literature would seem entirely out of place in a Chinese setting, as if an obvious display
of feeling were contrary to a universal law of moderation or an
act of disobedience to some moral force ruling over the order
of the cosmos.[2] The Chinese could, of course, give way to action
inspired by violent passions; they could be moved to fanaticism
or mob hysteria like other peoples without revealing much of
their feelings in facial features, which made them unpredictable
to the European and therefore mysterious and untrustworthy.
This was not a pose on the part of the Chinese; it had been
developed in accord with traditions far older than Confucius, in
conformity with what they believed to be man's proper relation to the universe to whose order he himself was an important contributing factor. The sanctions laid upon convention
by their ancestors made it so much more forceful in the present.
The way of the universe, always regarded as the right way, and
the way of man could be kept in harmony only by the proper
observance of traditional convention.

The Chinese lived in a concrete world where things could be
seen, heard, and felt, and his relation to these things was
important. Far from being simply dead, these things were inhabited by spirits[3] that identified themselves with the concrete;

---

2. When emotions are expressed in such a way as to contribute to a
state of equilibrium, earth and heaven maintain their proper positions and
all things are nourished (E. R. Hughes: *The Great Learning and the
Mean-in-Action*, New York, 1943, p. 106).

3. E. D. Harvey: *The Mind of China*, New Haven, 1934, p. 4.

even the dragon, the unicorn, the phoenix were concrete beings which certain men had seen on certain occasions. The supernatural, the transcendental were realities the Chinese was not ready to deny, but since he could not configurate them in a sense experience, he was unwilling to say anything definite about them. Heaven, to his ancestors, was not far above the earth; it was the sky, it was blue in color and as solid as the earth that supported him; there were gods in the wind and mountains who never lived apart from their native elements; heaven and hell of Buddhism and Taoism were located in definite places in certain directions; ancestors also inhabited dwellings either in heaven or between heaven and earth where they could observe what was happening below their level. There was, consequently, a strong emphasis on the positive at the expense of the unknown and intangible. For the scholar and thinker this was epitomized by Confucius when he said he could not consider it advisable to learn about death before he knew something definite about life; for the Taoist, the Buddhist, and others, as we have seen, a definite location was created for afterlife; a mystic realm for self-identification with a supramundane absolute or the condition of nirvana meant little in Chinese religion. The paramount relation between man and other men as well as concrete things made his life a very practical one. This meant he was much more interested in the moral aspects of life than in speculation about the ultimate, and Chinese thinkers, perhaps for the same reason, were primarily concerned about government and how its relation to the governed would contribute to keep man in harmony with the macrocosm.

After this preliminary sketch of the Chinese's relation to his environment we can try to reconstruct his viewpoint to see how he looked at his world. Like so many others, he found himself beset with all kinds of danger in a finite world. Everything points to a predominance of the agricultural over the pastoral in his way of life, and as a farmer he was concerned about his crops, about excessive heat or rain, storms, and floods from the rivers; there were also human enemies who brought destruction to his home and family, who ruined his irrigation facilities. He too sought for some kind of permanence in the midst of change, in the face of uncertainties, and found it, not in the beyond, but in a more positive reconstruction of his own experience. His search for the infinite is brought to mind by the paintings of the solitary thinker brooding over a landscape teeming with life and movement. Since the early Chinese showed no sign of introspection, we cannot say he was looking for the infinite within himself. He saw heaven above whence came the sunlight and the rain for his crops, the earth beneath with its fertilizing power, and man between the two, and so constructed his infinite or security on the basis of the relations between the three. If he was to experience any self-identification, it had to be related to something outside himself, somewhere between the Brahman of the Hindu and the exalted divinity of the Hebrew. The peasant saw the sun rise in the morning and set in the evening; he saw a regular pattern in the change of seasons, the movements of the moon and stars. He also observed how the earth responded to the cold of winter, the spring rains, the heat of summer; the rivers swelled in spring and ran low in summer; the wild beasts, the birds of the air lived out their lives to harmonize with the movements of nature. There were also upsets like an eclipse in the heavens, violent storms, and earthquakes that appeared as irregularities in cosmic harmony, and since man was strongly subjective in his self-esteem, he believed he could, by his own actions,[4] exert a favorable or adverse influence on the harmony between himself and his universe.[5] Man had within his own grasp the happiness of his destiny.

Chinese religion was, then, a way of regarding the sensory manifestations of his experience, of acting upon them, and keeping them in control. Everything that came in contact with his senses became an object not only of religious consideration in worship but also of religious importance because of its bearing on his life, an attitude which forbade him to neglect nature

---

4. Virtue was equated with power (G. Misch: *The Dawn of Philosophy*, London, 1950, p. 96).

5. Cf. M. Granet: *Chinese Civilization*, New York, 1951, p. 185.

or put her manifestations down as deceptive; no man could hope to achieve happiness in life, either here or in the beyond, by divorcing himself from nature or raising himself beyond her reach. The Chinese drew up an elaborate program of acting and thinking which extended itself into all his relationships with things and men so that these connections with his universe became primarily moral in character. One must groove his motives along definite channels of conformity and, somewhat like a Puritan, sacrifice personal and individual considerations to the dictates of duty—what one ought to do became first a matter of necessity and then of pride and satisfaction. Man should live along with nature, and that harmony could be upset easily by wrong thought or action.

The infinite in which the Chinese found his security was located, not in the exalted heaven of Yahweh, not in a metaphysical construct, nor in a retreat from life, but in the proper adjustment of man's ways to those of nature at large—a harmony between the operations of the microcosm and those of the macrocosm. As in Egypt, the infinite permeated the finite where the possibility of bringing about a harmony lay in the hands of man himself, and in this sense the Chinese was a potential creature endowed with a certain measure of responsibility in a potential universe, even if the area of his responsibility was circumscribed. But was the relationship set up between man and his universe a balanced one or was it largely subjective in character? The latter seems to be more true for two important reasons: the fragile crystal of perfection of which the Chinese boasted was built up on a way of life prescribed by subjective dictation, far different from the growing imperfections cropping up on the horizon of the objective thinker; moreover, the Chinese was too certain about the way of the universe and how he could act in harmony with it. Without emphasizing other evidence which will reveal itself later in our discussion, it seems that what was meant to be a well-balanced harmony between man as a subject and the universe as an object, a harmony created and supported by man's right behavior, actually turned out to be a harnessed horse controlled and directed by subjective reins. In India the Hindu was so deeply grounded in the infinite he identified himself with it more completely by backing away from the finite; the Chinese found his infinite saturating everything his eye could see, his ear could hear, he reached out over nature with a strong subjective arm, set up a framework of moral law to control it, and cuddled himself within the limits of an institutionalized security. Both India and China tended to use nature, each in its own way, as a subjective means to gain a more permanent satisfaction.

The Chinese cast about for a more specific means to cement this harmony between man and the cosmos, and this he found in the institution of the family. Other peoples have put great store by the family to guarantee male descent, but in China it became a link with infinity by joining it to ancestor worship; he also found it could keep the individual in line with the established social and political order, all of which might be called an extension, beyond the family, of man's area of control over the cosmos. The family as an organization was much larger than the western unit. It required male descendants to prepare a proper funeral, to carry on the rites at the grave, for those surviving on earth were in need of the guiding hand of those who had passed on. By paying respect to and fulfilling all the duties toward elders the members of the family were conducting themselves according to ancient traditions and so doing their share to uphold the harmony between society and the cosmos. The solid structure of the family reached heavenward like a pyramid; it extended its influence by way of example to other families; it was the cornerstone of social happiness.

As a social unit the family also had its disadvantages: one family frequently failed to cooperate with another, and so whatever social happiness it achieved was a sheltered one based on the notion that "my family is better than your family and hence deserves a larger share of heaven's rewards." The authority of the family was final and unquestionable, it built up little responsibility in the individual member who learned to think and act with the whole family as if it were a small mob. It made filial piety the paramount virtue among the younger members, but it also made them helpless victims of conniving concubines, and the mother-in-law often made life miserable for the young bride. The family took credit for the work of the superior members and suffered along with its criminals, for blood evidently carried more in its stream than relatedness; the man who was unfaithful to his family became either a social outcast or had to take refuge, with the coming of the Hans, in a monastery. The family was frequently a stifling institution for its members, but in the hands of the ruler or the aristocrat it was a most effective tool; in preserving the solidarity of tradition through the ages it was China's greatest asset, and if it was occasionally a nuisance in the larger social pattern, this was not put down as a fault of the family as an institution but of men who failed to use it properly—it was a tool of magic to achieve certainty and security.

Another means by which human desire attained stability in a changing world was the emperor himself. Like the pharaoh of Egypt he was the acknowledged son of a divinity, in this case of Heaven, the foremost of the Chinese pantheon, and the ruler's connection with the superhuman made him an absolute monarch whose authority was not to be questioned and whose person was sacrosanct. Every man must kowtow before him, while the ruler recognized Heaven alone as his superior. In the event that the emperor was deposed by a revolution or a new dynasty the people were told that Heaven was so displeased with his son he had to be removed. The ruler was also the head of the great Chinese family, standing at the apex of the pyramid of families making up the Chinese nation, and as such he had heavy responsibilities to the people as a whole. He was morally obliged to offer his people a sound example in behavior, i.e., his own family should be a model for all. Since the emperor as the supreme subjective power in China was the representative of Heaven on earth, he could contribute much to the control over the movements of the cosmos for the benefit of the whole nation; as the head of the state he also exercised full power over the social relationships of his subjects, so that the dictates of his power and the influence of his moral example emanated along two parallel lines to maintain prosperity in the land.[6] Hence the great concern of Confucius and his followers about the behavior of the ruler. In practice, however, this moral responsibility does not seem to have weighed very heavily on the mind of most rulers, and disasters of every description were laid at the door, first of the emperor, and then of every official in the government. The European wonders why they never effected a change in the form of their government. To attempt anything of the sort would have meant acting contrary to the ordinance of Heaven and upsetting the parallelism in royal function, and this in turn would bring about untold calamities to the whole people.

Other devices of magic were also employed to maintain control over the cosmos; in fact, much of the attitude of the Chinese toward the objective, many of the institutions he fashioned to preserve a universal harmony were patterned after the procedure of magic. The structure of society was severely criticized by Mo-ti and others, but the subjective means to an end was not held to be so much at fault as the men who disobeyed its rules; many recognized the evils of the imperial government without entertaining a thought about a change of form. The Chinese method of testing a moral law was to mold it into a social practice; if it then became a tradition and was sanctioned by men of authority, it was held to be an immutable article of revelation, one of the eternal verities contributing to the welfare of man in his cosmos. The important consideration was the sanctity of the method whose practical ineffectiveness was laid to the failings of the agent—it was the Chinese's stubborn clinging to a subjective management of objective possibilities that nullified many of the more advanced ideas of Confucius and other thinkers.

We notice here, in contrast to India, less emphasis on a legal code; the reason is much the same as in Egypt: the divinity

---

6. M. Granet: *op. cit.*, p. 400; cf. also B. S. Bonsall: *Confucianism and Taoism,* London, 1934, p. 56.

of the emperor, whose word was not to be questioned, debated, or argued about, made a formal code less necessary.[7] Furthermore, a law suit was so expensive for the average man and he was so ignorant of court procedure he had little chance against dishonest government officials;[8] certainly the imperial court was not as interested in the dispensation of justice as in the collection of revenue or the levy of troops, and in periods of imperial laxity the official was granted a free hand. Apart from the scholars and officials there was hardly enough individualism to assert itself over against the head of the family whose patriarchal control was rather absolute. The family, then, had a lion's share in the administration of civil law, while tradition, more forceful than law, lent a helping hand.

So far we have been dealing with the Chinese viewpoint as it developed in the early days and as it was reinforced by the Confucians. Was there another viewpoint entirely different from the Confucian outlook emanating from the southern part of China or perhaps from India? We are told by one writer that the southern Chinese have always been different from their brothers in the north.[9] Another asserts that Confucius was not the only one capable of understanding the character of the Chinese.[10] Turner[11] refers to Taoism, which brings the other viewpoint to the fore, as a mere reaction to the disturbances of the feudal period. It hardly seems possible the Chinese were capable of holding fast to the Taoist viewpoint and, as we have seen, the later version of its doctrine belied the original ideas ascribed to Lao-tsu, but we must place the two side by side to diagnose the fundamental difference between them, for Taoism

7. Legalism and law codes came into the foreground as a substitute for imperial strength in times of weakness (Fung Yu-lan: *A History of Chinese Philosophy* (Trans. by Derk Bodde), Princeton, 1953, I, p. 38).

8. E. D. Harvey: *op. cit.*, p. 10.

9. Cf. K. C. Latourette: *The Development of China*, New York, 1946, p. 42.

10. C. P. Fitzgerald: *China*, London, 1950, p. 88.

11. *The Great Cultural Traditions*, New York, 1941, I, p. 433.

was, at least for a time, a Chinese viewpoint. Basically, there is no great contradiction between the two, even if the *Tao* of Lao-tsu seems to be more akin to the *Brahman* of India.

Confucianism as represented by its founder reaffirmed what had already been laid down by tradition in that it emphasized filial piety, family loyalty, the respect for ancestors, the authority of the emperor, the emulation of the past. Confucius then stressed the moral values to be associated with all man's thoughts and actions within a practical and positive sphere. Heaven he thought of as a moral force and therefore attached much importance to human example. He aimed at the self-cultivation of the individual within restricted limits, one who would be able to distinguish the mean or norm in conduct without much conscious effort and thus come as near to divinity as is humanly possible.[12] In stressing individual development, however, he was going beyond the past, and his assertions about the dignity of man and the potentiality of things brought him close to the fifth-century Greek, if not to the viewpoint of the modern. Thereby he reaped much admiration but little cooperation from his contemporaries. He was far ahead of Mencius, who saw that men are far different from one another by nature but would not concede to them equal opportunities implied in the dignity of man.[13] One important aspect of his doctrine Confucius failed to recognize: he gave his unqualified support to the emperor and family tradition, two means by which the Chinese sought to guarantee their security in a changing world, but he could not see that these two supports stifled the individual's dignity and power of decision, and at the same time he declared this individual ought not to be used as an instrument; the same factors ruled against the potentiality of things. We are told that all through his life he hoped, against all precedent, that the rulers of China would fall in line with the way of Heaven and at the same time grant the individual more freedom. It neither happened during his days nor through the subsequent years that continued the triumph of the subjective tradition.

---

12. Cf. E. R. Hughes: *op. cit.*, p. 124–30.

13. J. Legge: *The Chinese Classics*, Oxford, 1895, II, p. 256.

It never occurred to Confucius that an individual could not use his freedom or self-responsibility to its fullest extent as long as the revelation of religion or tradition (there was little distinction between the two) held a restricting hand over him. Confucius was free, in a sense, but not free to do much with anything; nor did it enter his mind to change the traditions of the past. Why? The conventional ways of doing things, proper ceremony, obedience to family and emperor, were originally designed as magical means to achieve a subjective end and, as we have seen in the procedure of other magic, the means or *modus operandi* is never questioned; in case of failure it is the agent who must be held responsible. As we have pointed out, many families behaved badly and many emperors were unworthy of their office, but the family as an institution and imperial authority remained sacrosanct through the ages. Security was always the first consideration, and the means for bolstering it, namely the right way of doing things through the proper channels, acquired moral power, social grace, a certain beauty and refinement but never lost its original magical efficacy. Freedom and self-responsibility, then, were given free rein only insofar as they did not violate the limitations supporting the roof of security over the head of the Chinese.

These are the essential features and consequences of Confucianism which appear, on the surface, to be different from Taoism. The other view we shall now proceed to examine.

H. G. Creel[14] stamps the encounter between Confucius and Lao-tsu as fictitious, and, we might add, there is no historical evidence for the existence of the latter. Still, the fact that such a viewpoint was prevalent for a time is important, and so we must deal with it. The Taoist, like the Confucian, tells us we must keep in harmony with the universe, but such a harmony is brought about in a negative sense, by relaxation, by assuming a passive attitude toward finite experience. As Turner[15] remarks, Tao bears a strong resemblance to the Hindu concept

---

14. *Chinese Thought from Confucius to Mao Tse-tung*, Chicago, 1953, p. 98.

15. *Op. cit.*, I, p. 430; cf. also M. Granet: *op. cit.*, p. 250.

of reality.[16] While the Taoist (and the same applies to the later Buddhist) resembles Confucianism by directing our attention to the same goal, the means for reaching it is far different. For the Taoist and the Zen Buddhist as well as the Hindu the infinite is all-embracing and all-absorbing; self-realization in terms of such permanence can be achieved only by a denial of everything positive and active. Perhaps we can clarify it still further by another statement: the Confucian can effect his harmony only by an active cooperation between subject and the object which is separated from the former in terms of the time and space of finite experience, whereas the harmony of the Taoist represents a complete identification of subject with an object within as well as beyond the agent, the thinker, or the subject himself. In each case *Tao,* the object of attention, is the way of the universe; in one case, harmony with *Tao* is achieved by active participation in the affairs of life, in the other by neglecting the same. Once this mystic union of subject and object becomes a reality, there is no more need for thought or action. Although both men were interested in *Tao* but reached for it in different directions, we can see how the legend of Confucius' meeting with Lao-tsu arose and why the former could never have understood the other. The original doctrines of Taoism and Buddhism were soon so altered by the practical Chinese that the later versions were, in some respects, a denial of the first. It is questionable, then, if we can attach as much importance to Taoism in the Chinese outlook on life as to Confucianism.

There is perhaps more talk about morality in China than in any other early civilization, much of which can be found in the teachings of Confucius and his followers. We have already seen, in the study of the Hebrew, that responsible action is based on a balanced subject-object relationship, one in which the object is treated with the same dignity as the subject; such a moral relationship was the covenant set up between the Israelites and Yahweh. Was there anything equal to this agree-

---

16. H. G. Creel (*op. cit.,* p. 191) also comments on this resemblance.

ment among the Chinese? The relationship between man as a subject and the family ancestors or the emperor carried a great deal of weight with Confucius and other intellectuals; it saturated literature, especially the drama;[17] but in practice it was not very effective for the majority of the people. A large number may have been good Confucianists in times of prosperity, but in days of stress they became victims of superstition;[18] they would also kowtow to anyone with the power to reward or injure.[19] A writer on painting declares one should watch a man secretly in a crowd to learn about his true character.[20] It seems unlikely that the average Chinese reached the level of Hebrew moral responsibility to his divinity; if he reached it anywhere, it was outside the family circle. Another indication of a lack of responsibility is the prevalent use of magic which inspires expediency in thought and action, or we may say the magician applies subversive tactics to the object whether it be an inanimate thing, a man, or a god, thereby robbing it of its dignity. The Hebrew covenant reduced the element of magic to a minimum, if we can judge by the authority of the Old Testament. The difference between the family ancestors and the Chinese emperor as moral objects, on the one hand, and the Hebrew Yahweh, on the other, is due to an all-pervading, omnipotent personality of a sublime divinity.

Magic, as we find it elsewhere, was also a means by which the Chinese sought to exercise control over constant change, to regularize cosmic motions for the benefit of man; this method was resorted to in addition to exhorting man to keep his actions in conformity with the way of Heaven. There is no nation in ancient times that developed so many varieties of divination to discover the will of Heaven in advance and invented so many symbols to help the magician render the will of the object more

---

17. The reader is referred to the Introduction (XXV) of H. H. Hart: *The West Chamber,* Stanford, 1936.

18. E. D. Harvey: *op. cit.,* p. 7.

19. E. H. Parker: *Studies in Chinese Religion,* London, 1910, p. 7.

20. O. Siren: *The Chinese on the Art of Painting,* Peiping, 1936, pp. 60–61.

pliable. Every concrete object, from Heaven to the smallest stone, had an indwelling spirit which could easily be controlled by the right formula or technique for the benefit of the all-powerful subject.

The government of China, as we have said, was dominated by an absolute ruler holding his position by virtue of his descent from Heaven. Its whole structure, like that of Egypt, was pyramidal in form: the emperor at the apex, the mass of people at the base, and magistrates, officials, scholars, and tax collectors between the two. The citizen at the base was told to look up to the emperor with unquestioning loyalty, to be ready to defend him with his life; in most cases he had no time to learn to read, no occasion to learn to think independently. So many people who associate religion with a temple or church call the Chinese lacking in religious feeling because they fail to realize how mundane and practical their religion was, how sacred the emperor and the whole structure of government. In view of the monarch's absolute authority, the helplessness of the subject, and the usual lack of any moral responsibility on the part of anyone in government, it is hard to think of the typical Chinese as democratic.[21] A good share of the writings of Chinese thinkers has been devoted to the way their government ought to be run from the apex of the pyramid, or at least from the position of the government official, instead of starting with the common man at the base, because the authority of the emperor and the form of the government were too sacrosanct to be changed.

What was the meaning of knowledge for the Chinese? Since he was a practical man living within the framework of a positive experience, he must have learned much from observing what transpired in his environment. The peasant was well acquainted with the land he tilled, the hunter knew his game and its haunts, the warrior was versed in the lore of horses and weapons, the poet and painter knew much about the phenomena of nature, but in spite of all the information they may have gathered, they developed very little of what we call scientific

---

21. Cf. O. & E. Lattimore: *China,* New York, 1944, p. 29.

knowledge. A certain amount of information came by way of divination and from the decrees of the emperor, but there was nothing like the prophetic revelations of the Hebrews from a transcendent deity. The most reliable information came from the traditions of the past—the legends of the early emperors, the famous classics, the *Analects* of Confucius, all of which was accepted as authority from on high. This latter type of knowledge far outweighed in importance any information gleaned from the wayside, if we can judge from the scholars' examinations at court. And how did they pass on their knowledge to others? Like so many orientals they were fond of the symbol and the analogy, especially to convey the moral lesson they applied so frequently; instead of using what we call reasoning from cause to effect or from a general law to a particular the Chinese preferred the juxtaposition of two vivid images as a substitute for forceful arguments. The writer[22] made good use of similes, most convincing in their outlines, but the details were left unexplored by both the writer and reader; in most cases the writer's customary brevity gave him an added reason for both vividness and lack of exactness. All this was very well for art, literature, and moral precept but hardly adequate for the scientific description of an object or process.

Was the Chinese able to think in terms of a subject-object relationship in which the object was allowed to speak in its own right? Was he capable of dealing with objects without dictating to or tyrannizing over them? Was he fully aware of all the implications in the relationship of the whole and its parts? Did he know anything about argument other than analogy? There is plenty of evidence that he was able to think clearly in his own way, if not in the direction of scientific exploration, but living, as he did, in a compactly self-sufficient civilization where most of the fundamental questions had been answered by approved tradition, most of Chinese thinking was directed toward morality and government. In this field it turned out a great number of variations on the same theme without much effect in practice,

---

22. E. R. Hughes: *op. cit.*, p. 93.

because the framework of his thinking, the limitations of his subject had been fixed again, in the good old days. A problem, we have learned, is a conflict of difference between subject and object, between what the subject wants and what it may have from the object. Magic deals with a problem by oversimplifying the issue; it assumes the subject can have its way with the object without respecting its rights or investigating its true nature. Moreover, the Chinese's approach to problems, as we observe in his philosophy, his drama, and novel, was overshadowed by moral postulates (also tools of magic) which grooved the solution for a problem along a narrow channel; where moral precept could find no application, the thinker appeared to be out of his element. We may say the Chinese has been able to set up a balanced subject-object relationship for moral problems, but even here the object was not always treated fairly, and as soon as the constraint of moral tradition was removed, the subject shifted from one extreme to another. The archaeologist has had considerable trouble excavating ancient tombs and graves, because once poverty pushes out moral restrictions the Chinese plunder the graves.

The curiosity of the Chinese was never sufficiently sharpened to investigate all the practical implications and possibilities of what he discovered in phenomena. Indeed, he had the mariner's compass, gunpowder, paper, and printing at an early date, but what did the Chinese accomplish with these advantages? The mariner's compass was used to select the proper site for a grave, paper figures were burned as a part of the funeral ceremony, gunpowder frightened away demons.[23] This is not what we should call scientific procedure in spite of the interest in things that called forth these discoveries. The fact that the Chinese had at their disposal an excellent variety of white clay for the making of the world's finest porcelain does not mean they would ever have produced a Hippocrates. The authority of traditional knowledge and the religious sanctions attached to certain approved ways of doing things forbade a full freedom

---

23. E. D. Harvey: *op. cit.,* p. 2. I cannot agree with his conclusion that science could ever grow directly out of the use of magic.

of development both for the thinking agent and the idea. Instead of giving rise to the laws of motion or the quantum
theory it means that, by the method of magic or by following
the prescription of authority (both exerted the same influence
in practice), the thinker could only create a pseudoscience to
serve as an ornamental camouflage over the bedrock of con-
ventionalism. Science does not grow directly out of magic because its method is contradictory to everything required for the
foundation of the scientific view. Science is not produced from
an economic upheaval, a volcanic catastrophe, a change of government, or a chance discovery; it is produced by *men* who
know not only how to put things together by certain techniques
but who have learned how to use a balanced subject-object relationship in dealing with objects whether they are concrete
things, human beings, or mental concepts. This cannot be done
in a social or religious environment dominated by either magic
or authority suspended on high.

Subjectively controlled thinking, as it dictates to objective
nature, can achieve a stereotyped perfection which will continue to hold sway over man and his relation to the world
unless it is violently upset by contact with another viewpoint.
This perfection in China, created by his harmony between *Li*
and *Tao*, between man's way and the way of the universe, was
so much more obvious, in this case, because the whole viewpoint of the Chinese was directed to the concrete and practical
instead of including an abstract plane where it might create
opposition, as is often the case in the West, to the rule of practice. Plato could find a perfection in the world of ideas opposed
to their reflection in phenomena, Plotinus could find a sublimated
glory in the "one," and Augustine found it in the Heavenly City
of God, but in China there was no such a contradiction between
two worlds; there was an approved way of thinking and acting,
and he who conformed and he who fell by the wayside were
on the same plane of experience. This may also be a reason
why the Chinese never realized that his globe of perfection
was as fragile as one of his porcelain vases. Scientific thinking
with its balance between subject and object could drive no

wedge into this compact self-sufficiency, for the examination of an object per se might threaten traditions approved for so many generations; change could only be a variation on an old theme man was afraid to discard. Gunpowder and the compass were remarkable discoveries, but how could they become anything more than dispensable refinements in a scheme of things that was already right as right could be?

The Chinese were more conscious of history than the Hindus without developing a comparative view of the subject. Rather than exact dates for certain periods of time or the reigns of emperors, they preferred to remember definite events attached to great personalities.[24] Perhaps this was initiated in prehistoric times when certain legendary events made a strong impression on the mind, e.g., the subjects of the Han tomb reliefs. Historical perspective suffered, of course, from a disparaging comparison with other peoples which, as in Egypt, points to an overdose of confidence in self-perfection. Their tolerance was never put to a rigid test, because as soon as another group settled in their midst, that group found it economically and socially necessary to adopt the Chinese way of life. There was, however, no consistent persecution of foreign religious sects; in general, we may say, the foreigner was free from intolerant treatment as long as he was willing to kowtow to the emperor and aimed no threat at the Chinese social and political system, which was never seriously challenged until recent times.

There was evidently a certain awareness for the element of tragedy in Chinese cultural expression. We find some trace of it in the novel and drama, and if we look at Chinese life from the cradle to the grave, there was plenty of occasion for lamenting what we call misfortune; but misfortune can easily build up a compensation in the mind which is contradictory to tragedy. We have already explained, in our account of India, why the Buddhist found no room for it; the Confucian no doubt had enough confidence in the continuity of family life into the next world to discount tragedy as a threat to his happiness. A sense

24. A. Waley: *The Analects of Confucius*, London, 1948, p. 78.

of humor the Chinese certainly had, although, again as in Egypt, it was sheltered within the protective institutions of his social security; had the shell of his assumed superiority over others been shattered, it is debatable how well this humor would have held up.

Art also, according to those who wrote commentaries, came under the influence of morality, although it is hard to believe anything of this nature was uppermost in the mind of the painter at work. In one passage we are told that paintings are mirrors of conduct,[25] reflecting the way of Heaven for the benefit of the observer; again, it is claimed, poor paintings are laid at the door of efforts working against the laws of nature,[26] all of which may very well imply that the artist who, by his own thought and attention, has not brought himself into harmony with nature could neither understand her ways nor reproduce them in his art. Once more we are presented with analogies which would have been a joy to Ruskin but which are not explained in detail. The difference between the Northern and Southern Sung schools of painting apparently corresponds to what we might expect of the northern and southern temperaments;[27] the latter favored the sudden flash of intuition for creative work, the other preferred the more patient, gradual method, which probably means it was not as subjective in identifying the artist with his subject matter. It is interesting to note that the personality of the artist was brought far enough into the foreground to leave us a large number of names.

At this point we are in a position to say something more definite about the democracy of the Chinese viewpoint. What are the requisites for a democratic viewpoint? First, a balanced subject-object relationship in thinking, then a government in which the unit or individual part counts as a potential citizen capable of making his own decisions in a potential world; further, we should include a moral man capable of assuming responsibility for his thoughts and actions, a comparative pers-

25. O. Siren: *op. cit.,* p. 226.
26. *Ibid.,* p. 137.
27. *Ibid.,* p. 103.

pective of history, an attitude of tolerance, an awareness of tragedy as a part of life, and a sense of humor. In China the moral side of the picture was theoretically developed to a high level, but in practice the responsibility of the individual was hemmed in by an absolute form of government and the religious sanctions of the family; the same factors worked against a subject-object balance in thinking. Beyond these points we find nothing outstanding in favor of democracy except a sense of humor. It cannot be denied that Confucius, within the framework of tradition, went farther in the direction of the democratic viewpoint than anyone in the Near and Far East by stressing the dignity of man and the potentiality of things, but he was unable to break away from the human longing for certainty and stability he found in the family, the worship of ancestors, and the office of the emperor. The large majority of Chinese succumbed to the overpowering desire of subjectivity that sacrifices the hope for individual freedom to immediate security; that it would mean the ultimate ruin of the subject they could not understand. A few Chinese raised themselves high on the ladder of individual achievement, but the walls of tradition rose up equally as high to limit their sphere of influence.

INDEX

(Roman numerals i *and* ii *refer to Volumes I and II, respectively.)*

p 160 - bt s Kelfull blend of
historical fact.
myths + legend, +
modern criticism

The Text is densely packed,
full of information + valuable
synthesis.

Distilled essence of a great deal
of reading + thinking.

Summary of ostracism good 164

transition from confederacy to
empire 167 - 68 good.

C, Whitman has carried
the discussion of Herodo
forward of ch 177 - 78

p. 189 - "Errors" of Socrates,
are not so much his
errors as our own ??

Summary of the
Gods 195 - 76

195 - 96 Herodo
etc
blends
literary with
social + eco-
nomic history

197 - Discussion of
Pindar God, with
Beethoven + not
Brahms for
comparison ?